Food and Femininity

Kate Cairns and Josée Johnston

Bloomsbury Academic
An imprint of Bloomsbury Publishing Plc

B L O O M S B U R Y
LONDON • NEW DELHI • NEW YORK • SYDNEY

Bloomsbury Academic

An imprint of Bloomsbury Publishing Plc

50 Bedford Square	1385 Broadway
London	New York
WC1B 3DP	NY 10018
UK	USA

www.bloomsbury.com

BLOOMSBURY and the Diana logo are trademarks of Bloomsbury Publishing Plc

First published 2015

© Kate Cairns and Josée Johnston, 2015

Kate Cairns and Josée Johnston have asserted their rights under the Copyright, Designs and Patents Act, 1988, to be identified as Authors of this work.

British Library Cataloguing-in-Publication Data
A catalogue record for this book is available from the British Library.

ISBN:	HB:	978-0-8578-5552-7
	PB:	978-0-8578-5664-7
	ePDF:	978-0-8578-5774-3
	ePub:	978-0-8578-5556-5

Library of Congress Cataloging-in-Publication Data
A catalog record for this book is available from the Library of Congress.

Series: Contemporary Food Studies: Economy, Culture and Politics, Vol. 1

Typeset by Newgen Knowledge Works (P) Ltd., Chennai, India
Printed and bound in India

Contents

A personal food prologue

When we told people we were writing a book on "food and femininity," we received a few puzzled looks. Were we doing historical research? How is such a book relevant today? We live in times of shifting gender norms when it comes to food. Male celebrity chefs dominate our television screens—Jamie Oliver, Gordon Ramsay, Bobby Flay, the list continues. Many people can think of a man they know who enjoys cooking or who watches what he eats to avoid gaining weight. At the same time, it is not difficult to imagine a woman who hates to cook and instead goes out for dinner. Rather than opting for salad, she may even order a big steak or a juicy burger with french fries. Prioritizing pleasure, rejecting diets, and avoiding kitchen drudgery—these all seem like options for today's women. So why write a book about something as old-fashioned as women and food?

We responded to these puzzled looks and queries with questions of our own: *Who feels primarily responsible for feeding children healthy meals? Who is trying the latest juice cleanse or expressing concern for animals through veganism? Who is buying cookbooks, and managing weekly meal plans? Who is insisting on organic milk for the kids or making the trek to the weekly farmers' market?* There are certainly some men who do these things, but our research suggests that the answer to a lot of these questions is "mainly women."

To be clear, our interest is not simply women, but femininity. By femininity, we refer to collective ideas about how *to be and act* feminine, and signal our gendered identity to others. We perform femininity through our clothing, physical cues, and manner of speech, but we also signal it through our food choices and the ways we relate to food. In this book, we argue that food continues to signal femininity, even if it is not the straightforward performance of the 1950s' housewife. Despite the important changes that have occurred, food and femininity remain tightly intertwined in our collective imagination and in our emotional lives.

To demonstrate the connections between food and femininity, consider this thought experiment. Imagine a woman who *does not appear to care about food* and consider the social judgments that follow. Think of a woman who is thought to have "out-of-control" food habits and faces the stigma of being "fat." Consider the "bad mother" who sends her children to school with Kraft lunchables and is seen loading bags of potato chips and frozen meals onto the grocery store conveyer belt. Imagine a woman who does not make home-cooked meals that bring her family together at the table each evening. Consider who gets blamed when a child is seen to be overweight. Picture the woman who buys cheap meat at the grocery store and is seen to be unwittingly contaminating her children's bodies with antibiotics and growth hormones. What these examples all illustrate is that "failing" at food also means failing at femininity. Women's food choices continue to be closely examined under the social microscope and are harshly judged when they are deemed inadequate or ill-informed.

Parsing the enduring connections between food and femininity is not easy at a time when most people endorse gender equality and women are seen as empowered consumers able to make savvy and independent food choices. A postfeminist sensibility suggests that women's oppression is a thing of the past, which leaves women to manage food-related pressures in their individual lives. One of the key issues we hope to convey in this book is that many seemingly *personal* food struggles and stresses arise from the *social* challenge of successfully performing food femininities: the nurturing mother, the talented home-cook, the conscientious consumer, the health-savvy eater. These are not easy tasks to pull off, especially if one wants to achieve them in a relaxed, seemingly "effortless" way that avoids the impression of excess. As we show in the pages that follow, women are also judged harshly for caring *too much* about food: think here of the puritanical vegetarian, the joy-killing health nut, or the overprotective mother.

It appears that there is a relatively narrow band of acceptable food behaviors for today's women: successful food femininities involve considerable investments in "good" food practices while simultaneously avoiding the impression that one is a neurotic dieter or a preachy food zealot. As a result, even the most privileged women we spoke with (women with stable middle-class incomes and racial privilege) did not feel as though they were doing their absolute best when it came to food. They worried about whether they were making the right food choices to sustain the planet's ecosystem and about whether their family diet had caused their child's health problems. They worried about socializing their children to develop healthy and adventurous eating habits and about the equitable division of foodwork in their intimate relationships. Collectively these worries suggest that food is essential to understanding femininity and that this is a topic laden with intense emotions for many women.

As feminist scholars, we believe it is important to briefly situate ourselves within the story we are telling in this book. Even as we look critically at the interplay between food and femininity, we are not outside of these processes—our own identities are deeply bound up in the issues that we study. For instance, while conducting discourse analysis of food media for this book, Kate recalls subconsciously patting herself on the back when she discovered that her own lunch included quinoa and kale—two of the "superfoods" praised in the article she was analyzing. Clearly, feminine food ideals have a seductive pull, despite our critical reflexivity toward these ideals in our work. Indeed, Josée can think critically about the association between femininity and "sweet" foods (see Lupton 1996: 104–5), but she continues to experience satisfaction from baking, especially when she discovers a new DIY trick (e.g., homemade marshmallows). In our meetings, we invariably worked alongside a plate of Josée's latest baked treat, a trend that struck us both as funny and as a reminder of our own investment in particular food femininities. (Thank you Deb Perlman, of Smitten Kitchen, for your amazing granola bar recipe!)

Food and femininity have long been bound up in our lives. For Josée, the pressure to perform femininity through food has felt both attractive and fatiguing, especially given the example she was shown as a child. Her mother performed femininity through traditional foodwork that was extremely labor-intensive: grinding her own flour for homemade bread, planting a giant garden, cooking virtually everything from scratch (including yoghurt and pasta), and hosting large meals in a seemingly effortless, relaxed manner. Growing up, Josée learned a lot about food, gardening, and cooking, but she still wonders how it is possible to host a large holiday dinner in a way that is not exhausting. By contrast, growing up in a house with two working moms, Kate was exposed at an early age to nontraditional ideas about how foodwork can be shared within the home. She started making her own lunch at the age of ten and learned early on about the importance of feeding herself. Kate does not feel the pressure to cook elaborate dinners from scratch—she regularly (and happily) makes quick and easy meals. Even still, food is important to her identity, including the fact that she has been a vegetarian for ten years.

Despite our different childhood food experiences, we have ended up sharing a lot of the same food values and practices that seem to dominate our urban Toronto neighborhoods—a setting where organic butchers, farmers' markets, and urban beekeepers thrive. We both feel inspired by the collective food projects initiated by Toronto's various community food organizers—some of whom we speak with in this book. Another thing we share (along with virtually every woman we know) is the enduring pressures that surround ideals of feminine embodiment, even though our experiences have been less severe than many other women in our lives. Nonetheless, we have felt emboldened by activist efforts to destigmatize fat and to delink thinness and health in our collective imagination—an issue that we both work to foreground in our teaching.

While food is a source of both joy and stress in our lives, the stories of our participants remind us of how much more difficult the food-femininity nexus can be in the context of poverty. While daily foodwork continues to present its share of challenges for both of us, these challenges pale in comparison to the intense struggle of feeding children on a severely restricted budget—an everyday reality for millions of North American women. The central goal of this book is to understand women's food stories within the contexts of their lives—including the social, political-economic, and cultural processes that shape the food that is available, and the meanings it holds. Food practices speak to personal tastes, political commitments, and gendered identities, but they also illustrate gross levels of inequality. Our hope is that the food stories shared throughout this book will encourage a renewed interest in the feminist politics of food and shed light on the various forms of inequality that are reproduced and challenged in our everyday food lives.

Acknowledgments

Like many authors, we feel deeply indebted to the behind-the-scenes friends, family, colleagues, and research participants that helped turn an idea into a real-life book. This may seem like a cliché. To that we say, just try writing a book without intellectual or emotional support! It would be impossible. And even if it were possible, it would involve twice as much time and half the fun.

We owe a huge intellectual debt to everyone who helped us gather data, read drafts, and develop ideas. Invaluable research assistance was provided by Merin Oleschuk, Ali Rodney, Katelin Albert, Lance Stewart, Kerstin Giannini, and Elizabeth Lun. Thinking about the role of children and mothering (and the "organic child") cannot be separated from our collaborations with Norah MacKendrick, as well as with Kim DeLaat and Shyon Baumann. Thanks also to the following people who rigorously read drafts and provided invaluable feedback: Shyon Baumann, Jennifer Carlson, James Cairns, Rick Cairns, Ali Rodney, Athena Engman, Katarina Kolar, Sarah Cappeliez, Merin Oleschuk, Michelle Szabo, Bonnie Fox, and Deborah McPhail. Thanks also to anonymous reviewers and editors at *Theory and Society*, who helped us develop an earlier journal article exploring the idea of the "do-diet." We have presented aspects of this research at various conferences over the years and are particularly grateful for the feedback we received from colleagues within the Consumers and Consumption section of the American Sociological Association.

The editors of this book series—Mike Goodman and David Goodman—played a very large role helping this book come to fruition. We want to thank Mike for planting the seed that this project could become a book and both of them for their intellectual support and useful comments on draft chapters.

I (Kate) would like to thank Josée for first inspiring me to think sociologically about food when we met back in 2007 and for the many years of mentorship and feminist collaboration that followed. Thank you, also, for keeping me so well nourished during our day-long meetings at your kitchen table. Huge thanks to James for always being excited to think through ideas, to my Dad for catching even the tiniest grammatical error, and to the rest of the Cairns/Parliament/Dougan crew for the endless support. Thanks to Corey for the balance and humor that help me put things in perspective and for turning every new challenge into an adventure.

I (Josée) would like to thank Kate for her "brightsiding" in dark moments, steely resolve to meet deadlines, and unfailing intellectual camaraderie. I have learned so much from you. Also, thanks to the Ontario Early Researcher Award and the Social Sciences and Humanities Research Council for funding my collaborations with Kate. I would also like to thank my kids, Bram and Lucy, for being so patient when meals were arriving late and for believing that popcorn can be a real dinner. Thanks to Shyon for feeding me in many "hangry" moments and for your astounding patience, solidity, and smartness.

Finally, we both would like to thank the women and the men who generously opened up their homes to us and spoke so candidly about the place that food plays in their lives. We are so grateful for your honesty and hospitality, and we remain inspired by the energy, passion, and commitment you bring to daily meals.

Chapter 1

Caring about food

We live in mercurial times when it comes to food. Consumers are swamped with information telling them to *care more* about what they eat—to "connect" with local farmers, to teach children where food comes from, and to stave off obesity by substituting "real food" for processed junk. While some people are accused of not caring enough about what is on their plate, others are regarded as food-obsessed—they read about it, blog about it, and watch countless hours of food television. While there are certainly people who see food simply as "fuel," a large number of North Americans view food as key to their daily rituals, personal identities, and body projects.[1] Indeed, when we held focus groups and interviews discussing the role of food in people's lives, we heard many passionate stories of caring about food. Consider the following five food stories shared by Kerri, Marissa, Shannon, Alyssa, and Carmen.

Kerri insists that food shopping is not really a chore, as long as she has time to enjoy it. A white occupational therapist in her mid-thirties, she delights in the opportunity to peruse the aisles, read labels, and select fresh produce. In fact, she and her friend Brenda sometimes meet for midnight "dates" at a 24-hour grocery store, so they can "float around" and "really take your time." Turning to her partner, Brad, Kerri says, "it's different than going with you." When Brad rolls his eyes, Kerri laughs, adding, "you'd be clippin' on my heels." Indeed, Brad articulates a very different ideal shopping experience: "Nothing pleases me more than being able to go in and out . . . know what I want, get it, nail it, check out and be in the car within fifteen minutes." Kerri laughs and says, "[he] gives me a little lecture before we go. 'We're just getting this.'" By contrast, Kerri approaches food shopping as a reflexive process. "I like to peruse the aisles. I like to read the labels. I like to think about stuff I've been learning about, and reading about, and researching," she explains. "But I would say that when I'm with you," she turns to Brad, "I don't look at them. I'm looking at more price when we're together."

Marissa makes clear that food is about much more than fuel. The 43-year-old, black project management consultant views food as the foundation for not only our personal well-being but also the well-being of our society and planet. For this reason Marissa describes ongoing efforts to "educate" her husband about the health and ethical issues related to food choices, particularly when it comes to eating meat. "At first he was just like, well, animals are there to be eaten," she says, describing how she tried to help her husband understand the relationship between human health and industrial livestock: "animals that are anxious all the time can't release any good thing in their bodies." Similarly, when her husband expressed disdain for the term "organic," Marissa responded, "let's not use the word organic in this house. Let's talk about slow grown." When asked if her husband currently expresses skepticism regarding her food beliefs, she says "mild, but he likes to keep me happy because that keeps him happy." Marissa laughs and continues: "But again, I think about the ethics to some extent, but him, not at all."

"I've always loved to cook," says Shannon. "To me, that's my therapy, my getaway." Yet, despite her love of cooking, food is a major stress in Shannon's life. A white single mother living on social assistance, she must devote immense time and energy in an effort to nourish her daughter on their very limited income. "I coupon big time," she explains. "I am definitely a spend-time-with-the-flyers-on-Thursday-night girl." Shannon has developed a range of strategies for making food last, but there are issues beyond her control that leave her frustrated. "It's sad that the stuff that takes more chemicals to produce is costing less than stuff that doesn't," she says. Shannon is concerned about the health and environ-mental impact of pesticides, hormones and antibiotics, as well as the "carbon footprint" of imported food. However, prioritizing local and organic products is not an option for her; instead, she must focus on meeting her daughter's basic nutritional needs. Shannon sighs: "Yes, there are better options out there and I would love to choose them, but I can't afford to cover them." She scoffs at public figures who declare their quest to live below the poverty line for a week. "You need to get these politicians to walk into a food bank and see how degrading that feels," she says. "It pushes us to make decisions we don't want to make."

Alyssa admits that, as an actor, she has to watch what she eats. Even still, she refuses to allow career pressures take the fun out of eating. "I don't want to miss out on really enjoying food because I have to stay small for being in thea-tre," she explains. The white 22-year-old has tried plenty of diets over the years and describes the Weight Watchers experience as "all these slaps on the wrist." By contrast, Alyssa says her current vegan diet facilitates pleasurable eating even as it allows her to maintain the body size she desires as an actor. She is delighted to have found an approach to healthy eating that means "I don't have to make sacrifices,'cause I love food so much!" Alyssa rejects her father's accusation that she has become body-obsessed and insists that she eats healthily by choice. "[My dad] is like, 'you think too much about what you put in your body,'" she says. "And it's like, Dad, do you not understand that I put things in my body that I want?"

Seated around Carmen and Peter's dining room table, the week's meal plan is visible on the wall. "All the planning is like having another part-time job," says Carmen (33, Chinese-Canadian), as she reflects upon the place of foodwork amid their hectic work schedules and caring for a 16-month-old son. While Peter is game to run from store to store gathering ingredients, the planning work is Carmen's territory. "I write up the list and then I send Peter on various missions," she explains. "But I also super micromanage everything." This goes for cooking, too. The couple describes how Carmen will plan and prep a meal and then email Peter detailed cooking instructions to begin when he gets home. "So he is kind of doing the cooking, but it is more like the assembling," she explains, adding, "We call it cooking through avatar." While this system generally serves them well, they have encountered a few road bumps. Carmen says, "I came home one time and there were instructions for a cauliflower soup. And he had poured out the water that the cauliflower had cooked in!" As their friends gasp, Peter says sheepishly, "It was the worst soup of all time." As Carmen continues, it is clear that the memory of this failed cooking project is getting her worked up all over again. "I went ballistic!" she says, her friends laughing. "It was insane, the level of my rage."

Kerri, Marissa, Shannon, Alyssa, and Carmen all care deeply about food. We heard their impassioned food stories when we held focus groups to explore the role of food in people's lives. At the outset of this research, we were not focused on gender. At a time when consumers are flooded with food advice—*Buy local! Cook from scratch! Teach your child where food comes from!*—we wanted to understand how people manage these wide-ranging food ideals in their everyday lives. We know from previous scholarship that food is closely connected to identity, joy, love, and struggle (e.g., de Solier 2013; Lupton 1996; Probyn 2000). Australian cultural studies scholar Deborah Lupton aptly describes food and eating as "intensely emotional experiences that are intertwined with embodied sensations and strong feelings . . . They are central to individuals' subjectivity and their sense of distinction from others" (1996: 36). We saw those themes in our focus groups, but what we had not fully anticipated was the striking significance of *gender* within these discussions. Food and gender have a long, interwoven history, of course, and we had explored themes of gender in our previous work on foodies (Cairns, Johnston, and Baumann 2010). However, we were surprised by the continuity with previous decades of feminist struggle in the stories we heard—a discovery that ultimately motivated us to write this book. Gender was not just a side in these food discussions—it felt like the main dish.

First, there was the issue of recruiting participants: when we put out the call for focus group hosts, we encountered many, many more women than men who wanted to talk to us (and their friends) about food. And then there was the content of the conversations. Carmen and Peter's story of "cooking through avatar" resonates with a trend that we heard repeatedly throughout these discussions: while many men were supportive with grocery shopping and cooking, women typically performed the *planning* work of researching and guiding family food decisions. When explaining this arrangement, many women told us that they simply *care more* about food, so it made sense for them to take the lead on things like making grocery lists, planning healthy meals, or teaching children about the environmental implications of their food choices. In fact, some said they *cared so much* about food that they actually enjoyed a lot of this food labor—or, at the very least, it was so important to their sense of self that they could not imagine *not* doing it.

Food was an emotional topic for many of the women we spoke to—a source of joy, guilt, hope, and anxiety. It was also a site in which they invested key aspects of their identities—as mothers and caregivers, health- and body-conscious eaters, informed foodies, and socially and environmentally committed citizens. In this research, we deliberately spoke with people who expressed an interest in food and recognize that others have a more casual relationship to their daily diet. We think that these stories of caring about food reflect a broader gender dynamic within a food-obsessed North American landscape, a dynamic that shapes both the standards that women face and the practices by which they struggle to embody them in their everyday lives. Studying food helps us understand contemporary standards for being a good mother, a responsible caregiver, a healthy woman, a discerning consumer, and an ethically mindful shopper—standards that do not always feel easy to achieve, particularly when money and time are tight.

As feminist scholars, we wanted to better understand the gendered dynamics and class inequalities reflected in these food discussions. These discussions were rarely straightforward and contained a blend of continuity and change. We spoke with men who were much more involved in foodwork than their fathers. In addition, many women described allocating tasks to their partners, and few women did *all* of the shopping, cooking, and clean-up. At the same time, many women felt personally responsible for food tasks in the household and experienced a pressure to handle food in ways that minimized risk and maxi-mized family health. This sense of responsibility generated strong feelings of guilt and shame for women when standards were unmet, as well as pride and joy when foodwork goals were achieved. It was these gendered observations that kept bringing us back to the following question: *Why do so many women care so much about food?* This question has led us to explore others. Which women get to care about food? Which ways of caring about food are most socially valued? How is the emotional experience of foodwork shaped by access to resources? How do poor women find ways to care through food when their choices at the grocery store are limited?

As we introduce this book, it is important to state that we ourselves care about food—not only in our personal lives but also as feminist scholars. We support struggles toward gender equality and do not believe that this requires women to reject the significance of food in their lives—to throw in the apron, so to speak. We certainly do not want to diminish the history of women's food labor, knowledge, and love in the kitchen. Although food is deeply personal, we see food as more than a matter of individual taste. Sociologically, food can be viewed as a lens into pressing questions in our contemporary world—questions about the inequalities fostered by corporate-dominated capitalist economies (Goodman et al. 2011; Guthman 2011; Nestle 2007), the struggle to promote well-being amid seemingly pervasive health risks (Lupton 1995; MacKendrick 2010; Murphy 2003; Szasz 2007), the shifting understandings of childhood and family (Beagan et al. 2008; Bugge and Almas 2006; Cairns et al. 2013, 2014; Cook 2009b) and the way toward a more environmentally and socially just future (Carolan 2011; Goodman et al. 2010; Johnston and Cairns 2012; Micheletti 2003). We propose that *caring about food* provides a starting point for engaging with these struggles, and we seek to contribute to a feminist food studies that builds from women's food identities and experiences.

Scholars have known for some time that food is a way for women to express their femininity (e.g., Avakian and Haber 2005; Beagan et al. 2008; Bordo 1993; DeVault 1991; Hollows 2003a; Inness 2001b). In the oft-repeated words of femi-nist food scholar Marjorie DeVault, "by feeding the family, a woman conducts herself as recognizably womanly" (1991: 118). In this book, we investigate the contemporary contours of this relationship. How are food and femininity connected today? Our interest in food includes the unpaid foodwork[2] that goes on in the home (and sustains capitalist economies), as well as the ways that food is consumed to construct an identity. Food is about getting the daily meal on the table, but it is also about expressing creativity, seeking pleasure, connecting with others, nourishing (and controlling) the body, and enacting politics. Throughout the book, we explore how these food practices are gendered and show how food femininities emerge in the context of intersecting dynamics of race and class privilege. Our research reveals that living up to feminine food standards is profoundly shaped by access to economic and cultural capital. Because food plays into so many aspects of women's lives, we theorize food femininities as multiple and performative, laborious and emotional, culturally articulated and embedded within material structures. Our goal is to make clear why food and femininity remain intricately connected topics that require open-minded kitchen table discussions as well as critical research.

In the next section, we pay homage to past feminist food research and raise new questions about the current moment of food and femininity. After situating our research in historical context, we outline our study and the chapters that follow.

1. Food, femininity, and feminism: A very brief history

> Women have [historically] been the caretakers of our stomachs. Men have cooked for aristocrats and kings, but it was women who devoted extraordinary energy to finding, growing, preparing, and serving food to the better part of the human race. (Schenone 2003: xii)

Ideas about food and femininity are not what they used to be. Some women reading this book may not consider themselves "caretakers" of anybody's stomach but their own. Still, the connection between women and foodwork has a striking degree of historical and cross-cultural consistency, especially in modern times. Sociologists Patricia Allen and Carolyn Sachs note that "in most societies women continue to carry the responsibility for the mental and manual labor of food provision" (2007: 1). Food and culture scholar Sherrie Inness writes, "Food and its preparation are strongly coded as feminine" (2001b: 1; see also Lupton 1996: 39; Schenone 2003: xii–xiii).[3]

Throughout much of modern Euro-American history, the idealized woman was one who cooked delicious, nourishing meals for her family, and maintained a smiling face in the midst of this domestic labor. In Colonial America, women's cooking was a necessity for survival. Writer Emily Matchar describes this as a time of "extreme DIY" where a largely rural population learned to make what they needed to get by (2013: 30). Even though foodwork involved drudgery, survival skills and repetition, historians suggest that Colonial women also saw it as a site of joy, pride, and empowerment, particularly since it was vital for many families' survival (Schenone 2003: 50–1). With capitalist industrialization, daily necessities gradually moved out of the household and into the industrial realm. With this movement, domestic cookery became less about producing all the daily necessities within the home and opened up a space for culinary distinction for white middle-class families. As men moved into the industrial workforce, a cultural dichotomy emerged where men "worked" outside the home and women stayed inside to "make" the home through domestic labors like cooking.

By the second half of the nineteenth century, Victorian women's domesticity was not just a separate sphere from men's labor but was put on a pedestal, associated with self-sacrifice and feminine purity. Domestic reformers believed that a shared ideal of feminine domesticity could provide an "antidote" to class difference (Shapiro 2001: 34–5), and teaching cooking was a key way that the "masses" could be "civilized." Describing the emerging programs to develop "scientific" cooking practices in public school, Shapiro writes that "[a] kind of democratic leveling was believed possible in the school kitchen, where the great rules and responsibilities that lay behind the perfect boiling of an egg were equally pertinent to females of all social classes" (2001: 135–6). Class differences invariably appeared, however, given the necessity for working-class women to labor outside their own home (Stansell 1987). Idealized domestic femininity was clearly most relevant to the middle- and upper-class woman, for whom the "most impressive duty was to make her home a heaven in miniature, herself the angel ready at the end of each day to receive and revive the weary worker" (Shapiro 2001: 14). Great pride was taken in the ability to host delicious meals with mouth-watering desserts, even if those dishes were, in fact, made by the hands of domestic servants (Dorfman 1992: 23; Inness 2001b; Levenstein 1988: 61).

By the twentieth century, an idealized connection between culinary standards and middle-class femininity was firmly established. Recipe books from the 1900s showed women "not only the right way to make tea sandwiches or decorate teacakes but also how to be feminine and ladylike" (Innes 2001b: 53). These recipes for femininity were clearly classed and raced, creating visible symbols of privileged white heterosexual femininity. At the same time, the connections between food and femininity reached beyond upper-middle-class white women, shaping the identities of women with less social power. As Innes (2001a: xi) aptly summarizes,

> For women without access to other forms of creative expression, preparing a superior cake or batch of fried chicken has been a way to display their talent in an acceptable venue. But foods and the stereotypes attached to them also have been used to keep women (and men, too) from different races, ethnicities, and social classes in their place.

To be clear, throughout modern Euro-American history, many women have felt locked into foodwork. Historically, women were largely unable to shift the burden of this daily labor to male members of the household, although privileged white women could transfer hands-on labor to a racialized serving class (Glenn 1994). While it is critically important to examine food as a source of oppression, it is also important to acknowledge that making delicious food—a pound cake or a piece of fried chicken—has also given women a source of meaning, power, and identity (Gantt 2011; Kelly 2001; Schenone 2003: xv; Williams-Forsom 2001: 179, 183).

Until relatively recently, women's domestic foodwork was a necessity for most eaters. Some processed foods became available in the 1920s (e.g., Wonderbread, Velveeta cheese, Gerber baby food), but a wide variety of mass-market, ready-to-eat foods did not appear on supermarket shelves until the 1950s, a decade when women were encouraged to develop their creativity in the kitchen but also use "modern foodstuffs" like "freeze-dried mashed potatoes" (Inness 2001b: 142). Reading through historic cookbooks, the level of assumed cooking knowledge would likely surprise the contemporary reader.[4] Ingredients were simply listed in vague terms, with the expectation that readers knew *how* to combine and cook them into a palatable dish (e.g., Schenone 2003: 61; Wellesley 1890). The imagined readers of these cookbooks were women, as Western men historically refrained from significant involvement in "unmanly" food-related tasks (L'orange 1997: 442). Men may have made the odd Sunday breakfast or barbecued burgers on the weekend (Adler 1981), but, by and large, the domestic kitchen was historically considered women's domain.

Gendered expectations about foodwork began to change in the 1960s and 1970s. The economic crisis of the 1970s made one-income families less viable and pushed more middle- and upper-middle-class women into the paid workforce.[5] At the same time, the second-wave feminist movement shook expectations about domestic work, including foodwork. Betty Friedan's famous text, *The Feminine Mystique* (1963), critiqued the idea of the "happy housewife"—an ideal fueled by the assumption that "women cook to please men" (O'Sullivan et al. 2008: 64). Friedan and other liberal feminists suggested that women's talents and energies were wasted in the home cooking dinner, a task associated with low status, low value, and low intelligence (Friedan 1963: 244–5).

There are two important caveats to this brief story of feminism, foodwork and women's paid employment. First, it is important to emphasize that feminism did not *cause* the demise of women's "from-scratch" cooking, nor did it push women into the workplace. Feminism offered women a language to critique inequitable domestic expectations, but certainly many women had embraced processed foods and disliked cooking long before feminism (Matchar 2013: 112–13; Shapiro 2004: 131–57). For example, Peg Bracken's bestselling *I Hate to Cook Cookbook* was first printed in 1960 and sold more than three million copies. The feminist movement did not kill women's love of cooking, but it *did* raise questions about the expectation that women should work outside the home and complete the mainstay of domestic work, including dinner preparation. The second important caveat to this story of second-wave feminism involves the intersection of gender, race, and class. Not all women were equally empowered by the second-wave feminist movement, which was predominantly white and middle class. Privileged women's entry into formal employment was, and continues to be, facilitated by the paid foodwork performed by working-class women and women of color—the nannies who prepare lunch, the fast-food workers who enable meals on the go, the lunch ladies who work in school cafeterias (Allen and Sachs 2007: 25; Glenn 1994).

Regardless of the role feminism actually played in women's relationship to cooking, the second-wave feminist movement came to be popularly understood as a flight from the home and the stove. As Matchar writes, "The idea of the feminist abandoning her children to TV dinners while she rushes off to a consciousness-raising group is unshakable" (2013: 112). Domestic work, including cooking, became linked to patriarchal oppression and emerged as the "Other" to feminism (Hollows 2007: 34). Not surprisingly, many feminist women developed an ambivalent relationship to foodwork, and a similar ambivalence developed within the academy. Avakian and Haber argue that until recently women's studies scholarship neglected cooking, "as if it were merely a marker of patriarchal oppression and therefore, not worthy of attention" (2005: 2). Not surprisingly, a love of cooking came to feel like a dirty secret for some feminist-identified women. Central to this ambivalence toward domestic cooking was its connection to inequitable gender relations. Arlie Hochschild's landmark sociological work, *The Second Shift* (2003 [1989]), documented the unpaid labor that women performed in addition to paid employment and pointed to the "stalled revolution" that kept full equality out of reach.[6] In her book, Hochschild aptly captured the pressure many women felt to earn a wage *and* clean the house, bathe the kids, and cook a delicious and nutritious dinner. Although women now worked outside the home, the feminist revolution had "stalled"—leaving women stressed, without "social arrangements that ease life for working parents" and lacking "men who share the second shift" (2003 [1989]: 13). Hochschild's research brought particular insight into the emotional strain women experience as a result of feeling primarily "responsible for home and children"—even those who were committed to ideals of gender equality.

While Hochschild's research exposed the emotional strain of women's enduring responsibility for domestic labor, Marjorie DeVault's (1991) research focused
specifically on issues of foodwork. In her classic work *Feeding the Family*,
DeVault documented the extensive, often invisible work that women put into
food preparation. Her research showed how this care-work is not just practical but works symbolically to constitute understandings of family and femininity.
DeVault argued that foodwork may be rewarding and meaningful for women,
but simultaneously "burdensome and oppressive" (1991: 232). Like Hochschild,
DeVault paid tribute to the meaning of domestic work for her research subjects
while simultaneously connecting women's domestic (culinary) labors to broader
issues of gendered social inequality. She suggested that women's unques-
tioned connection to foodwork may work at a structural level to inscribe women's
secondary status:

> A continuing identification of women as family cooks has consequences
> for equality at home that reach beyond the practical. It means that women
> continue to be the ones who take account of others in the household and who
> strategize about pleasing others, attending carefully to tastes so as to present
> a pleasing meal . . . It still seems relatively rare for men to cook for women in
> the same way that women cook for men—with assiduous attention to their
> needs and preferences, carefully working to please, day after day. This kind
> of asymmetry reinforces a gender distinction . . . Specifically, the gender rela-
> tions of feeding and eating seem to convey the message that *giving service*
> *is part of being a woman, and receiving it fundamentally part of being a man*.
> (1991: 234; emphasis ours)

When reviewing the classic works of Hochschild and DeVault, the question arises: Just how different are things today? At first glance, the Western
landscape of food and gender has clear markers of change. For one, it
has become culturally acceptable for men to show interest in food beyond
BBQ'ing; some men are avid cooks (Sobal 2005; Szabo 2013: 623). Men
self-identify as "foodies" and may spend considerable effort perfecting
their signature dishes (Cairns et al. 2010). Male chefs like Jamie Oliver and
Gordon Ramsay have become prominent food personalities, not just for their
role as professional chefs (a position long dominated by men) but also for
their enthusiastic interventions into everyday meal-making. At the same time
as men seem to be more involved in the domestic kitchen, women cook less
than they did in previous generations, especially as their formal labor participation has expanded and convenience food options have become readily
available.[7]

Despite significant shifts in the cultural and material connections between food and gender, important continuities persist. When it comes to celebrity chefs, there is still a sharp divide between the nurturing, home-focused female *cook* and an aggressive, professional male *chef* (Johnston et al. 2014; Naccarato and LeBesco 2012: 43–5). In home kitchens, women still do the majority of household labor within heterosexual relationships, including the two most time-consuming tasks: cleaning and everyday cooking (Lachance-Grezela and Bouchard 2010: 768; Szabo 2013: 624). Matchar reports that "women cook 78 percent of all home dinners, spend nearly three times as many hours on food related tasks as men, and make 93 percent of the food purchases" (2013: 26). Men do cook more than they did in the 1960s, but often specialize in leisure cooking, like weekend breakfasts or showcase meals for guests (Cairns et al. 2010; Szabo 2013: 624). Put differently, the second shift remains a reality for many women, and Hochschild's "stalled revolution" stills seems a salient description of the current gender landscape. In a Canadian study, food scholar Brenda Beagan and colleagues (2008) found that even as women rejected the idea that cooking is "women's work," the majority of the foodwork still tended to fall on their shoulders. To make sense of this distribution of labor, the women in their research gave alternate rationales, saying that they had higher food standards or greater interest in health than their male partners, or wanted to avoid the conflict that comes with asking family members for help.

While battles over foodwork simmer below the surface in many relationships, some women have reclaimed foodwork as a site of pleasure and empowerment. Instead of rejecting a homemade dinner as a sign of oppression, old-fashioned domestic skills—like canning, making jam, baking pies—have been reframed as hip, handy, and fun. As Emily Matchar explores in her book *Homeword Bound* in the late 1990s, "domestic DIY became hip again" (2013: 44), and cooking has been "subject to a total makeover" (2013: 100). In Matchar's words, "if a jar of home-canned tomatoes was once a sign of poverty, it now became a sign of an enlightened attitude toward food and the environment. If an apron was once a symbol of oppression, it was now a kitschy-cool reminder of the joys of cooking" (2013: 45). Responding to the same trend, *New York Times* writer Peggy Orenstein (2010) coined the term "femivores" (think feminist meets locavore) to describe the trend of educated, feminist-identified women who turn away from paid professional employment and embrace domestic homemaking and food provisioning in the spirit of sustainable consumption (think backyard chicken coop).

What are we to make of this resurgence of women's interest in cooking and food provisioning? It may appear like a simple, romanticized swing of the pendulum back to feminine domesticity, but this reclamation of the domestic realm has some important political and social underpinnings. Matchar argues that the "new domestics" have roots in third-wave feminist efforts to revalue femininity, as well as the "radical homemaker" movement of the early 2000s, where DIY projects had critical, proenvironmental, anticorporate underpinnings (2013: 43–4; see Hayes 2010). While the widespread interest in domesticity today may seem disconnected from these politicized projects, for many women the reskilling and revaluing of homemaking emerges from a critique of alienated workplaces and industrialized food systems and a desire to create lifestyles that are more sustainable and socially just. As the author of *Radical Homemaking*, Sharon Hayes, writes, "Making a commitment to cook sustainable, local foods for one's family, rather than relying on processed foods and take-out menus, entails re-attuning our palates and tastes . . . [and] the rebuilding of a food culture based on principles of ecological sustainability and social justice" (2010: 236–7).

While many projects for domestic reclamation involve a critique of capitalist economies and their alienating, sexist workplace cultures (e.g., Hayes 2010), this is not all that is at stake in contemporary feminine domesticities. Matchar points to a common moralizing undercurrent of contemporary appeals for healthier, sustainable ways of eating, which mourn the loss of (women's) home-cooked meals. This is a theme that feminists have critiqued in the writing of food guru Michael Pollan, who has linked feminism with the loss of cooking skills and the consumption of processed foods (Bowen, Elliott, and Brenton 2014; Hardin 2009; Hope Alkon 2013; Matchar 2013: 111; Szabo 2011). Yet as Matchar says, "[t]he historically inaccurate blaming of feminism for today's food failings implies that women were, are, and should be responsible for cooking and family health. And, unsurprisingly, women are the ones who feel responsible" (2013: 114). Even though Matchar's "new domestics" (2013) and Orenstein's "femivores" (2010) are clearly influenced by third-wave feminist insights, the renewed interest in home-cooking holds contradictory implications for the interplay between food, feminism and femininity.

Most critically, the contemporary interest in feminine domesticity has clear connection with popular currents of postfeminism. As we discuss in Chapter 2, the term "postfeminist" has become central to recent feminist cultural critique, although its meaning varies (Gill and Scharff 2011: 3). When we speak of postfeminism, we refer not to a periodization (i.e., something that comes *after* feminism), but rather a postfeminist "sensibility" that requires analytic interrogation (Gill 2007). A postfeminist sensibility takes the gains of feminist struggles for granted and assumes that gender equality has been achieved, rendering collective feminist movements passé (McRobbie 2004). Because we are all assumed to be equal players at the gender table, women are framed as individuals who freely "choose" to "empower" themselves with activities previously linked to femininity's subordinate status—including shopping and cooking. Work on postfeminism to date has focused on women's relationship to beauty and sexuality (e.g., Gill and Scharff 2011; Lazar 2009), but has not paid significant attention to foodwork (but see Hollows 2006). This gap needs to be addressed, particularly since individualism, choice, and empowerment are key themes in contemporary food discourse—themes we explore in the chapters that follow.

Food is commonly framed through the lens of individual choice: you can *choose* to eat healthily; a mother *chooses* to feed her baby organic food; a woman *chooses* to make dinner each evening because cooking is an activity she enjoys. This individualized framing appeals to a popular desire to experience agency, but draws attention away from the structural obstacles that shape and stratify individual food choices—especially in a neoliberal context where the state has transferred responsibility for food onto individual consumers (e.g., the expectation that mothers seeking to protect their children from pesticides and chemicals must purchase expensive organic produce; Cairns, Johnston, and MacKendrick 2013). In this context, women may prioritize cooking because they feel they alone are responsible for mediating a toxic and unhealthy food system and getting safe, healthy meals on the table. Indeed, Matchar's "new domestics" demonstrated a love for home-cooking but also a tremendous amount of fear when it came to the safety of the food system; in the words of one committed home-cook, "the only way to know what's in your food is to make it yourself" (Matchar 2013: 106).

*   *   *

In this first chapter, we have deliberately sought to introduce the story of women's foodwork in a broad-brush fashion, especially as gender inequities are so frequently glossed over in postfeminist culture. However, as the book proceeds, we shift from a general narrative to attend to the diverse ways that food and femininity come together in women's lives. Rather than viewing femininity as a singular phenomenon, we draw insight from feminist scholarship that challenges universalizing stories of gender and feminism. Women come to food from different social locations that emerge at the intersection of race, class, sexuality, and food history, in addition to personal interests and experiences. For example, Becky Thompson's classic work on food and eating issues, *A Hunger So Wide and So Deep* (1994), critiqued the extrapolation of white women's eating problems (e.g., anorexia) as though they were universal. Thompson's work not only brought in neglected perspectives—those of working-class women, women of color, and lesbians—but argued that eating problems were fundamentally linked to the systematic barriers that differentially positioned women experienced, such as racism and poverty. This differentiated view of women's food problems has been continued in more recent scholarship. For example, Saguy and Gruys' (2012) work on media depictions of eating disorders shows that thin, anorexic white bodies are more likely to be viewed as blameless "victims," whereas media depictions of fat bodies reinforce stereotypes about the slothful, out-of-control character of poor people and women of color.

Women do not relate to food in one universal way, and throughout the book, we explore a multiplicity of food femininities. As Gill and Scharff argue (2011: 12), speaking of *femininities*—in the plural—is a way to focus analysis on the construction and performance of gender and to avoid essentialism. While recent gender scholarship has yielded rich accounts of multiple masculinities, Gill and Scharff point toward "a relative lack of interest in femininities," as opposed to studies of "women and girls" (2011: 2). Their work highlights the need to treat masculinity and femininity as polyvalent concepts, rather than statements of an essential gender character. Eager to map out the diverse ways that women engage with food, we now turn to our study and the chapters that follow.

2. The study

We did not originally set out to study food and femininity. Our research for this book began with questions about how American and Canadian consumers negotiate food decisions in their everyday lives—what they eat, where, when and why they buy it, and how they think and feel about it. These questions arose from our interest in consumption and food politics and the growing pressure to consider the social and environmental implications of our food choices (Johnston and Cairns 2012). Josée had recently explored these questions through a survey distributed to 1,200 shoppers at grocery stores and farmers' markets throughout Toronto. This research provided a snapshot of some broad trends—for example, who buys local or organic foods, who identifies as a "foodie"—and inspired us to talk to people about how they think through these issues in their everyday lives, especially as they negotiate pressures of time, convenience or eating on a budget.

Our research was informed by a feminist, interpretive methodology that views participants' understanding of their everyday lives as a lens into broader structural processes (Reinharz 1992; Smith 1987). The participants engaged in our research were a fairly diverse group, although they were united by a common, special interest in and passion for food. Our entire sample included 129 food-oriented consumers, consisting of 89 focus group participants (69 women, 20 men) and 40 in-depth interviews with women (11 of whom were specifically targeted as prominent Toronto food activists). Of these participants, 31 were people of color and 98 were white, 79 were middle/upper middle class, and 50 working class/poor. Our sample also includes some variation along the lines of relationship status and sexual orientation: 77 participants identified as married or partnered, and 21 identified as gay, lesbian, bisexual or queer. Participants' age ranged from 20 to 70 years.

In terms of our research process, our first step was to carry out focus groups investigating everyday food perspectives (see Appendix B for focus group prompts). Focus group participants were selected through a combination of snowball sampling and purposive sampling. As a first step, we recruited focus group hosts through the initial survey as well as through postings in stores, community centers, and food-related listservs. We then asked that person to invite three to five friends or neighbors who might like to join a group discussion about food. Later, we complemented this snowball sampling with purposive sampling, in an effort to increase the representation of lower income participants in our study. In total, we conducted 20 focus groups that included 69 women and 20 men. Our focus group sample is not representative of the general population, especially since we specifically targeted those with a keen interest in food. However, we did talk with people from a range of class and racial/ethnic backgrounds, as well as different age groups and living arrangements, allowing us to gain insights into food practices and experiences emerging from various social locations (see Appendix A).

Holding the focus groups in participants' homes made for a relaxed, comfortable setting. Seated around the kitchen table or on couches in the living room, these discussions had the feel of a conversation among friends, often with plenty of laughter. We brought treats from a local bakery, and the host served tea or juice (or wine and beer in a few evening groups). Welcomed into people's homes, we had the opportunity to cuddle with cats, play with children, and admire backyard gardens. This setting also meant adapting to the stuff of life, unlike research conducted within a university office. One particularly memorable group involved three young mothers and their energetic toddlers, making for a slightly hectic discussion punctuated by frequent crying bouts and loud interruptions from the voice of a Cookie Monster doll under the table. On another occasion, the host's parrot landed on Kate's shoulder and remained there for several minutes of conversation. Rather than viewing these sorts of surprises as barriers in the data collection process, we felt that each new setting helped us get to know our participants better. We are extremely grateful to the hosts who welcomed us into their homes and to all of the participants who generously shared their food experiences, ideals, and struggles with us.

It was our feminist perspective that prompted us to organize the focus groups within preexisting social networks. Feminist scholars have promoted focus groups as a setting in which participants can raise issues for discussion, facilitating the co-construction of knowledge and providing opportunities for critical reflection (Pini 2002; Wilkinson 1998).[8] Our hope was that coordinating discussions among friends would not only foster a more comfortable research setting but also create the potential to generate meaningful conversation that could continue outside of our study. Participants frequently commented that they enjoyed the focus group experience and that they wished they had the chance to talk about these issues more often. As we were wrapping up the discussion at her house, Kerri said, "I think it's the one thing that everybody has an opinion on, is what we eat and you know, what we put into our bodies and how it affects us . . . And in a way, meeting with a group of people that we do know is kind of like, I've never been part of a book club or anything like that, but it was kind of like that." Her friend Brenda nodded and said: "We should do one of those once a month nights where we share food." Kerri's face lit up: "I think that's a great idea!" Brenda added, "because it was so much fun, honestly."

While the focus group inspired Kerri and Brenda to organize a monthly food night, these discussions were not all laughter and lighthearted conversation. Talking about food means probing into intimate aspects of daily lives, and this sometimes made for stories of struggle or awkward silences. Participants not only laughed together, but also consoled, supported, and reassured each other. For instance, when Tara (a single mother living on disability support) expressed guilt that she sometimes sends her teenage son to the grocery store when she is not feeling up to it, her friend Rosita suggested that this is providing him with valuable experience. In one group of close friends, three young women bonded over the shared experience of being told they were too "fat" by mothers and grandmothers, laughing lightly over what were clearly hurtful comments. In various other groups, participants who had immigrated to Canada connected through the shared feeling of longing for food experiences from "home," including ingredients that were either unavailable or prohibitively expensive in Toronto. There were also times when discussion became heated, such as the debate on food politics that erupted at Carmen and Peter's house. One member of this group espoused a very principled approach to food ethics and insisted that individual consumers have a responsibility to make ethical choices. (For instance, she stated that she only eats bananas when she is in countries where they are grown.) Others in the group critiqued this stance as an expression of privilege and argued for greater attention to race and class dynamics that shape available food options. Over the course of a 2-hour discussion, this same group of friends shared moments of both laughter and tension—a reflection of food's emotional salience in their lives.

In order to probe more deeply into women's personal food narratives, we followed up our focus groups with in-depth interviews with 40 women (who had not participated previously in focus groups). Eleven of these interviewees were targeted specifically as prominent Toronto-based food activists; the rest responded to our call for women living in Toronto who view food as significant to their identities, and we used purposive sampling to increase the representation of low-income women in our sample. When we distributed our call for participants through various food-related listservs, we were overwhelmed by the response. "Showing people that vegan food is delicious and beautiful brings me great satisfaction!" wrote one woman. "I would love to participate in the study as I am very passionate about nutrition (especially with kids) while being conscious of a budget and time constraints with a young family," wrote another. "I could probably talk to you for days about my relationship with food!" read yet another response. In addition to the sheer volume of potential participants, we were struck by the enthusiasm with which each woman responded to our research. These were women who cared deeply about food and who felt a strong desire to share their food stories.

To say that the women in this study all care about food is not to suggest that they relate to food in the same way. On the contrary, these women imbue food with distinct meanings that reflect their own identities, values and commitments. Carol told us that "healthy food means I'm being a good parent." For Alejandra, food "is culture, it's love, it's your roots." Bronwyn, a food activist, said that food is "a particularly amazing way to bring people together . . . gardens, markets, kitchens, food projects—they're all like staging grounds for new things to happen." Like others we spoke to, each of these women invests food with a distinct set of meanings that express central priorities in their lives. These meanings were not simply an outcome of personality differences, but were rooted in the particular opportunities and constraints of each woman's social location. For instance, while we saw some common meanings given to foodwork by mothers, these meanings were differently articulated depending on class position; working-class mothers seeking to promote their children's healthy development on a limited budget face a unique set of challenges when it comes to living up to standards that are generally set by upper-middle-class women.

While women give meaning to food in the context of their everyday lives, this meaning-making process is informed not only by social position and privilege but also by broader cultural discourses. In order to understand the kinds of messages that circulate about women and food today, we supplemented our interviews and focus groups with a discourse analysis of food blogs and magazines (see Appendix D for a listing of sources). Our participants' stories are at the center of this book, and we are careful to situate their lives within a particular geographic and historical context. We also want to contextualize their food narratives within a broader discursive landscape of popular media relating to food and femininity. We conducted this additional discursive research to allow us to better understand how idealized conceptions of food and femininity inform women's everyday food practices and identities.

3. The chapters ahead

The book is organized around key sites in the performance of food femininities: shopping, mothering, health and body, politics, and pleasure. These sites emerged inductively as research themes that speak to the ways food and femininity are connected in daily life. While they were not equally important for each woman we spoke to, these food femininities help us better understand the complex ways food and femininity are intertwined within contemporary consumer culture. Together, they tell a story of food as an essential part of constructing feminine identities.

The second chapter lays the theoretical foundations for the book and outlines the conceptual "toolkits" that inform our analysis. To analyze the connections between food and femininity, we pull from interdisciplinary perspectives, including gender studies and feminist theory; critiques of neoliberal governmentality; and sociological approaches to culture, consumption, and social change. In this chapter, we engage with theoretical debates that animate our research—debates about femininity, postfeminism and emotion, the lived experience of neoliberalism, and the tension between the politics and pleasures of consumption. Drawing from these theories, as well as the living, breathing world of women and food, we outline a social theory of *food femininities*.

In Chapter 3, we shift to our empirical research and explore the powerful feelings associated with the seemingly banal task of shopping for food. To our surprise, many women we spoke with emphasized the pleasurable aspects of

grocery shopping—a practice that fostered a sense of discovery, joy, and satisfaction. We suggest that the positive emotions tied to purchasing food reflect
cultural associations between consumption, femininity, and care (Johnston and
Cairns 2014). While food shopping is clearly a component of food labor, buying
food gives many women an opportunity for a kind of domestic leisure and also
signals their competence and ability to care for others. At the same time, the
emotional rewards accrued by the successful female shopper are far from
universal. For women living in poverty, grocery shopping is a stark reminder of
the difficulty of caring for one's family with limited resources. As so many women
in our study made clear, food and love are deeply connected in our cultural
renderings of femininity. To be denied access to good-quality food is not only a
material deprivation but a site for emotional struggle and gendered hardship.

Chapter 4 continues to explore the emotionally salient connections between
femininity and foodwork, but shifts to feeding children. This chapter features
mothers' creative efforts to sneak vegetables into kid-friendly dishes and to
socialize children to make "good" food choices. Analyzing diverse narratives
of nourishing and socializing children through food, we highlight the emotional
potency of maternal foodwork. Getting dinner on the table is not just a practical task, but involves a range of emotions that emerge from social standards of
"good" mothering as well as mothers' intense feelings toward their children. We
build upon feminist scholarship on intensive mothering and social reproduction
and show how many North American mothers face a new maternal ideal: raising
an "organic child" (Cairns, Johnston, and MacKendrick 2013). Many mothers in
our study described efforts to protect their children from harmful chemicals and
food additives and felt that this required careful, conscientious consumption.
Raising an "organic child" often resulted in feelings of stress and anxiety—
particularly among poor and working-class mothers who struggled to negotiate
these pressures on a limited budget. We demonstrate how the organic child
ideal is informed by neoliberal notions of individual responsibility, positioning
mothers as *personally* responsible for shielding their children from the risks of the
industrial food system. At the same time, we argue that critics must not dismiss
food-focused mothers as neoliberal dupes. Maternal discourse is constituted
through neoliberal logics, but is embodied and enacted through food traditions
that have deep roots within feminine and maternal identities.

In Chapter 5, we move from the foodwork of child-rearing to food and the
care of the self. Feminist scholars have long demonstrated how women are
constrained through dieting discourse and oppressive conceptions of the
female body. In this chapter, we explore the workings of a new healthy eating
discourse that we call the "do-diet," which frames women's eating through

a lens of empowerment and health, rather than vanity and restriction (Cairns and Johnston 2015). The term "do-diet" is drawn from *Chatelaine*, a Canadian women's magazine that offers advice on diet "do's" as opposed to "don'ts." This emphasis on healthy eating as a positive choice was frequently articulated by women in our study, who tended to eschew restrictive diets as a thing of the past and emphasized the intrinsic rewards of making healthy food choices. Yet, we demonstrate in the chapter that even as the do-diet emphasizes choice, this discourse still demands diligence, self-regulation, and corporeal control. This contradictory discourse is particularly challenging for women who encounter the do-diet from marginalized locations and face heightened fat-phobia and classed barriers to the idealized practice of "choosing health."

In Chapter 6, we explore another gendered site of caring through food, namely, making "ethical" food choices to express care for other beings and the environment. Here we engage with recent debates about making change in the food system—debates that have certainly involved women, but which curiously lack a feminist agenda (Allen and Sachs 2007: 5). Drawing from our conversations with women consumers and food activists, we examine how women think through the politics of food choices at an individual and a collective level. In past work, we have highlighted some of the tensions that are obscured by the dominant food narrative of "eating for change" (Johnston and Cairns 2012). We build on this work by analyzing gendered care-work that is demanded, but seldom acknowledged, in contemporary appeals to consumer food politics. Given that women are primarily responsible for food planning and shopping, the push to consume ethically tends to fall on their shoulders. Central to this process is a neoliberal conception of consumer politics that positions women as *individually* responsible for solving social and environmental injustices. Yet, we find that this issue is not simply resolved with a shift to collective food politics. Instead, our interviews with food activists reveal how the gendering of foodwork may be reproduced in the public sphere, where community gardens and food security projects are coded feminine and the realms of food policy and agricultural leadership are dominated by men. These divisions are also raced and classed, necessitating an intersectional investigation of how progressive efforts to change the food system may inadvertently reproduce structural divides.

In Chapter 7, we explore the complex relationship between femininity and food pleasure, focusing on the pleasures of eating and cooking. Pleasure occupies an ambivalent space in the landscape of food femininities. Given that femininity has historically been associated with personal sacrifice and dietary restraint, for women to openly pursue pleasure in food holds feminist potential. However, given its self-oriented connotations, pleasure rubs up against socially valued aspects of the femininities explored in previous chapters—food femininities characterized by care, self-control, and ethics. This can create tension for women who prioritize pleasurable food experiences, as seen in the experiences of female foodies. What's more, we examine the class-and-race dynamics that shape the performance of foodie femininities and thus complicate the feminist potential of embracing food's pleasures. In the second half of the chapter, we examine women's ambivalent relationship to cooking—an act historically associated with drudgery and oppression for many, but which has undergone something of a cultural makeover in recent years. We examine the gendered distinction between "everyday cooking" and "leisure cooking," as well as the struggle to find pleasure in foodwork when money and time are tight.

In the concluding chapter, we return to some of the big-picture issues that have arisen throughout the book. Drawing insight from our participants, we outline our vision of a feminist politics of foodwork. Priorities for moving forward include, first, a respect for the meaning that women find in food and a careful effort to avoid devaluing women's foodwork as retrograde. Second, and more ambitiously, a feminist politics of foodwork requires a commitment to structural critique and collective efforts to redress enduring inequalities. Privileged women must do more than enjoy the pleasures of food; they must think critically about what inequalities these pleasures reproduce and what injustices undergird their daily meals. Finally, building a feminist politics of foodwork also means forging greater connections between feminist movements and food movements, both within the academy and beyond. This is by no means a modest menu, but our ambition is inspired by the passion we witnessed in our conversations with women—women who differed from each other in many ways, but who all emphasized how deeply they cared about food.

Notes

1. The "mainstreaming" of foodie culture is widely noted. Krashinsky (2013) notes the influence of foodie trends on mainstream foods and grocery stores, and Hadlock (2013) discusses a "nation obsessed with food" and suggests that half of the American population identifies as foodies.
2. In this book, we do not look at women's paid work in food production. For an overview of this literature, see Allen and Sachs (2007: 6–9). We use the term "foodwork" to refer to all of the labor that goes into procuring and preparing food, including food shopping, cooking, and clean-up, as well as the mental and emotional labor of writing lists, planning meals, and ensuring that others' needs are met.
3. While there are strong cross-cultural and historical connections between women and foodwork, we do not want to diminish the complexity or the variety of these

relationships. Even the classic assumption of premodern societies—that women gather and men hunt—has been problematized in key anthropological texts (e.g., Bodenhorn 1990; Brightman 1996).

4. We acknowledge that it is difficult to know how these early cookbooks were used (and by whom). See Short's study of British home-cooking (2006), where she cautions against a romanticized view of historical cooking that sets up contemporary cooks as hopeless and unskilled.

5. While white women started to work more outside the home in the 1960s and 1970s, it is important to note that black women (including middle-class black women) had a longer history of working outside the home (Matchar 2013: 40).

6. While Hochschild's work was exceptionally influential, socialist feminists had offered an earlier gender critique of domestic work and identified the necessity of social reproduction for the functioning of the larger capitalist economy (e.g., Luxton 1980).

7. Compared to the 1960s, women today do significantly less cooking and food clean-up. In the United States, the number of hours spent on cooking and cleaning-up each week was 13.8 in 1965 and only 5.5 in 2011. For men, this number increased slightly from 1.8 hours in 1965 to 2.2 hours in 2012 (Bianchi et al. 2000; US Bureau of Labor Statistics 2012). Of course, this work has not simply disappeared but has shifted to more marginalized women. As Allen and Sachs write, "much of the preparation and serving of food has now been transferred from women's reproductive labor into the home to other women, often poor women of color, who prepare food in processing plants, grocery stores, and restaurants" (2007: 4). A full 77 percent of US food workers are women, and many are in precarious, part-time positions; significantly, women make up less than 20 percent of jobs as head cooks and chefs (2007: 7–8).

8. Our approach was similar to food scholar Meredith Abarca's (2007) "Charlas Culinarias" ("Culinary Chats"), a concept she developed through research with working-class Mexican women in their kitchens.

Chapter 2

Thinking through food and femininity: A conceptual toolkit

In this chapter, we outline the core concepts that inform our thinking throughout the book and help us to understand shifting dimensions of food and femininities. We hope this chapter will appeal to readers with an interest in gender, food, and consumption scholarship. This chapter is theoretical, but not disengaged from "real" food struggles and experiences. We follow food sociologist Michael Carolan's perspective on "lived experience," which challenges scholars to "*enliven* social theory by injecting living, breathing, feeling bodies into social methods and conceptual frameworks" (2011: 9).

Our theoretical approach draws inspiration from French philosopher Michel Foucault's metaphor of a theoretical "tool box" (1994a: 523), as well as Anne Swidler's (2001) notion of a cultural toolkit that people draw from to give meaning to their lives. Just as the participants in our study draw upon available cultural toolkits to navigate the relationship between food and femininity,[1] we use an interdisciplinary range of theoretical resources in our analysis. Below we outline three distinct but related conceptual toolkits that we draw upon throughout the book. The first toolkit involves concepts we employ for theorizing food femininities. The second toolkit theorizes the emotional dimension of our relationship to food and femininity in neoliberal times. The third toolkit conceptualizes femininity in relation to food's dual role as a source of social status and a catalyst for social change. We engage with feminist scholarship throughout, including theoretical approaches to femininity, embodiment, emotion, care-work, and social reproduction. Our intended contribution is to weave these ideas together in new ways and to make explicit how these concepts can illuminate the shifting landscape of food and femininity.

1. Food femininities: Embodied ways of doing gender

In their introduction to *New Femininities*, British cultural theorists Rosalind Gill and Christina Scharff articulate their efforts to "open up questions about the ways in which gender is lived, experienced and represented" (2011: 2). They suggest that "speaking of 'femininities' [in the plural] is a way of highlighting the social production and construction of gender and avoiding essentialism" (2011: 2). Embracing Gill and Scharff's approach in this book, we examine how femininities are enacted through food ideals and practices, building on research documenting long-standing associations between food and femininity (e.g., Charles and Kerr 1998; Devault 1991; Inness 2001; Lupton 1996; Swenson 2009). This leads us to the following question: How are femininities—in the plural sense—enacted, reinscribed, and contested through contemporary food practices, like shopping, cooking, eating, and feeding others?

We explore this question in this section by drawing from feminist theories of embodiment, the idea of "doing gender" as a social practice, as well as theories of power, consumerism, and postfeminism. (In our third toolkit, we incorporate additional insights from socialist feminist traditions exploring the political economy of care-work.) These theories help us understand how gendered food patterns are embedded in institutions and material structures, as well as daily routines, emotions, and body practices. Together, they crystallize into *food femininities*, which we conceptualize as the food-specific ways feminine subjectivities are embodied and enacted in daily life. Food femininities are not singular or static, but multifaceted and evolving expressions. Some women may incorporate food within a femininity oriented toward corporeal restraint and body work oriented toward thinness. Other femininities are constructed through foodwork that communicates love and care through home-cooked meals. These are not bounded, internally coherent performances. Rather, women must negotiate multiple competing feminine ideals in their daily food practices, a finding in keeping with Jennifer Carlson's (2011) contention that contemporary femininity is fundamentally multiplicitous, fragmented, and expansive.[2] Our research reveals how women enact multiple, and sometimes contradictory, food femininities as they express their own complex relationship to food—one that weaves together personal tastes, familial obligations, political commitments, and body projects, to name just a few of the emotionally charged sites where food and femininity meet.

Doing gender and embodied food practices

In our analysis of food femininities, we approach gender not as something that we possess but as something that we *do*. The concept of "doing gender" was developed in a seminal work by American sociologists Candace West and Don Zimmerman in 1987, to theorize gender as an ongoing practice that is performed in everyday life.[3] While this concept has received a number of important critiques,[4] we believe that drawing analytic attention to the link between gender and social practice continues to have tremendous relevance, especially given recent arguments regarding the utility of practice theory (see Shove et al. 2012). Thinking of gender as something we enact through daily practices helps debunk the idea of gender as a fixed identity, or a biological output. The concept of "doing gender" illuminates how femininity (and masculinity) is a social achievement shaped by social interaction and affirmed through institutions and structures. In short, we argue that food practices, ideals, and habits[5] are key facets of the way we "do gender" on a daily basis.

Food is a key part of the way we "do" or "perform" gender, but this does not mean that gendered food practices are always well thought out or deliberately rehearsed. Rather, many feminine practices become so engrained in our ways of being and relating in the world that we are often unaware of them (e.g., Blair-Loy 2001; Ridgeway 2009). Further, to say that gender is socially constructed is not to suggest that there is no connection to physical bodies. To the contrary, doing gender frequently occurs through embodied practices (Messerschmidt 2009: 86–7). Femininity, more specifically, is enacted through all sorts of corporeal cues and practices related to food and eating. Think here of our food cravings and habits (e.g., do we order a salad or chicken wings?), the way we hold our posture (letting our stomach relax, or pulling it in?), the embodied labor of cooking a meal or the pleasures and anxieties we associate with food (e.g., how comfortable are we facing an empty fridge, or a child who refuses to eat the meal we prepared?). While the body is irrefutably connected to femininity, biological sex does not determine the femininities we enact in daily life or the femininities available at a collective cultural level.

Our sociological approach to food femininities examines the connection between individual interactions and broader gender regimes. When we "do gender" through food, we are performing femininity at an interpersonal level, but we are also interacting with social structures and institutions (West and Zimmerman 2009: 114). As we discuss later, the food femininities explored throughout this book are situated within a capitalist economy where women are disproportionately responsible for social reproductive labor (Armstrong and Armstrong 2001; Ferguson 1999; Fox 1988). Here, it is useful to remember that structures are not anonymous, distant forces but are constituted through gendered ideals and practices. Ridgeway and Correll emphasize the significance of "gender beliefs" in the reproduction of social structure, which, drawing from Sewell (1992), they understand as "jointly constituted" by "cultural rules or schemas" and "distribution of resources" (2004: 511).

Thus, while food femininities are enacted through embodied interactions in everyday life, these interactions unfold in specific social-structural contexts and involve a complex interplay of cultural schemas and material resources. For example, we may perform femininity by ordering salad or sushi, dishes that are often culturally coded as feminine for Western eaters (Lupton 1996: 104–11; McPhail et al. 2012). This seemingly individual taste preference is connected to myriad gendered structures and institutions (e.g., media depictions of gendered food tastes, gendered workplace cultures). Similarly, women may derive emotional rewards from feeding family members, but the fact that women are more often responsible for this foodwork is clearly linked to the gendered organization and hierarchies of labor markets (Gupta et al. 2010; Lachance-Grzla and Bouchard 2010: 771–2). What's more, the performance of food femininities will vary in different institutional settings that hold us distinctly "accountable" for our gendered conduct (West and Zimmerman 2009: 114). In certain settings, we may be able to redo gender in ways that deviate from dominant cultural schemas about femininity (e.g., at a potluck with women's studies students). In other contexts, compliance with dominant expectations may be required to establish an accountable gendered self (e.g., baking cupcakes for a child's party; see Ridgeway 2009: 151). This raises the following question: In what circumstances do food practices allow women to do gender in ways that reproduce, or *disrupt*, hegemonic gender scripts? (2009: 150).

Hegemonic femininity and power

In this book, we are interested in the performance of food femininities in all of their complexity and multiplicity, including the way gender scripts are challenged. At the same time, we also seek to understand how and where power congeals: How are food femininities shaped by *hegemonic* gender ideals? Here we draw insight from Raewyn Connell's (1995) concept of hegemonic masculinity, which has been hugely influential within gender studies and which highlights the need to study not just gender difference but gendered forms of power. As Deutch writes, "[m]en have more say, and they get more money, more attention, more interesting work, more status, and more leisure. Masculine pursuits are given greater value" (2007: 117). While there has been little research into hegemonic femininity to date (Gill and Scharff 2011: 4; but see Pyke and Johnston 2003; Scharff 2007), we argue that the concept is useful for theorizing food femininities.

Connell states that "hegemonic masculinity is not a fixed character type, always and everywhere the same. It is, rather, the masculinity that occupies that hegemonic position in a given pattern of gender relations" (1995: 74). Thus, hegemonic masculinity is fundamentally *relational* (Connell and Messerschmidt 2005: 848). Building on this approach, we understand femininity to be constructed in relation to masculinity and within the context of particular institutional arrangements that reproduce gendered power differences, such as the heterosexual nuclear family. Connell argues that femininity can never be hegemonic, given that it is always subordinate to masculinity (Connell and Messerschmidt 2005: 848). While we understand this point, we believe that a theory of hegemonic femininity has analytic merit, especially if we think of hegemony in neo-Gramsian terms—as the way inequalities are rationalized and made commonsensical. We find the concept of hegemonic femininity useful for theorizing feminine identities in relation to broader power hierarchies. Here, we build on Mimi Schippers' call to put femininity "back into" the analysis, "without losing Connell's invaluable conceptualization of hegemonic masculinity" (2007: 89).

The defining feature of hegemonic femininity is its relation to an unequal gender order where power is inequitably distributed. As Schippers states, "Features of masculinity and femininity provide the hegemonic scaffolding for relationships between men and women as 'naturally' and inevitably a relationship of dominance and submission" (2007: 91). Schippers argues that not all aspects of femininity are hegemonic (2007: 97)[6]; rather, she defines hegemonic femininity as "the characteristics defined as womanly that establish and legitimate a hierarchical and complementary relationship to hegemonic masculinity" (94). In our research, we seek to identify how food practices are shaped by and sustain hegemonic expressions of femininity. At the same time, we argue that food femininities are not *necessarily* hegemonic; not every performance of food femininity upholds an inequitable gender order. In fact, we believe that food practices are a potential site through which to resist hegemonic gender beliefs (think here of a woman who reclaims the BBQ as a site of culinary pride and pleasure, or a father who does the daily grind of making meals with young kids underfoot). Nevertheless, hegemonic femininity can hold significant appeal as it becomes entrenched in common sense. Throughout the book we show how the performance of hegemonic food femininities can engender social and emotional rewards for women—as seen in positive evaluations of the "good mother" who carefully monitors and regulates her child's diet. At the same time, femininities become hegemonic precisely because they serve to uphold patriarchal relations of power—such as the expectation that women are "naturally" caring and thus primarily responsible for the labor of social reproduction, prioritizing the needs of others before their own needs.

Together, Connell and Schippers show how particular ways of doing gender are rendered hegemonic—made to seem natural, desirable, and common sense within particular contexts, and in ways that legitimize or obscure unequal gender relations. Adding to this understanding of gender hegemony, Cecilia Ridgeway contends that certain "rules" of gender become hegemonic when (1) they are institutionalized (e.g., enshrined in mass media or work structures), and (2) the content of these beliefs is put forward as universal, even though it represents the experiences of dominant groups (i.e., "white middle-class heterosexuals"; 2009: 149–50). Throughout the book, we examine how women negotiate the relationship between hegemonic food femininities idealized as "natural" and "universal" and the gendered food practices they manage in daily life. We find that food is deeply implicated in the construction of hegemonic femininities linked to care-work, maternal devotion, and bodily discipline. At the same time, we identify multiple instances where food is used to push back at gender hegemony—to carve out space for counterhegemonic femininities that resist masculine power and to contest harmful aspects of hegemonic femininity, like compulsory thinness or perpetual self-sacrifice.

While this book centers on food femininities, our analysis cannot be limited to power enacted through gender relations. Instead, we situate the performance of food femininities within wider power inequalities. Because dynamics of race, class and sexuality afford different opportunities for doing gender in relation to food, an intersectional approach to inequality is essential. This means not just including women from different subject positions, or avoiding the long-standing tendency to see white, middle-class women's experiences as universal. It also means unpacking the intersectional relations that shape the way femininity is understood and experienced (see Choo and Ferree 2010: 145). As Schippers insists, hegemonic femininity should not be posited as a universal constant, but should be empirically investigated in specific contexts, paying careful attention to how it is "refracted through race and class difference" and may be "folded in to support race and class hegemony" (2007: 99).

An intersectional approach to food femininities requires interrogating how hegemonic femininities privilege some women while restricting, shaming or marginalizing others. Food is used to construct femininity in multiple domains (e.g., through shopping, mothering, body work), and these feminine practices are refracted through patriarchal[7] gender beliefs as well as institutionalized racism and class inequality. The intersection of multiple systems of inequality means that hegemonic food femininity is simultaneously a site of privilege and oppression. This raises questions like the following: How do "ethical" shopping spaces like farmers' markets feel more or less inviting to women depending on their race and class position? How do gender, race, and class intersect in the search for an "authentic" dining-out experience? How do cultural constructions of the "good mother"—a woman who feeds her children the freshest, healthiest, organic home-cooked foods—assume access to cultural and economic resources? Carrying out the research for this book, we were particularly struck by how social class enables and confines the performance of food femininities. Often, this axis of inequality was signaled not simply through the "facts" of widely varying grocery budgets but through expressions of *emotion*—feelings of entitlement and disgust in a discount supermarket, or the anger that comes from not being able to afford quality food for family meals. Throughout the book, we show how analyzing emotion in women's food narratives generates new insights into the lived experience of class privilege and constraint (see Pugh 2013).

To fully understand the emotional landscape of food femininities, we need to briefly unpack two ideological contexts that fundamentally shape hegemonic food femininities—consumerism and postfeminism.

Femininity, consumerism and postfeminism

Understanding food femininities requires an analysis of consumerism, an ideology that promotes commodity consumption as a primary means for crafting identity and achieving the "good life." Among the core elements of consumerism is the enduring association between shopping and femininity (Currie 1997; Williams 2006: 147; Zukin 2004: 35–62). Critical scholars of consumer culture have shown how the association between femininity and consumption was historically articulated in negative terms: irrational consumer femininity was defined in opposition to the (masculine) rational consumer ideal (Slater 1997: 34; see also Zukin and Maguire 2004: 175). These cultural associations of femininity bolster the stereotype of the woman shopaholic, mindlessly stockpiling purses and shoes. Not surprisingly, women can and do feel ashamed and pathologized for shopping—at the same time they continue to feel responsible for getting the shopping done.

While the link between consumption and femininity has detrimental conno
tations, when we look specifically at the feminine *food* shopper, a more
nuanced picture of hegemonic femininity and consumerism emerges. The
female food shopper is socially valorized as a nurturing figure, somebody who
carefully researches the best values and brings home nutritious food for loved
ones. While women's self-oriented consumption has been pathologized as
indulgent and illogical, women's caring consumption can be constructed as
"educative and transforming" (Miller 1997: 38) and is designed to "fulfill moral
obligations" (Zukin 2004: 30). More specific to food, women's shopping can
fruitfully harness the pleasure of "good" food, especially if these goods (e.g.,
local apples, organic broccoli) are seen to have social and environmental
payoffs (Biltekoff 2013: 87–8). In Chapter 3, we show how food shopping
facilitates the performance of consumer femininities that align with cultural
ideals of familial care, rather than socially disparaged schemas of feminine
consumer indulgence. Throughout the book, our focus on multiple food femininities allows us to explore how food consumption is constructed through
distinct but interrelated landscapes of care and responsibility—ideals that are
deeply gendered. These include self-care and work on the body, familial care-
work in the domestic sphere, and caring for distant others through ethical
consumption in a global food economy. Conversely, the cultural connections
among consumption, care, and femininity can engender strict penalties for
women who are excluded from this hegemonic ideal. For instance, Elaine
Power has shown how single mothers living on welfare are stigmatized as
"flawed consumers"—a pathologized femininity that emerges at the intersection of gender and class (2005: 651).

In addition to analyzing the gendered dynamics of consumerism, our
understanding of food femininities also interrogates contemporary currents of
postfeminism. As Gill (2007) and other feminist scholars have noted, a postfeminist "sensibility" valorizes women's agency and choice (Gill and Scharf 2011:
4), but is characterized by the "double entanglement" of feminist and antifemi-
nist ideas (McRobbie 2004: 256). British feminist Angela McRobbie argues that
"post-feminism positively draws on and invokes feminism as that which can be
taken into account, to suggest that equality is achieved, in order to install a
whole repertoire of new meanings which emphasise that it is no longer needed"
(2009: 12). Thus, while celebrating feminist ideals of empowerment, postfeminism works ideologically to suggest that gender oppression is a thing of the
past, as contemporary women are free to exercise agency through their personal
"choices"—that is, the *choice* to eat an organic, vegan diet or to cook nightly
dinners for loved ones. How are these seemingly personal choices shaped by

hegemonic gender ideals? How are they refracted through dynamics of race, class and sexuality?

An important outcome of the postfeminist focus on individual choice is a shift away from collective understandings of feminism as a social movement struggling for social justice. British feminists Jessica Ringrose and Valerie Walkerdine argue that in the context of postfeminism it has become "difficult to formulate feminist critiques capable of reading both a class and gender analysis of 'oppression' back onto this supposed easy and celebratory 'feminization' of consumption and desire" (2008: 231). Existing scholarly critiques of postfeminism have focused primarily on media and popular culture (Banet-Weiser and Portwood-Stacer 2006; Gill 2007; Hollows 2003; McRobbie 2004; Salvio 2012) and have usefully demonstrated how a postfeminist sensibility reframes (hetero)sexual attractiveness as a site of empowerment. We contribute to critical literature on postfeminism by exploring how women negotiate postfeminist ideals of consumer choice, pleasure, and individual empowerment through food, keeping in mind feminist goals of collective action, solidarity, and social change. Can women derive pleasure from *choosing* to labor in the kitchen, when domestic foodwork has historically constituted a site of gender oppression? Are women free of the pressures associated with feminine body ideals if they are equipped with a critique of the diet industry? Throughout the book, we explore how women engage with, negotiate, and sometimes reject postfeminist ideals as they negotiate food femininities.

Calibration: The balancing act of food femininities

While a postfeminist sensibility suggests that women are now empowered to choose freely in their everyday food practices, our research reveals the subtle, yet powerful, regulatory pressures surrounding the performance of food femininities. Throughout our focus groups and interviews, we were struck by a remarkably consistent theme: an aversion to extremes. When discussing a variety of food topics, women worked to present a moderate relationship to food ideals and were careful to distance themselves from displays of excessive commitment. For instance, when describing their healthy eating practices, women frequently told us that while they are health conscious, they are not "obsessive" in their food choices. Similarly, mothers emphasized that while they carefully monitor and regulate what their kids eat, they are not "crazy" in their approach to feeding children. Ethical consumers insisted that while they are conscientious, they are not "fanatical" about the politics of their purchases. Analyzing these narratives, we identify a recurrent practice of discursive positioning that we call *calibration*. By calibration, we refer to the process through which women actively nego-tiate hegemonic food femininities and position themselves as reasonable, informed, and moderate.

Calibration is not just about the common tendency to position oneself within the "middle ground." We argue that calibration is analytically and politically significant because it reveals the sharp boundaries surrounding food feminini-ties and persistent gendered social pressures. Food is a culturally valued site for the performance of femininities, but our research suggests that there is a thin line between hegemonic and pathologized femininities. As a result, the woman who seeks to enact a hegemonic food femininity (e.g., the caring mother and consumer, or the health-conscious shopper) must tread lightly to avoid associa-tion with feminized pathologies (e.g., the over-involved mother, the obsessive health nut or the self-righteous ethical consumer). As feminine figures character-ized by irrationality and a loss of control, these pathologized femininities can be understood as contemporary articulations of the "hysterical" woman of history (Moore 2010: 108).

Despite significant social change in past decades, women continue to feel scrutinized and judged for their relationship to food. Under the social microscope, it is not enough for today's woman to simply care about food. She must hit the "sweet spot," enacting a hegemonic femininity that shows she cares about food but does not care *too* much. A woman who is health- and body-conscious, but able to enjoy a piece of birthday cake without obsessing over calories. A woman who makes organic meals for her toddler, but does not freak out if he eats a hot dog at his grandmother's house. The concept of calibration draws attention to patriarchal processes that make the performance of hegemonic femininity difficult to fully enact, involving a constant balancing act of effort, restraint, and self-consciousness. Given the fine line between hegemonic and pathologized femininities, it is not surprising that food generates strong emotions in women's daily lives.

2. Feeling neoliberalism

Our second conceptual toolkit situates gendered food practices within a broader context of neoliberalism. While the term "neoliberal" has been used so widely (and sometimes vaguely) that it risks losing meaning, we argue that there are important reasons to retain this term. Most pressingly, the ideology of neoliberalism—with its idealization of market relationships and aversion to collectivist state interventions—continues to shape societal relations globally. Geographer and social theorist David Harvey provides a useful definition of this term:

> [neoliberalism is] in the first instance a theory of political economic practices that proposes that human well-being can best be advanced by liberating individual entrepreneurial freedoms and skills within an institutional framework characterized by strong private property rights, free markets, and free trade. (2005: 2)

Neoliberal ideas operate ideologically when they obscure the structural underpinnings of inequality (e.g., blaming poverty or sickness on moral failure) or offer market-driven solutions that naturalize corporate interests while jettisoning state regulation (Cairns and Sears 2012: 67).

In this book, we examine how neoliberal imperatives come to structure feminine subjectivities: put simply, how the entrepreneurial neoliberal self takes on a specifically feminine form. Our goal is to illuminate distinctly *gendered* aspects of neoliberal governmentality. Situating our analysis of food femininities within a neoliberal political-economic context, we pay particular attention to dominant discourses emphasizing self-reliance, consumer choice, flexibility, and individual responsibility.

To make the connection between neoliberalism and everyday emotions and embodiment, we draw from Foucault's work connecting power operations to the body in late modernity (1977, 1982, 1994b). In Foucault's groundbreaking conceptualization, power was not simply about *repressing* bodies but was itself *embodied*. Power relations are seen as "having an immediate hold on [the body]; they invest it, train it, torture it, force it to carry out tasks, to perform ceremonies and to emit signs" (Foucault 1977: 25). Extending this conception of power as productive and embodied to the context of neoliberalism, scholars have drawn insight from Foucault's (1991) concept of governmentality (e.g., Cairns 2012; Dean 1999; Rose 1999). Governmentality studies explore how conduct is shaped not only by formal political rationalities but also by the mundane ways individuals govern themselves in everyday life (Foucault 1994b). Neoliberal governance operates through technologies of "responsibilization" that download collective responsibility for health, well-being, and happiness onto self-regulating individuals (Cruikshank 1996; Lupton 1999). Thus, neoliberal governance is not externally imposed onto bodies, but operates *through* the embodied actions of the free subject—often through market mechanisms or actors. For example, the self-governing subject purchases organic foods to protect her children against food system risks (MacKendrick 2010, 2014). To fight breast cancer, she regularly eats broccoli and participates in a corporate-sponsored "run for the cure" (King 2012).

While governmentality studies emphasize embodied surveillance and discipline, neoliberalism also operates at the level of emotion, as structural problems are individualized as private burdens to be managed through work on the self (Cairns 2013; Cairns, Johnston, and MacKendrick 2013; Illouz 2008). Drawing from women's food stories, in the chapters that follow we analyze the *emotional and embodied* dimensions of neoliberal discourses—how they come to be understood in daily life as part of one's caring, respectable self. The emotional resonance of neoliberalism can be seen in the anxiety, guilt, and frustration experienced by many mothers who feel they are individually responsible for protecting their children from harmful food additives and chemicals—a responsibility that they manage through careful, informed, and expensive food purchases. We want to emphasize, however, that neoliberal discourses are not always experienced as oppressive and constraining in the performance of food femininities; consider, for instance, the feelings of satisfaction and pride that may result from actively promoting one's health through careful food choices. Given that conceptions of feminine agency are constituted through available discourse, the neoliberal invitation to express agency through food choices can yield emotional rewards in women's lives—particularly in the context of a postfeminist sensibility that promotes "choice" as the key to feminine empowerment.

In short, theorizing the embodiment of neoliberalism requires attending not only to *work on the body* performed by the self-regulating subject but also to the *felt experience* of neoliberalism in everyday life. While emotions are commonly understood to reside within the individual, we draw insight from feminist scholars who explore emotions as "collaboratively constructed and historically situated, rather than simply as individualized phenomenon located in the interior self" (Boler 1999: 6). From this perspective, emotion provides a lens on the ways neoliberalism is experienced, reproduced, and challenged through everyday food choices, habits, and labor. This approach avoids rationalist binaries of cooptation and resistance and draws attention to the connection between lived experience and "big picture" questions of oppression and inequality.

Throughout the book, we demonstrate how feminist perspectives can support an analysis of the embodied dimensions of neoliberalism—one that incorporates Foucauldian insights, but avoids an overly deterministic analysis that straightforwardly manufactures disciplined subjects. We think of this totalizing tendency as a kind of "Foucault Machine": the analyst identifies a social agent and (unsurprisingly) discovers disciplined subjects (Cairns and Johnston 2015; Johnston and Cairns 2013).[8] While we are wary of the Foucault Machine tendency toward theoretical determinism—that is, input empirical data and churn out preset governmentality explanation—our own research suggests that Foucauldian insights on neoliberalism's productive power cannot be easily dismissed (Cairns 2013; Cairns, Johnston, and MacKendrick 2013; Johnston and Cairns 2013).

Indeed, our interviews and focus groups suggest that neoliberal discourses *do* have a powerful presence in women's consciousness, especially in relation to everyday food habits. At the same time, women are not passive dupes of some neoliberal leviathan. We demonstrate how women engage with neoliberal discourse through the process of calibration, whereby women negotiate food femininities while avoiding pathologized extremes. Feminist Foucauldian scholarship has made the important contribution of theorizing subjectivity formation as a socially situated process, analyzing how neoliberal discourse is negotiated in the context of gendered, classed, and racialized relations of power (Cairns 2013). Our analysis of food femininities shows that embodying neoliberalism involves an ongoing and emotionally demanding process of calibration—a process where women must concurrently maximize their consumer choices while exhibiting self-control.

In sum, while drawing upon Foucauldian insights about discourse and power, our emphasis on *feeling neoliberalism* facilitates a feminist analysis of the way women negotiate the contradictory discourses available to them, allowing for resistance, complexity, and even change. This feminist approach is also attuned to the significance of social location, as we speak to women with varying degrees of agency in the food system—women as consumers with varying access to resources and also women who perform food femininities as public-sphere actors and activists.

3. Consuming status/Eating for change

In our third toolkit, we draw out the connections between food femininities and two seemingly disparate realms of food scholarship: food as a source of status and distinction and food as a catalyst for political change. We begin by laying out the sociological tools that connect food consumption and social status. Then, we explore how food can simultaneously serve as a focal point for individual and collective projects for social and environmental change. While we take private consumption seriously as a site for political reflection (and potential collective action), we believe it is important to resist romanticizing this realm—especially in neoliberal times where consumption is put forward as a solution for mammoth structural issues like climate change (Shove 2010).

Food acts as a focal point for many projects for social change—community gardens, school lunch programs, biodynamic and organic agriculture. At the same time, cultural sociologists and consumption scholars suggest that consumption—including food consumption—works to naturalize class disparity. This finding was a key contribution of French sociologist Pierre Bourdieu's seminal work *Distinction* (1984), which has generated numerous subsequent studies on the classed nature of consumption, including food consumption (e.g., Cairns et al. 2010; Carfagna et al. 2014; Johnston and Baumann 2010). The meaning ascribed to consumption habits frequently denigrates working-class people as having bad taste—as in the equation of white bread with "white trash" (Bobrow-Strain 2012). At the other extreme, social elites are positioned as food connoisseurs with excellent taste who naturally gravitate toward ethical foods and cosmopolitan dining experiences (Cappeliez and Johnston 2013; Johnston, Szabo, and Rodney 2011). Not only are food tastes stratified by class, but elites have a disproportionate influence over what foods and cuisines are considered high status, even in an omnivorous cultural age where outright snobbery is eschewed. Indeed, British sociologist Douglas Holt argues that elites have "the power to set the terms through which tastes are assigned moral and social value" (1997: 95).

At the same time that we see food shopping as a clear instance of classed consumption, it is important not to reduce foodwork to simply a matter of distinction. Food frequently acts as a vessel where people channel their hopes for social and environmental change. It has become commonsensical to view food shopping as a political act with collective implications—"buying local" in order to support local farmers, or paying extra for "happy meat" that has been humanely raised. Yet, scholars continue to debate the political efficacy of popular appeals to "eat for change" (Johnston and Cairns 2012). Some point toward the transformative potential of collective food movements that empower citizens and promote ecological and social justice (Baker 2004; Carolan 2011; Lockie 2009; Star 2010). Others suggest that seemingly progressive initiatives may mask processes of neoliberalization, where state responsibility for the safety and security of food systems is transferred to self-regulating individuals (Allen et al. 2003; Guthman 2008; Maniates 2002; Szasz 2009). Critical voices suggest that these "educated, responsible" consumers are not only valorized as morally superior but are framed as the "hallmark of good neoliberal citizenship" (Biltekoff 2013: 93; Guthman and Allen 2006). While these debates have been productive, scholars have increasingly questioned this binary of collective food citizen versus individualized consumer dupe and have sought to unpack the shifting balance of forces that make up the citizen–consumer hybrid in specific empirical instances (Banet-Weiser and Mukerjei 2012; Johnston 2008). Willis and Schor critique a "naïve aggregationist" approach that assumes individual shopping choices can add up to alter structural forces, but argue that ethical consumption still holds value as "one in a toolkit of actions available to people and groups that are trying to make social change" (2012: 166).

The implicit and explicit politics of ethical food consumption continue to generate rich debate—is this a classed practice of consuming status or a political act of eating for change?—yet gender issues have been a relatively minor theme in these conversations (but see Judkins and Presser 2008; Kimura 2011; Little et al. 2009; MacGregor 2006; Vins 2009). This is noteworthy given that women do more household shopping than men and are the most common purchasers of "ethical" products like organic foods (Bellows et al. 2010; Gonzalez 2009; Lea and Worsley 2005; Magnusson et al. 2001). In this book, we contribute to these debates by unpacking the *gendered* dimension of ethical consumption. Contemporary food choices are imbued with moral significance as they embed consumers in relationships with a range of human and nonhuman actors in the food system—a phenomenon that Goodman, Dupuis and Goodman dub the "commodification of care" (2012: 207). Using Goodman et al.'s concept as a springboard for our analysis, we theorize ethical consumption not only as a form of care but as a form of *gendered* care-*work*. Here we build upon feminist scholarship that sees feminine care-work[9] as a form of labor that is "often invisible, usually accorded little value and only sometimes recognized as skilled" (Armstrong and Armstrong 2001: 1), but critical to sustaining patriarchal capitalist power relations (Vinz 2009: 172).

To better understand how foodwork can be seen as a form of invisible care-work in capitalist economies, we draw insight from Canadian feminist scholars' emphasis on the material inequities of political economy, labor and embodiment (e.g., Eichler 1997; Ferguson 2008; Fox 2001; Luxton 1980; Smith 1987).[10] Continuing this tradition, Canadian sociologist Andrea Doucet (2013) argues for analyses that see gender not *only* as a social construction but as part of embodied, material practices. To be clear, in arguing that ethical consumption extends women's gendered care-work, we are not suggesting that women are "naturally" more caring or connected to nature. Rather, we argue that gendered foodwork is rooted in both cultural discourses of femininity and structural gender relations (e.g., inequitable work environments), which together position women as more domestically oriented than men and prima-rily responsible for caring through food—within the home and beyond.

If ethical consumption extends women's gendered care-work, what does this mean politically, for both food and gender politics? This question involves a tension between critiques of neoliberal governmentality, on the one hand, and feminist visions of the personal as political, on the other. Even as we are critical of how ethical consumption can further the individualizing tendencies of neoliberal-ism, we are wary of how such critiques can work to dismiss women's politicized foodwork as a mere technology of neoliberalism. This dismissal reproduces a historical gender binary that restricts politics to the (masculine) public sphere and denies the political significance of women's social reproductive work in the realm of home and family. This dichotomy has been challenged in the work of Swedish political scientist Michelle Michelletti, who notes that "opposition to smart shopping as political action rests on a conventional, common, and narrow view of politics" (2003: 19). We argue that attending to the complexities of women's food narratives can help us to move beyond such dichotomies, in order to theorize the political dimensions of food femininities as they are negoti-ated in everyday life.

4. A feminist approach to food and "eating for change"

This chapter has presented a range of conceptual tools that can shed light on the complex relationship between food and femininity. We have argued that food is integral to multiple realms where women "do gender"—shopping, mother-ing, relating to the body, and expressing care—and that these practices are shaped by a patriarchal gender order as well as intersecting structures of racism and class inequality. Food femininities are reproduced within everyday gender relations at the same time that they are shaped by structural forces, includ-ing a neoliberal ethos that valorizes individual market solutions over collective action, and a postfeminist sensibility that positions feminist struggles as a thing of the past. In this context, women are encouraged to enact food femininities that emphasize their consumer power, mobilize care and concern through food shopping, and valorize choice as a symbol of feminine empowerment.

In the following chapters, we explore how food femininities are performed in the realms of shopping, mothering, healthy eating, ethics, pleasure, and foodwork. Across these sites, our research reveals the striking persistence of food-related gender inequities, despite many women's commitment to feminist principles. Gender equality is a near-universal goal, but the way to use food to achieve equality is uncertain. This tension leads us to emphasize the deep ambivalences within contemporary food femininities. Many women articulate a commitment to gender equity in their public and private lives, but find themselves structurally constrained by and *emotionally invested* in food practices that reproduce oppressive gender relations. Women are disproportionately responsible for care-work, and this can generate guilt, anger, and resentment; at the same time, many women in heterosexual relationships are attached to the role of household manager and often believe they are more qualified to make decisions about food and health than their male partners. Similarly, many women vehemently critique the social pressures put on women's bodies, yet find it difficult to resist seeing thin bodies as symbols of control, health, and responsibility. Caring about food can be a source of power, self-worth and pride, but it can also be a way that femininity remains tightly linked to problematic idealizations of care-work, consumerism, thinness, and intensive mothering.

While the notion of "eating for change" has widespread popular appeal, we argue that it is important to reframe this challenge in feminist terms. This means asking questions like the following: To what extent do our efforts to "eat for change" reproduce or challenge historical understandings of food and femininity? How might we envision a feminist vision of "eating for change" that challenges hegemonic gender ideals and works toward more equitable food practices—from the kitchen to the grocery store, to community food activism? We consider these questions in the chapters ahead and take guidance from our participants' stories of negotiating food femininities within their everyday lives.

Notes

1. We use the term "femininity" (in the singular) when referring to the gendered category and "femininities" (in the plural) when describing the multiple ways this category is enacted.

2. We refer readers to Jennifer Carlson's insightful article (2011) to better understand how femininity is constituted through multiplicity. Carlson is not simply arguing that there are multiple femininities, but that the process of performing femininity itself requires the negotiation of multiple norms and expanding domains. Our contribution to research on femininities is slightly different than Carlson, as we focus on mapping out the multiple norms and domains that relate food to femininity. However, we agree with Carlson that the performance of femininity involves a complex balancing act that is often difficult or impossible to achieve (see our concept of "calibration" in this chapter).

3. There are many points of similarity (and a few key points of difference) between West and Zimmerman's idea of "doing" gender and Judith Butler's idea of gender "performativity." We are influenced by both theories and share Butler's interest in understanding how subjectivities are constituted through discourse. To compare these two approaches, see Moloney and Fenstermaker (2002).

4. Scholars have critiqued the concept of "doing gender" and the way it has been taken up by researchers. In particular, this trajectory of research has been critiqued for neglecting structure, social change ("undoing" gender), feminist critique, embodiment, the relationship between gender and sex categories, as well as the role of nonreflective actions in "doing gender" (Deutsch 2007; Messerschmidt 2009; Risman 2009). These critiques are instructive, yet we believe it is possible to use the concept while avoiding certain myopic tendencies (e.g., understanding micro-interactions through a "doing gender" lens while still paying attention to the ways political–economic structures support or undermine these practices). See West and Zimmerman (2009) for a response to some of these critiques.

5. Many feminine food practices—such as, ordering salad, or holding in one's stomach—operate at the level of habit. We believe an appreciation of practical consciousness (Vaisey 2009) or "habitus" (Bourdieu 1984) is vital for understanding everyday food choices (Johnston and Cappeliez 2012) and moving beyond the "if they only knew" attitude toward food and social change (see Guthman 2008). Messerschmidt argues that appreciating nonreflexive behaviors is also key to understanding how people "do gender" (2009: 87).

6. Deutsch similarly asks whether gender difference necessarily reproduces gendered inequality (2007: 117). She suggests that difference can exist within a heterosexual relationship where work is equally shared, but a couple specializes in work that they find enjoyable (e.g., woman cooks and man cleans), but she usefully questions whether this individual gendered specialization may collectively reinforce inequality by reproducing stereotypes (e.g., about women caring more about food).

7. Some feminist scholars have argued for doing away with the term "patriarchy" in an effort to break from a tradition of white feminist scholarship that implies a static and universalizing understanding of women's oppression (see Patil 2013). We draw insight from these critiques, but feel that an analysis of patriarchy is crucial to understanding the structural dynamics of intersectionality—an approach that moves beyond an additive understanding of oppression to examine how capitalism, (hetero)patriarchy, and white supremacy work together to sustain inequalities (hooks 2004; Razack 1998; Smith 2005; Spade 2013). This approach differs from a simplistic conception of patriarchy as *overt* gender inequality privileging men—as *individuals*—over women. Instead, we understand patriarchy as a social system of hierarchal gender relations. A structural understanding of patriarchy is crucial for analyzing the way gender inequalities are naturalized and thus obscured. As bell hooks argues, "we cannot dismantle a system as long as we engage in collective denial about its impact on our lives" (2004: 24).

8. The idea of the "Foucault Machine" originally emerged out of conversations between Kate and her brother, James Cairns. We are thankful for the contribution he made to this early conceptualization.

9. We acknowledge the complications of the term "care," as well as the important distinction between "nurturance" and "reproductive labor" helpfully unpacked by Duffy (2005). Briefly, Duffy argues that nurturing work is a specific subset of a broader category of reproductive labor and uses census data to show that white women tend to occupy the more financially valued "nurturing" occupations.

10. While a critique of the capitalist underpinnings of social reproduction is now taken for granted in much feminist scholarship, this analytic insight has roots in socialist feminist scholarship theorizing social reproduction not as a separate realm where men oppress women but as embedded within material relations of capitalism (Ferguson 1999; Fox 1988; Luxton 1980; Seccombe 1992).

Chapter 3

Strolling the aisles and feeling food shopping

"It doesn't feel like a chore," said Gail, a white, 33-year-old acupuncturist, reflecting on the process of food shopping. "Every week I sit down and I plan what I'm gonna make in the week. And I make a list and I go out and get the food. I like the whole process of it." With her female partner at home on maternity leave with their second child, Gail derives great satisfaction from purchasing and preparing food for her family. "It's definitely a nice way for me to mother," she said. Yet, Gail makes clear that the shopping experience feels quite different in different venues. "I hate going to No Frills [a discount grocery chain]," she said with a sigh, "by the time I get out of there it's like, 'Oh thank god I'm done here.'" Gail contrasted the experience of this discount grocer to "wandering around the market and going into a little shop." She then went on to describe the joys of shopping at an organic grocer in her neighborhood: "It's just a really nice friendly neighborhood kind of feeling. Rather than a corporate feeling." Gail maps out diverse shopping spaces— from enduring a crowded, "corporate feeling" discount grocer to leisurely wandering the farmers' market or a "friendly neighborhood" shop. Ultimately, though, she describes food shopping as an enjoyable experience. Gail's comments resonate with the shopping narratives shared by many women in our study and speak to the contradictions embedded in the emotions of food shopping.

In *Building a Housewife's Paradise*, Tracey Deutsch documents "a widely resonant discourse of women and supermarkets" that emerged in post-war America (2010: 183). This was a time when "celebrations of women's food shopping were ubiquitous," articulated through the "refrain that women were thrilled with the new, streamlined, and aesthetically pleasing supermarkets" (2010: 183). Fifty years later, the association between femininity and the supermarket remains—women continue to do most of the food shopping—but the celebratory rhetoric has been disrupted. A trip to the grocery store is commonly perceived "as mundane and as a chore" (Cockburn-Wootten et al. 2008: 414), and food shopping is listed alongside housecleaning within scholarly investigations of housework (e.g., Kroska 2004; Vijayasiri 2011). As noted in the introductory chapter, women are still responsible for most of this labor in North American households (Statistics Canada 2011; US Bureau of Labor Statistics 2011). Given this inequitable division of food labor, we might expect that women would dislike food shopping and might even *resent* the time they spend at the grocery store. However, when we asked women about the food shopping experience, we often heard expressions of pleasure and satisfaction, like those shared by Gail above. "I do like shopping," said Claudette. "I like the tactile experience and determining if something's good. I don't think of it as a chore. It's a pleasure." Contrary to the common construction of grocery shopping as a mundane chore, many women described trips to the supermarket as "fun," "exciting," and even "therapeutic." How do we understand the emotional rewards that women find in grocery shopping?

Emotion is not something we normally associate with groceries. Yet, it was a prominent theme in our food conversations, especially when it came to the salient connections between food and femininity. Put simply, we found that food shopping gives women an opportunity to perform an idealized and emotionally rewarding femininity—to be the woman bringing home a healthy, tasty, nutritionally satisfying bounty. Yet, not all shopping experiences generated positive emotions, as detailed in Gail's comments above. Here we draw on the Bourdieusian concept of habitus—the internalization of one's position in a larger social structure—to help us understand the classed processes underlying participants' embodied, emotional experiences of comfort and discomfort in various food shopping spaces. More broadly, the concept of the habitus can illuminate the lived experience of consumers in a neoliberal context where individual choices are highly valued, such that shopping can come to feel (for some) like a kind of freedom (Slater 1997: 35–7).

In this chapter, we use our interview and focus group data to explore the pleasures and places associated with a privileged habitus of food shopping. We argue that these shopping experiences are analytically significant for the ways that they allow women to perform a desirable consumer femininity. However, for women with limited resources, the potential pleasures of food shopping are undermined by material constraints, a situation that generates feelings of frustration, guilt, and anger.

1. Theories of food shopping: Gender, class, and place

Despite signs that men are taking a growing interest in food culture and cook-ing (Szabo 2012), women in heterosexual relationships continue to perform the majority of domestic foodwork, including grocery shopping (Beagan et al. 2008; Cockburn-Wooten et al. 2008; Coltrane 2000; Kroska 2004; Lachance-Grzela and Bouchard 2010; Warde and Martens 2000). Overt appeals to gender roles may be less common today than in the past, but gendered schemas of foodwork persist (as we will see below). Even as expectations regarding masculinity and femininity have shifted somewhat, "the feminization of consumption in our collective imagination remains relevant in the twenty-first century" (West 2009: 286).

In this chapter we explore food shopping as a way of performing a socially valued consumer femininity—one that aligns with gendered notions of feminine care and nurturing and stands in opposition to the irrationality and indulgence of a pathologized consumer femininity (Slater 1997: 34; Zukin and Maguire 2004: 175). Feminists have long shown the significance of women's foodwork in the performance of caring femininities and the reproduction of the heteronorma-tive family (DeVault 1991), and food purchasing is a central component of this gendered practice (Koch 2012). In his ethnography of shopping, anthropologist Daniel Miller found that "even when men are heavily involved there is a strong tendency to distance themselves from identification with the act and concept of shopping" (1998: 39). Miller argues that as a result "the female shopper is ideo-logically inscribed as the norm, irrespective of the statistics that demonstrate a diversity of practice" (1998: 39).

In framing our argument about food shopping as a site for doing gender, it is important to clarify that we are not making an essentialist claim about gender differences at the grocery store. This is not about suggesting that "Men Buy Groceries Like This, Women Buy Groceries Like That" (Marcotte 2011). Instead, our focus is on understanding *how* women experience food shopping as pleas-urable (or frustrating) and how these emotions relate to the performance of femininities. In previous research with foodies, we found that many women food-ies struggled to enact femininities that satisfied competing discourses of care and pleasure; these women embraced self-oriented aspects of pleasurable food experiences even as they continued to regard food as a site of caring for others (Cairns et al. 2010). In the analysis that follows, we consider how women's narratives of food shopping pleasures may work to resolve this tension, as they enact a consumer femininity that satisfies ideals of both pleasure *and* care. The pleasurable element of grocery shopping problematizes conventional gender boundaries that position women's social reproductive work as distinct from leisure (Cockburn-Wooten et al. 2008). While women may derive pleasure from strolling the aisles of the grocery store, it is important to consider how the ongoing association between femininity and food shopping works to legitimize and reproduce a gendered division of domestic labor (DeVault 1991).

Even as we consider the transgressive potential of a consumer femininity that challenges gendered categories of work and leisure, pleasure and care, it is imperative to critically analyze how feminine pleasures are shaped by, and may inadvertently sustain, patriarchal relations of power. Feminist scholars have drawn attention to food's emotional significance as well as the complex relationship between pleasure and gender subordination (e.g., Black 2004; Bordo 1993; Lupton 1996). However, few have extended this analysis to contemporary food *shopping*, and "very little research to-date has focused on the relationship between class relations, emotion, consumption and senses of well-being" (Rafferty 2011: 241). Building on what Pugh calls the "stratification of feeling" (2009: 26), we analyze shopping narratives of pleasure, disgust, anger and guilt as expressions of the "the ways in which class and gender become incorporated into embodied selves" (Lawler 2004: 110). Grocery shopping generates a range of emotions, and these different emotions reflect broader relations of power. As we will show below, an intersectional analysis reveals that some gendered foodwork can be pleasurable, but these pleasures are facilitated by class privilege.

While drawing on a feminist perspective, we employ Bourdieu's concept of habitus to understand how practices of "doing gender" are shaped by social class. The concept of habitus provides a way of understanding how class and gender structures become internalized as part of everyday pleasures, discomforts, and common sense. Habitus suggests that "in quite subtle ways, through discourse, practices, and institutions, and through interactions with others in their environment, principles are set up for the individual about what matters, what is noticed, how one comports oneself physically, socially, emotionally, and much more" (McLeod and Yates 2006: 90). Central to the concept of habitus, and a key part of its utility for feminist scholars, is an emphasis on embodied ways of being (Krais 2006). As sociologist Diane Reay puts it, "Bourdieu has developed the concept of habitus to demonstrate the ways in which, not only is the body in the social world, but also, the ways in which the social world is in the body" (1995: 354).

Throughout our focus groups and interviews, we were struck by how participants' descriptions of food shopping were heavily laden with sensory narratives

and emotion. Habitus offers a key theoretical tool for understanding how embodied experiences of food shopping are shaped by the interplay of structural
processes and social practice. Grocery narratives are not simply banal accounts
of personal purchases but provide a surprisingly rich account of how the social
world enters the body and becomes visible through food likes, aversions, and
emotions. As such, analyzing the emotional dimensions of food shopping can
deepen our understanding of habitus as an "embodied sedimentation of the
social structures that produced it" (Bourdieu and Wacquant 1992: 19).

A place-sensitive analysis of shopping emotions—investigating who
feels comfortable where—also illuminates the *spatial* dimension of habitus.
Emotion-laden narratives of consumption reflect the interplay between the
habitus of the consumer and the place-specific element of the experience. In
Bourdieu's words, habitus yields "a 'sense of one's place' which leads one to
exclude oneself from the goods, persons, place and so forth from which one
is excluded" (1984: 471). In one of the only existing studies of emotion and
grocery shopping, a geographic analysis revealed that place, risk and emotion
were deeply intertwined in the shopping process and that many "consumers
wish to make their purchases in places where they can minimize encounters
with people and things that are unknown to them" (Williams et al. 2001: 216).
People like to shop among "familiar strangers" in "local places" where they feel
at home (2001: 216). Relatedly, other scholars have demonstrated the pleasures associated with shopping in localized food venues, like farmers' markets
(Smithers et al. 2008; Thompson and Coskuner-Bali 2007). The assumption
that often accompanies discourse about alternative food shopping is that
shopping becomes pleasurable only when consumers engage with the local
and leave the industrial, corporate food sector behind. While some women *did*
speak fondly of the pleasures of shopping at farmers' markets, our data challenge a simple dichotomy between the pleasure of local eating and the "chore"
of routinized supermarket shopping. As will be clear below, different classed
spaces foster different kinds of emotions, and these emotional responses
reflect a gendered and classed consumer habitus.

2. The emotional experience of food shopping

Kate: How do people feel about the experience of food shopping? Is it
          something that's a chore to you, is that something that . . .

Julia: It's how I relieve stress.

Mai: Same here. I love it.

Kate: Really! So what do you love about it?

Mai: I love food, so this is just how I'm getting food. I'll just go up and down the aisle, be like "Look at that! That's on sale! I'm gonna get that!" But it's just, like you said, it's relaxing. I've been with people who just hated it and just wanted to get in, get what they wanted and get out. And I'm like, but then you're gonna miss, you know, maybe there's a sale or maybe they have raspberries for once or something.

This kind of enthusiasm toward food shopping was common among women in our focus groups and interviews. Women distinguished the pleasures of food shopping from other types of shopping pleasures and even distanced their own shopping femininity from one associated with consumer culture more generally. For example, Ruth clarified that while she loves *food* shopping, "I don't like shopping at all . . . I don't like going into stores and buying things . . . It just makes me feel awful." On the other hand, she said, "food shopping I love. I love the experience."

Mindful of Miller's (1998) caution that the discourse of shopping does not necessarily reflect shopping practice, we do not interpret participants' narratives as evidence that food shopping is *always* enjoyable. Nor do we claim that this discourse was articulated without exception. We spoke with men who reported that they enjoyed grocery shopping, and some women said they greatly disliked the shopping experience. For example, Natalie, a 27-year-old editor, declared "I hate grocery shopping" and explained how she struggles to squeeze in trips to the grocery store with her busy work schedule. Other women expressed disinterest in food shopping, describing it as something that they neither loved nor despised. Even with these exceptions, however, we did observe gendered patterns in our data that speak to and reinscribe hegemonic femininity—as caring, familial, and skilled at consuming. While our analysis reveals a gendered ideal across classes, we also show how access to this performance of femininity is sharply differentiated by material resources and powerfully shaped by social class.

Food shopping femininities: "I'll just cruise the aisles . . . and he just goes bananas"

"I like grocery shopping," shared Lois, a retired nurse. "When we go away to Florida one of the highlights of the trip is going into different grocery stores and seeing what they've got." Lois derives pleasure from the element of discovery involved in grocery shopping, while her husband does not: "I'll just cruise the aisles to see what there is, and he just goes bananas . . . He wants to go in, he wants to get what he wants, he wants to get out." Lois's account of the different approaches she and her husband bring to the grocery store reflects a broader gendered pattern observed throughout our focus groups and interviews. While individual feelings about shopping varied, participants consistently contrasted the methodical yet leisurely approach of a contented female shopper with the time- and cost-oriented approach of an impatient male shopper.

This relational articulation of shopping femininities and masculinities was not limited to focus groups involving both men and women; participants commonly articulated their own gendered performances in opposition to some real or imagined Other. In a focus group involving four men, Eric, a 41-year-old musician, described his weekly shopping trip as a "chore." Eric was one of the few men in our study who did most of the shopping for his wife and children, and he expressed frustration regarding various obstacles to his standardized shopping routine:

> It's the people in there that go to the middle of the row and they leave their fucking cart, and then they walk halfway down and they're looking around, and no one can get past their cart . . . And I find that, not to make the stereotype, but I actually find that women are the worst at this. They leave their cart like, fucking sideways! Everyone's trying to get by! Like, what the hell!

Eric encounters several barriers to a quick shopping experience, but chief among them is the leisurely female consumer who is not facilitating proper "traffic flow." Here we see how shopping femininities and masculinities are relationally constituted. There were no women participants in Eric's focus group, yet he enacted his own shopping masculinity in relation to an imagined female consumer.

At the same time, this efficiency/leisure binary did not always map onto male- and female-identified participants, particularly within gay and lesbian relationships. "[My partner] always says I'm like the world's fastest shopper," said 60-year-old Joanne, who is retired. Joanne contrasted her own approach to her partner's: "she likes to meander up and down the aisles and I'm like, 'Okay, I'm here for five things, let's get them and get the heck out of here.'" Despite her emphasis on speed and efficiency, Joanne did acknowledge a pleasurable component to food shopping. "I mean, I enjoy it," she said. "But I do tend to kind of go up and down the aisle fairly quickly."

In addition to the desire to peruse options, women frequently linked the pleasures of food shopping to the joys of feeding others, invoking a hegemonic femininity associated with care and nurturing (DeVault 1991;

Lupton 1996). Notably, this was not limited to women who were feeding partners and children. Tiffany, a university student, enjoys a trip to the grocery store when she anticipates feeding others, but said "it's almost disappointing if I'm having a week where I'm only cooking for myself." She contrasted the "euphoria while I'm gathering all these wonderful things" to the "sad" reality days later when facing a refrigerator full of wilted vegetables. Many women articulated a similar contrast between the pleasures of shopping for others and the dissatisfaction of purchasing food solely for oneself. In doing so, they enact consumer femininities defined by ideals of care and connection and distance themselves from the self-oriented consumption of an indulgent female shopper.

While we observed strong linkages among femininity, food shopping and care-work, there were important nuances in these relationships. For some women who were primarily responsible for the routine grocery shopping in their families, the caring element of foodwork was described as simultaneously pleasurable and tedious. Beth (60, semi-retired) declared "I love grocery shopping" but drew a distinction between the kind of shopping she enjoys and the monotony of daily care-work. "My son is back home again, so I feel like I am in the 1950s again," she said. "June Cleaver?" joked Beth's friend Daniella.[1] Beth laughed, "Yeah, I feel like I'm part of that." She continued: "I do get a little tired of the everyday, you know, we need bananas, but that's why I go to different stores to make it a bit of an adventure." Beth and Daniella's reference to the 1950s' housewife reveals a reflexive relationship to historical gender roles; while Beth recognizes elements of this caring femininity in her everyday shopping practice, she seeks out opportunities for "adventure" to enact a femininity that is distinct from this hegemonic ideal. For many women we spoke with, finding novelty and pleasure in food shopping appeared to serve as a strategy for managing the gendered burden of foodwork and establishing distance from the unattractive trope of the beleaguered housewife.

While most women engaged with gendered notions of care, there were multiple instances where our respondents deviated from the stereotype of selfless consumer femininity. Women clearly experienced food shopping as an opportunity for pleasure and leisure—not just sacrifice. Deb (43, unemployed) spoke fondly of the "discovery of going up and down the aisle and finding something new that you might really like." Participants wove rich descriptions of the sensory experience of selecting food. "I like finding fresh stuff," said Marissa, a 43-year-old project manager, "I like colours, I like smelling them." While women focused on different aspects of the shopping experience, it was not simply the items in their cart that brought them pleasure. Rather, it was the process that they invested with emotional significance. Significantly, a common obstacle to enjoying grocery shopping was not having enough time to enjoy the process. In the words of Sue (40, family support worker), "I don't actually find it fun because everything is crammed into a day. So it's just like, ahh! But you know, when I'm not rushed and it is nice and leisurely and I have time to go and check all the tomatoes, that is really nice."

In addition to this sense of discovery, food shopping also afforded opportunities to perform *successful* femininities, and the associated sense of accomplishment was an additional source of pleasure for many women. This successful feminine shopper performed complex calculations about health, cost, family preferences, and ethics (Koch 2012). Kelsey, a 27-year-old law student, framed this capacity for planning as a natural extension of femininity: "I think women are better at multitasking . . . So I think that it involves a lot of, you know, planning for different things and scheduling." This image of the well-organized female shopper was also articulated by men in our study. Aidan, a 27-year-old architect, contrasted his own spontaneous grocery shopping with his partner's more disciplined approach. "What my girlfriend does is make lists," he said, and then joked more generally, "I'm pretty sure that's all she does." As made clear in Kelsey and Aidan's comments, successful shopping femininity is contrasted with a less skilled masculine shopper, a pattern observed in previous research (Lake et al. 2006). In his ethnography of shopping, Miller demonstrates how the construction of men as bad shoppers works to affirm their masculinity. Such criticisms suggest that "although he may shop, he is not a natural shopper" and thus function "as praise for his natural manliness" (Miller 1998: 25). This gendered dynamic was pervasive among heterosexual women in our study, who frequently lamented or joked that their partners were clueless when it came to food shopping. "Sometimes my husband is happy to help with shopping," said Nina, a 42-year-old editor, "but he comes home with lots of unauthorized purchases." Christine described going to great lengths to support her husband's infrequent trips to the grocery store:

> He'll go if I say, "You know what? I'm not up to going into a grocery store today, this is what we need." And I'll make him a list, but usually it's a shorter list, and I'll describe exactly what it is that I want him to look for . . . "Okay, if you pick out a cereal, make sure it has at least three grams protein and three grams of . . ." [laughter] Because he'll come home with something that I won't touch. Like, if it's like, a sugary type thing that's masked as a healthy food but it's actually not, because of all the labeling, right? He'll see just the flashy label that makes it look like it's healthy, whereas I actually read.

While the figure of the unskilled masculine shopper facilitates the performance of successful femininities, he also generates additional work for women, who are positioned as naturally capable shoppers with greater capacity for planning and concern for family health (Beagan et al. 2008: 663).

Indeed, this oppositional construction of shopping femininities and masculinities was used to justify the gendered division of foodwork. Maria, a 32-year-old policy analyst, primarily shops for her partner and herself because "he doesn't kind of adhere so much to like, a standard of shopping that I do." Although Maria saw logic to this arrangement, she expressed uneasiness with the underlying gender dynamic:

> Now that we've moved in together I really see these gender roles coming out. And part of me is revolting and part of me is acquiescing . . . part of me wants us to be equally involved in all aspects. But sometimes it's almost like it's just easier for me to take on *something that I enjoy and that I'm good at*. (emphasis ours)

Maria reflects critically on the gendered division of labor she finds herself participating in, yet she remains invested in a femininity enacted through foodwork—a site in which she derives a sense of pleasure and accomplishment. Her thoughtful articulation of this tension reveals how the practice of doing gender is deeply ingrained in one's sense of self, even as it may also be the source of ambivalence (Adkins 2003).

Even as narratives of shopping for pleasure may work to naturalize women's responsibility for foodwork, women may also enact shopping femininities that subvert this power differential. This potential was evident in the way some women described food shopping as a source of personal time. Grace, a 53-year-old management consultant, spoke candidly about shopping as a break from the care duties associated with mothering. "I went shopping to avoid my children," she said, drawing laughter from her friends, "I got my ass out of the house so my husband could deal with the children." Grace described this as a deliberate strategy she used to create time to herself, sometimes incorporating other leisure activities in the period she had allotted for groceries: "I was doing a purposeful thing. And if I just happened to spend an hour, whether it was to go to the library or whatever . . . it was very much my down time." Grace's story of using shopping to create "down time" blurs the boundaries between labor and leisure in women's social reproductive work; while shopping is part of the care-work associated with food femininities, the actual experience of grocery shopping may afford women self-oriented opportunities for pleasure. Her story also highlights how the performance of femininities may simultaneously reproduce and rework hegemonic gender expectations.

Class, place, habitus: "It's a very different feel, it's a very different experience"

As evident in Gail's comments at the beginning of this chapter, the pleasures associated with food shopping were not universal and varied according to location. In this section we explore how class shapes food shopping femininities. We argue that the affective experience of shopping has a habitus dimension that relates to place (see also Johnston et al. 2012). While we acknowledge the material differences that structure various shopping spaces, we show how the emotional experience of these spaces is relationally defined; that is, shopping emotions are constituted through the interplay between specific shopping places and a gendered, classed consumer habitus. These emotions reflect and reproduce the classed boundaries that guide certain shoppers into (or away from) certain consumer spaces, revealing a core class dimension within the performance of shopping femininities.

Grocery store hierarchies

While participants associated varying levels of comfort and pleasure with different shopping spaces, there was a remarkable degree of consistency in the defining features attributed to different venues. At one end of the spectrum, discount grocers were described as "crowded" and "horribly organized," characterized by their fluorescent lights and "industrial" feel. The uninviting discount grocery environment was contrasted with the more aesthetically pleasing experience available at higher-end grocery stores characterized by their "wide aisles," and "attractive displays." And at the farthest end of the grocery spectrum are the "gorgeous," "relaxed" shopping experiences on offer in premium grocery spaces like Whole Foods Market. Many participants described this spectrum of grocery store atmosphere and related this spectrum to their enjoyment of the shopping experience. "Some stores give you a different vibe," said Cynthia, a 55-year-old who works part-time in retail. "And some of the more upscale stores I'm thinking, okay, why is it so much more relaxed to shop here? I think it feels like it might be a sense of décor, better lighting, more attractive displays, instead of you know, industrial shelving or something." Participants articulated the same defining features of each shopping environment with notable consistency. This point might seem predictable, but what is more sociologically significant is how participants' emotional experience of each venue varied in ways that reflect their class position and habitus.

While certain shopping venues were widely regarded as pleasurable settings, the sense of one's capacity to participate in, and thus derive pleasure from, such spaces clearly varied according to the class position of the consumer. For example, Judy, a 56-year-old who works for a legal publisher, described her dislike of grocery stores, but described her experience at a farmers' market in very different language: "[t]o go to the [farmers'] market is TRULY a joyful experience for me," she said. "The interaction with the people, how beautiful everything is, just the whole vibe of the other people shopping . . . It's a very joyful experience." Although Judy attributed these pleasures to the farmers' market setting, she acknowledged that this "joyful" shopping experience requires considerable material resources. "I spend a tremendous amount of money on food," she said, adding that since shifting her shopping to farmers' markets, "my food expenses just psssht shot up." Judy's frank account of her own costly food shopping habits highlights an important, yet often unstated, class dimension shaping food shopping emotions: access to the "joyful" experience of shopping at farmers' markets requires that one has the resources needed to participate in this space and experience these kind of pleasures.

Despite the positive feelings attributed to farmers' markets, these were not always experienced as inviting; some working-class and poor participants described feeling out of place there, unable to perform this high-status shopping femininity. Syd, a 26-year-old aspiring actor, said that while she would love to shop at farmers' markets, "I actually end up feeling really intimidated when I go in those sort of places, 'cause money is a huge stress for me at all times." Women in various income brackets acknowledged the appeal of shopping in "feel-good" venues like farmers' markets and specialty stores, but women with limited material resources often saw this high-status shopping femininity as unattainable.

Disgust, aversion, and deals: Classed responses to discount grocers

Feeling out of place as a shopper was related to a lack of resources in affluent shopping environments, but privileged women also experienced discomfort in certain venues, especially discount grocers. "There's a Food Basics near me that I would never go in because it's a hole," said Ellen, a 47-year-old high-income nurse practitioner. She continued: "There might be good deals there but I am not going to go in there and have that sort of experience. It's disgusting." Many middle-class consumers said they were repelled by a perceived lack of cleanliness in discount grocers, a finding that is in keeping with previous research exploring "the stereotyping of abject spaces as defiled, dirty and polluted" (Williams et al. 2001: 15). These expressions of repulsion call to mind what Lawler calls "middle-class disgust" (2004: 119). Examining how narratives of disgust work to delegitimize the working class through "the signifiers of a pathologized working-class existence" (120), Lawler argues that "it is the authority instantiated in a middle-class habitus that can make such judgments stick" (120). For many affluent women, the discount grocer constituted an offense to their middle-class sensibilities and breached their sense of entitlement to pleasurable consumption.

Nevertheless, the ability to reject and avoid "disgusting" shopping spaces reflects class privilege. Many low-income women agreed that discount grocers were not particularly inviting, but financial pressures trumped these aesthetic concerns. "I don't mind food shopping at all," said Nadine, who is 48 and lives on disability support, "but it depends on where I go." She explained:

> Sobeys [middle-end grocer] is much more pleasant. It's cleaner, aisles are wider, the décor is nicer, but again it's pricey. Food Basics [discount grocer], I don't love it so much. It's not as clean, décor isn't much to speak of, I don't find the people who work there are very friendly, but it's cheaper. So it's sort of a six of one, half a dozen of the other. But the actual process of "oh I've got to get groceries," no I actually, I love picking.

Contrasting the experience of Sobeys and Food Basics, Nadine acknowledges the very same features identified within narratives of middle-class disgust, yet she articulates a different emotional response. Rather than rejecting the discount grocer as an offense to her senses, she tolerates these features as a normalized aspect of food shopping—one that does not necessarily detract from the overall pleasures of her consumer experience and especially her ability to "pick," to make choices. Finally, for some women, saving money at discount venues was enjoyable in its own right. "I like going to No Frills," said Nadia, a 27-year-old substitute teacher with a low income. She explained: "I'm one of those people that look for how I can save money. So most of the time I feel like I get a pretty good deal there." Contrast Nadia's satisfaction with getting a "good deal" with Ellen's comment that "there might be good deals there but I am not going to go in there and have that sort of experience." These divergent responses of satisfaction and repulsion speak to how shopping emotions vary depending on privilege. To be sure, the enjoyment of getting a good deal is not limited to low-income shoppers, but the disgust and aversion to discount grocery stores was something we observed exclusively among privileged participants.

Comfort and luxury: Relative and relational

Across our focus groups and interviews, we were struck by how the same middle-brow grocery stores dismissed as unremarkable by middle-class respondents were depicted as *luxury* experiences by low-income respondents. For example, 26-year-old Kalise, who works in retail, described Sobeys (a middle-end grocer) as "supermarket heaven." At present, she shops almost exclusively at a discount grocer, but said that if money were not a concern, "I'd personally shop at the Sobeys store forever." Laughing, Kalise detailed the pleasures to be discovered in this shopping environment: "When I go in there, it's just like, wow. Everything is always fresh . . . you never see anything looking all grungy and gross . . . You want to just go in all the aisles." While venues such as Sobeys were viewed as a luxury for those accustomed to the discount shopping experience, more privileged women spoke dispassionately about these middle-end grocers. A privileged consumer habitus required a more exclusive shopping environment to create associations of pampering and luxury. "I like shopping at Whole Foods," said Lisa, a 42-year-old product developer. "I know I spend a lot more money when I shop at Whole Foods and I know it walking in the door. But I feel pretty good about it." This privileged shopping femininity derives pleasure spending *more* money in order to have a luxury consumer experience and calls to mind Bourdieu's association of upper-class distinction with distance from necessity.

A different expression of classed femininities was apparent in a shopping habitus based on a feeling of universal comfort—the feeling that one could comfortably shop *anywhere*. A small number of participants expressed an ease of access to *all* shopping spaces—discount, premium, and everything in between—displaying a sense of entitlement and mobility associated with high-status omnivorous food consumption (e.g., the foodie who will "eat anything"; Johnston and Baumann 2010). Carol, a white affluent producer in her early forties, explained that she prefers shopping at "upscale" venues like Whole Foods Market when accompanied by her daughter, but also enjoys hunting for deals and "ethnic food" at discount chains like No Frills:

> My daughter comes to the St. Lawrence Market with me or Whole Foods. But we don't go to the regular grocery stores together. So I guess to that end we only go to the sort of more upscale types of shop . . . But you know I do enjoy a No Frills or a discount grocery store too to see what they've got there . . . they often have a really interesting selection of produce. And some ethnic foods and such . . . I enjoy looking at it. But not with [my kids]. 'Cause I can see they do also have No Name white bread and you know all that kind of stuff that kind of grosses me out.

While Carol feels at ease traversing diverse consumption spaces, she limits her children's shopping experiences in ways that are revealing. Careful to restrict their exposure to only the "more upscale types of shop," she socializes her children into a middle-class habitus fostered through privileged consumer sensibilities. Articulating her desire to shield them from items such as "No Name white bread"—arguably one of the "signifiers of a pathologized working-class existence" (Lawler 2004: 120; see also Bobrow-Strain 2012)—she reveals her middle-class habitus, remarking that such inexpensive, processed food "kind of grosses me out."

While the distinction between shopping spaces tended to center on the sensory atmosphere, positive and negative associations were often extended to the kinds of *people* one expected to find in these stores. "I've seen things," said Gail, explaining her dislike of No Frills, "what people do to each other." She continued: "Like somebody got in somebody's way and she threw down her basket and started yelling at her. There was like, an extreme situation." Gail was not the only person to complain of the rude shoppers and employees who were understood to populate discount grocery stores; this assessment was contrasted with the "conscientious," "friendly" clientele in higher-end venues. When describing why she enjoys farmers' markets, Kelsey noted that you meet "very like-minded people" there. Thus, through narratives of shopping emotions, participants distanced their own consumer femininities from particular people and places and aligned them with others—those who were understood to bring the same disposition and tastes (or *habitus*) to the shopping experience.

Race and ethnocultural othering

In addition to markers of class distinction, our focus groups and interviews reveal the intersectionality of food boundaries, which includes stratification based on gender as well as race. In several instances, participants discussed the comfort of shopping for foods familiar to their racial-ethnic traditions, a practice that sometimes involved a "nostalgia factor" for foods eaten "back home." While food shopping preferences were a way to connect with ethnocultural traditions, they were also a source of ethnocultural othering. After stating that she "wouldn't go to No Frills," Alyssa, a white, 23-year-old actress, explained: "No Frills reminds me of the awful Portuguese girls on my soccer team when I was growing up. Just like that area of the city. They were very mean. Like, it reminds me of them. Just that. There is nothing wrong with," Alyssa hesitated, perhaps registering how her comments might offend others in the focus group. She continued from a slightly different angle: "I don't think I would have many options at No Frills. I know it's really cheap, like maybe I could get some organic brown rice, in a package." From the othering of Portuguese communities in "that area of the city," to the assertion that No Frills would offer few healthy or hygienic food options, Alyssa's narrative is one of distance. Alyssa assumes that her own diet is different from those who purchase food at No Frills and believes that she would be out of place in this shopping environment.

In other cases, racialized shopping boundaries were expressed through the desire to avoid unfamiliar food experiences, as seen in a focus group hosted in a predominantly white, affluent neighborhood. When Daniella mentioned how she enjoys shopping at T&T Supermarket, a Chinese grocery chain, Axel responded, "Do they speak English?" He explained: "'Cause I have a problem going [shopping] downtown . . . they are all Chinese and I think half of them don't speak English. They couldn't explain to me what I was looking for." Axel regards T&T as a space of Others; like Alyssa, he imagines that he would feel out of place in this seemingly foreign environment and thus restricts his own shopping to more familiar spaces. On the other hand, the racialization of consumption spaces also emerged through narratives about the allure of exoticized shopping venues. This form of racialization occurs through the performance of a privileged omnivorous femininity that is comfortable shopping and eating anywhere, moving fluidly across class and ethnocultural boundaries. For example, Beth spoke of the pleasures derived from shopping at a Middle Eastern grocer that is "like transporting yourself across the world 'cause even the cashiers are wearing veils and beautiful jewelry." Thus, in addition to having a gendered and classed dimension, the pleasures of food shopping may be linked to the cultural curiosities of a dominant white imaginary, which positions itself as the "center" and attains pleasure by relishing the tastes and delicacies of Others residing on the ethnocultural periphery (Cappeliez and Johnston 2013; Everts 2010; Heldke 2003; hooks 1998; Johnston, Baumann and Cairns 2009).

Class reflexivity and awareness

While emotional accounts of familiarity and discomfort were pervasive throughout our focus groups and interviews, explicit references to one's class privilege were rare. For the most part, privileged food shopping femininities were rarely and briefly connected to material privilege (see also Johnston and Szabo 2011).

One of the only exceptions to this tendency occurred in a focus group with four men who were very interested in food and who openly discussed their nonconventional masculinities. We speculate that these men's comfort level with their gender identities—combined with their status as white, "creative class" professionals—may have allowed them to openly reflect on class dynamics structuring the emotional experience of food shopping. The outspoken host,

Eric, wondered aloud whether his sense of comfort at Fiesta Farms (a high-quality, independent grocery store with a reputation for selling "ethical" products like "happy meats") may be a "class thing." He explained: "The people in Fiesta are more like me than the people in Loblaws, and definitely the people at Price Chopper or No Frills . . . The people in Fiesta are yuppies like me and *I feel more comfortable*. I know that's a totally jackass thing to say, but it's, like, they seem more polite and you can talk to people" (emphasis ours). Highlighting the way classed boundaries manifest emotionally, Eric said that shopping venues catering to low-income consumers feel "very very sad. There's a lot of sad people there, they're really broke . . . the whole thing makes me sad." Admitting that he was "being classist," Eric contrasted this "depressing" shopping experience with one he finds more uplifting. "I go to Fiesta and everyone's awesome! They've got their Audi's parked in the parking lot and everything's okay," he joked. Rob, a 32-year-old architect, suggested that perhaps this was an issue of *values* and the comforts of shopping alongside those who "have the same priorities" as he does:

> The people who shop at Fiesta [Farms] are there for the same reasons that I'm there, because the produce is nice, the prices are pretty good, and there's a good variety. And yes, that tends to be the same class of people, unfortunately or fortunately or whatever. But I don't know, I think that's why I get along with those people.

While there were important differences expressed by participants in this focus group, a careful reading of the overall discussion makes clear the high comfort level experienced by privileged participants in a privileged shopping environment where one is presumed to share common values. Eric stated this baldly; however, we also observed this sentiment in our conversations with privileged female shoppers, such as Kelsey's belief that farmers' market shoppers were "like-minded."

As explored earlier, the relationship between habitus and shopping venue was often expressed through emotional discomfort or disgust when a privileged shopping habitus came into contact with a low-budget grocer. While this kind of disgust was articulated from a place of material privilege, disgust can also signal an expression of critique or resistance, as evident in a focus group of five women held in a working-class neighborhood. When discussing different shopping spaces, the conversation turned to a new high-end grocery store that had recently hosted a grand opening. "Apparently they have four hundred variety of cheese," said Sitara, adding that while she probably would not shop there, "I wonder what kind of experience it would be to go into this place." In contrast,

Vicky was less curious and more appalled: "[i]t's too much! It's so decadent!" she said with exasperation, adding "It makes me disgusted." Vicky likened this extravagance to her one experience at an expensive fine foods store. "It was so awful! All these rich people were in there dropping hundreds and hundreds of dollars. All these fancy, way over the top foods . . . I was totally disgusted." Vicky's disgust toward the opulent elite food shopping experience shows how it offends her own consumer habitus. This impassioned critique of a privileged consumer habitus highlights how emotions may offer a lens into the classed dynamics of consumption—the frustration, disgust, guilt, and even anger embedded in the performance of classed and gendered subjectivities. It also reaffirms Skeggs' argument that class politics is often submerged in formal discussions, but observed at the level of emotion, in the "frustration that things are not fair, and a knowledge that they are unlikely to change in the future" (2004a: 90).

Class constraints and working-class consciousness

Cynthia explains that when she and her husband immigrated to Canada 25 years ago, they chose this neighborhood in order to be close to Chinatown, where they could find the foods they wanted for an affordable price. Now, seated around her dining room table, the focus group takes up most of the space between the kitchen and living room of her small duplex. The group consists of four women and one man—a mix of friends and acquaintances—and much of the discussion focuses on the difficulty of finding healthy foods for low-income shoppers. As we move to the question of how their shopping habits might change if money were not a concern, the conversation reveals a great deal about the classed and gendered nature of the shopping habitus. "I'd shop everywhere," declares Deb, laughing. She continues, "I would! I'd go to Whole Foods! . . . I love going in there. It's a gorgeous store, but I just about fall over in shock at how much things cost." Elaine nods, "I also like look- ing at Carrot Common," she says, referring to a worker-owned natural foods store, "but I don't actually buy anything while I'm there." Lois agrees, "I just think it's interesting." Like Elaine, Lois appreciates the allure of this exclusive shopping environment, but does not feel that she is a part of it. "I don't very often buy anything there because they are pricey," she explains. "And if you've not tried one of their products before, sometimes you're a bit leery of spend- ing that much money on something. But it intrigues you, you know?" Derek, the one man in the group, weighs in with a different perspective. "I don't think I would change much," he says, drawing looks of surprise from the women around the table. "I'm pretty happy with my place where I shop and with their products." Derek cannot conceive of a fantasy of pleasurable shopping and remains unconvinced by the women's enticing depictions of these exclusive and "interesting" venues. This contrasting response seems to be rooted in the fact that he does not value food shopping as a site of pleasure and discovery in the same way the women do; it is not an important site for the performance of his identity. Deb, Elaine, and Lois, by contrast, imagine a world in which they could visit expensive specialty shops not only as curious guests but as entitled consumers, moving through these exclusive spaces with a sense of ease and comfort.

Whether expressing disdain toward the elitism of a fine foods store, or desire for the gourmet delights of Whole Foods Market, less privileged women tended to speak of upscale shopping spaces in ways that conveyed a sense of distance—a distance that we interpret through the lens of habitus. While these women enact consumer femininities through the narrative of shopping for pleasure, they allude to the ways these pleasures might be deeper, or simply *easier*, if they had greater material resources. Our analysis reveals not only how class constrains the pleasures of shopping but also how working-class and poor women respond emotionally to the injustices of their disadvantaged class position. Poverty denies these women access to a relaxed, pleasant shopping experience that appears central to the experience of successful middle-class shopping femininities.

We encountered such emotions when discussing food shopping with working-class and poor women, even as they also described shopping as an activity they enjoyed. In fact, such negative emotions were often expressed even more intensely by those who identified most strongly with the pleasures of food shopping. "It makes me angry if I can't afford something," said Nadine. "Everyone should have access to decent food." Harsha, a 28-year-old living on social assistance, also spoke about how material constraints shape the emotional experience of food shopping, noting that buying food is "less enjoy-able when you're on a budget." The pleasures of food shopping are far outside of Harsha's material reality; instead, she describes her current approach to food as "survival mode."

Even as class constraints created emotional strain for working-class and poor consumers, many of these women articulated an ambivalent relationship to the gendered ideal of pleasurable consumption. "Before I lived on my own and I had a little bit more disposable income, I found it quite enjoyable," recalls Sarah, a 23-year-old student. "Now the challenge of grocery shopping has become a bit of a chore just because I feel more focused on trying to get the cheapest product . . . and planning out my meals way more carefully just because I have limited resources." Sarah reflected upon the ways in which her habitus has been shaped by her parents' struggles as refugees during the Vietnam War. "I think that grocery shopping is definitely a luxury," she said. "Having parents who were refugees and lived in refugee camps and never had food, I'm very aware of how ridiculous the concept of the North American grocery store is. To walk into a huge building that has piles of potatoes and crackers and everything you could possibly want, and you could have all of it. But I've always liked it." Even as she rejects the entitlements embedded within a privileged consumer habitus and struggles with the frustrations of shopping on a limited budget, Sarah continues to experience food shopping as a site of pleasure. Despite her ambivalence, she concludes that "overall, it's enjoyable."

Women also expressed frustrations that emerged at the intersection of gender and class, as they struggled to perform a caring consumer femininity in the context of material constraint. Shannon, a single mother living on disability support, lamented the challenge of feeding herself and her daughter on such limited resources. She said, "It frustrates me because I can't make the best choice that I think is available for my family." Shannon devotes significant time and energy to planning her weekly purchases around sales and coupons—evidence of how the gendered burden of foodwork is exacerbated by class—and still often feels as though she has failed. Toward the end of the interview, Shannon reflected upon the emotional rewards derived from class privilege. "If you could just go in the store and not look at prices and pick up anything and everything you wanted, how much less stressful would life be?"

3. Conclusion: The gendered and classed pleasures of food shopping

In this chapter, we suggest that understanding the perpetuation of domestic inequality requires asking questions about pleasure, class, emotion, and femininity. Is food shopping always experienced as a chore? Are certain women positioned to enjoy grocery shopping more than others? Drawing from our focus groups and interviews, we have developed an analysis of food shopping as a site for doing gender, as well as a place where class lines are drawn. Given that many aspects of consumption occur outside the realm of formal, instrumental rationality, we paid particular attention to participants' accounts of the emotional dimension of food shopping. Our analysis reveals how food shopping may constitute an opportunity for discovery for women, as well as "escape" from regular life and childcare duties, even as it is clearly a component of domestic foodwork. At the same time, shopping is highly stratified by social class, yielding emotional experiences that reflect the classed context of the shopping venue, as well as the class position of the consumer. Emotion provides a lens onto these intersecting dynamics of gender and class and the ways in which structural inequities are reproduced through the embodied, felt experiences of food shopping—the consumer habitus. Grocery shopping is indeed a major source of pleasure and discovery, but it is also a lightening rod for more negative emotions, like disgust, anger, and frustration.

Women alluded to several aspects of food shopping that they did not enjoy—from the crowded atmosphere of the grocery store to the stress of shopping within one's budget. Yet, despite the presence of negative elements, many identified strongly with shopping as a site of pleasure—a realm in which they enacted a socially valued consumer femininity and were able to make multiple consumer choices. While this femininity aligned with gendered expectations regarding women's care-work, it also afforded possibilities for discovery and satisfied desires for socializing and independence. This analysis helps us better understand the persistence of gendered inequalities within the home, since food shopping—at least for the food-identified women we spoke with—was not straightforwardly identified as burdensome or a source of oppression. It also sheds light on the felt experience of neoliberalism (see Chapter 2), which we have connected here to the gendered pleasures of enacting choice, responsibility, and competence in the marketplace.

Our research clearly demonstrates the profoundly gendered nature of food shopping, but it also speaks to the necessity of studying the classed dimensions of these practices and emotions. The hegemonic food shopping femininity—a woman who is a capable, conscientious consumer who values high-quality foods in a luxurious shopping environment—is not universally available. This does not mean that low-income women can be understood simply through their "lack" (Skeggs 2004a). Many working-class and poor women said that food shopping was enjoyable, even though it was often challenging and stressful. These contradictory narratives reflect the performance of a classed femininity. While the pleasures of food shopping have obvious financial constraints with negative emotional consequences, many working-class and poor women remain invested in the performance of this valued consumer femininity.

Privileged women, in contrast, are more able to invest in hegemonic consumer femininities by virtue of their cultural and economic resources. As part of their privileged habitus, they feel disgust at discount venues, an emotional orientation that enacts the boundaries between a respectable middle-class femininity and a pathologized working-class femininity (Lawler 2004; Skeggs 2004c: 102–3). While some middle-class participants acknowledged the increased consumer choice afforded by their material privilege, very few expressed awareness of the *emotional* dividends derived from experiencing a privileged consumer femininity.

While our research reveals how a desirable (and privileged) femininity is enacted through food shopping, we feel it is noteworthy that the men and women we spoke to did not make ideological statements about food shopping as a gendered responsibility (e.g., "women *should* shop for food"). On the contrary, some women reflected critically upon the gendered roles that they found themselves participating in. This disjuncture highlights the ambivalence that feminists have shown to be "at the heart of many forms of gender and sexuality reproduction" (Skeggs 2004b: 29) and supports the feminist argument that reflexivity alone does not guarantee an end to gender inequities (Adkins 2003: 35). Contrary to theories of detraditionalization that position reflexivity as the key to social transformation, Adkins argues that "reflexivity does not concern a liberal freedom from gender, but may be tied into new arrangements of gender" (2003: 34). This analysis resonates with the ambivalences contained within shopping femininities, as women engage in practices of doing gender that exceed the boundaries of a straightforward model of internalizing norms. Many women in our research reflected openly upon the gender relations in their home—including their disproportionate responsibility for food shopping—yet were unable to pragmatically or emotionally detach from these identity projects, especially since there are clear socioemotional rewards for performing a successful, caring, shopping femininity. As we explore in the next chapter, a similar dialectic of reflexive critique and emotional attachment emerged in mothers' narratives of feeding children.

Note

1. June Cleaver was a character on the popular American television show, *Leave it to Beaver*. She is often regarded as the prototypical 1950s' housewife.

Chapter 4

Maternal foodwork:
The emotional ties that bind

Carol's concise email revealed the efficient word choice of a skilled planner. "42. Married. Three kids—one girl and two boys. Age 7, 5 and 2." Briefly referencing her husband's business and her own career as a film producer, Carol condensed their busy lives into a few short sentences. "Always interested in feeding kids the best possible food. Worried about chemicals, hormones, antibiotics, etc." When we scheduled the interview, Carol requested a reminder one or two days in advance. "I have quite a few things on my plate these days," she explained, "and I need reminders."

Now, sipping tea at her dining room table, Carol's fast-pace life is momentarily paused as she smiles over a photo of her children. Each wall of the room features a large work of art, save for one that is the backdrop for a grand piano. Dressed in a loose-fitting white blouse and khaki capri pants, Carol brushes her blonde hair behind one ear and explains that this photo was taken at their local farmers' market. "We go there every Tuesday. And I let them pick stuff out. So yesterday we got local strawberries and a loaf of sprouted grain bread." Carol flips to the next photo, which features a skinny girl with braids grinning over a plate of pancakes. "This is my daughter," she says, smiling. "She loves pancakes so we rotate them around. These ones are papaya and quinoa. Papaya is supposed to have great stomach enzymes, especially for little kids." Carol describes her creative efforts to pack added nutrients into her children's meals, preparing their food from scratch. "Sometimes it's the fruit I have on hand. Sometimes it's vegetables, carrots and things like that and I make it with more sort of pumpkin pie spices to hide the vegetables," she explains. "Anyway, this day is papaya for her birthday."

As we discuss the significance of food in her life, Carol consistently brings the conversation back to feeding children. "I think healthy food means that I'm being a good parent. And that I'm giving the best possible opportunity to my kids," she says. Given the salience of this commitment, Carol admits that she sometimes scrutinizes other grocery carts with a "judgmental eye," particularly when she sees "really awful stuff going down the conveyer belt with kids there." Contrary to the common perception that kids are difficult eaters, she says, "I'm quite proud that my kids like to eat lots of good things." Despite these successes, her children's health has not been free of stress. Carol explains that her daughter was infected with a serious virus as an infant and, as a result, has always been "a little bit behind." In light of this history, Carol views her daughter's diet as an especially critical component of her development. "It is very important for me that she eats very well-balanced food to concentrate," she explains. "She'll be fine, she's just behind. And I feel sad and bad about that. So I want to do my best to give her a good running start to catch up."

Reflecting more broadly on food and mothering, Carol relates her feeding practices to the healthy development of her children and the environment in which they will grow:

> They always say that women make the best voters because you think about your kids all the time. And I don't want them to eat crappy stuff. I don't want them to be left with a crappy world. We have to be respectful. We're fortunate, we can afford good food and we have to be respectful of that too.

Carol might seem exceptional, as a committed mother who maintains a successful career while feeding her kids healthy, home-cooked meals and fostering their environmental consciousness. This is an impressive balancing act that few mothers have the time, resources, or even the desire to achieve. Yet, Carol's story contains core themes that echo throughout the narratives of the 47 mothers in our study. These include nutrition promotion and disease prevention, fostering healthy and diverse (not picky) food habits, and cultivating children's understanding of ethical issues. These themes resonate with critical scholarship on motherhood and foodwork, including DeVault's insight that family foodwork allows women to present themselves as "recognizably womanly" (1991: 118). We interrogate the contemporary relevance of this claim (made over two decades ago) and explore the specific kinds of food projects required of "good mothers" today.

We begin the chapter by unpacking the connections between foodwork, emotion, and the ideology of intensive mothering, which encourages women to selflessly invest their time and emotional energy in labor-intensive, child-focused parenting practices (Hays 1996). In the second section, we explore mothers' role as "guardians of health" (Beagan et al. 2008). Finally, we examine how the provision of "pure," organic food has become an essential part of middle-class mothering ideals, producing the idealized figure of the "organic child" (Cairns, Johnston, and MacKendrick 2013). Throughout the chapter, we show how the foodwork of "good mothers" is not only demanding and labor-intensive but is regulated through the emotional burdens and joys of feeding children. What was striking throughout our conversations with mothers was not simply the consider-able amount of maternal labor involved in addressing these concerns *but the emotional potency of foodwork.* Our analysis shows how women may engage reflexively with mothering ideals, yet remain enmeshed in the emotionally binding ties of maternal foodwork. These ties help explain the persistence of gendered parenting schemas, as well as the lived experience of mothering in a neoliberal context, shedding light on how women emotionally negotiate the transferring of health responsibilities onto individual consumers.

1. Mothering and foodwork: Emotional investments and intensive mothering

None of the mothers in our study felt totally secure in their mothering practices. Even those like Carol, who seemed to gracefully enact an idealized maternal femininity, still shared doubts with us. But it was not simply the fear of fail-ure that motivated maternal foodwork. Equally compelling was the promise of success and the emotional rewards of achieving or even approximating maternal ideals. These rewards were clearly articulated in our interview with Gail, who is white and middle class and whose female partner had just given birth to their second child. When asked about the significance of food to her identity, Gail describes the gratification of maternal foodwork: "probably the most visceral way is when I sit down across from my son and watch him eat. I'm so happy when he likes something. And I'm kind of proud of him and proud of myself." It is noteworthy that Gail describes this happiness and pride as a "visceral" experience. The gratification of foodwork is not limited to the level of rationality, but is deeply felt. Thinking back to her son's first meals, Gail says "there was that piece of, oh wow, he's eating, and that feels really good and I want to do that again." As Gail articulates, the pride and joy of successful foodwork has seductive appeal for mothers and exists in dialectical opposition with the shame and fear of failing at these tasks.

In this chapter, we focus on the emotional potency of maternal food-work. Extending classic feminist scholarship on maternal care-work, we shed light on some of the contradictory ways gender inequities are reformu-lated according to neoliberal ideals of choice and individual responsibility.

Children's food practices are widely seen to reflect the success or failure of mothers' socialization efforts. Resulting emotions range from the pride in raising adventurous eaters to the anxiety of navigating food system risks. The fact that Carol feels "sad and bad" about the developmental effects of a virus her daughter developed as a baby and actively works to compensate through a rigorous food regime demonstrates how mothers feel ultimately responsible for children's well-being—including aspects that are beyond their control. Some women we spoke to reflected critically on the gendered pressures placed on mothers, yet most remained emotionally invested in these food-care practices. Thus, we argue that while mothering ideals are both attractive and constraining for women with children, they are also emotionally binding—making them difficult to reject, even when they feel impossible to achieve.

While mothers in our study sometimes had partners who offered practical support with grocery shopping or food provision, these women tended to experience the mental and emotional labor of daily foodwork as a personal responsibility. Indeed, most of the partnered mothers we spoke to took the lead on foodwork in their household. Even women like Carol, who embraced feeding children as an important aspect of their identity, articulated the challenges of this gendered burden. Although her husband is skilled in the kitchen, Carol is the primary shopper and cook in their home. She attributes this division of labor to her husband's hectic work schedule, but also said, "I think women still do more cooking. And they still do more thinking about it. It's the *thinking* that is the heaviest burden." Carol likened the planning element of foodwork to her work as a film producer.

> Like I said to my husband a few times, I'm a producer . . . And a producer is an organizer. You look over the budget and you hire people and you delegate jobs and you manage all of that. And I feel like, I said, I produce at work and then I come home and I produce this house. Because I tell you to go buy this and if I'm out one night and he's home for dinner I'm like, "make this for dinner."

Carol's apt analogy of mother as "producer" evokes the feminist argument that women's foodwork constitutes a form of gendered labor that produces the heteronormative family (Bugge and Almas 2006; Charles and Kerr 1998; DeVault 1991; Parson 2014). This foodwork extends beyond the practical task of preparing food to include mental and emotional foodwork, like planning shopping lists, making sure that nutritional needs are met, and managing conversations at the dinner table. Research on the division of family foodwork within heterosexual relationships indicates that women's inequitable share of food labor often becomes more pronounced with the arrival of children, suggesting that this gendered burden is heightened with motherhood (Fox 2009).

In her seminal text *Feeding the Family*, American sociologist Marjorie DeVault (1991) describes how women are "recruited"into mothering discourses of nurturing the family through foodwork, such that they become personally invested in these practices as an expression of identity. This is not to say that women are "naturally" more nurturing or devoted to their children. On the contrary, we reject such essentialist notions and direct our attention toward the *social and discursive processes* through which foodwork is constituted as a site for performing maternal femininities. DeVault's concept of "recruiting" is useful for fostering a nuanced analysis of how women engage with mothering discourses—one that recognizes their agency, but emphasizes how mothers' emotions are impacted by cultural discourses that associate maternal love with foodwork. For many mothers, foodwork is not simply work, although it is certainly a form of labor. It is also a way to perform femininities by caring for family members and expressing love through food. As we demonstrate throughout the chapter, emotion is key to recruitment and *retention* in mothering and foodwork discourses; this occurs not only through the fear of failure but also the emotional rewards of successful foodwork. In the words of Agnes, a cashier with two young children, "I like opening up my fridge and seeing it full. Makes me feel good. I feel secure and I feel like, okay, my kids are alright."

Building on the emotional dimension of recruitment into foodwork, a gendered division of household labor can be further legitimized through rationales that do not explicitly name gender, but rely upon gendered assumptions. One such assumption is the idea that women are more interested in health. Using interviews with women from different ethnocultural groups throughout Canada, sociologist Brenda Beagan and colleagues find that in the absence of explicitly gendered discourses, "health becomes a central rationale for a gendered division of labour" (2008: 662). The white and African-Canadian interviewees in their study did not explicitly state that foodwork was women's work, but generally accepted the fact that promoting household nutrition was women's responsibility. Beagan et al. conclude that women, and especially mothers, are not only associated with family health but are held responsible when a household does not maintain a nutritious diet. Their study illuminates the cultural expectation that women act as "guardian[s] of health" (662), a responsibility that contributes to the intense emotions associated with feeding children.

Gendered conceptions of foodwork as an expression of care must also be understood as a component of "intensive mothering" (Hays 1996; see also Arendell 2000: 1194–5).[1] As an ideology, intensive mothering constructs the "good mother" as one who is selflessly devoted to her children and who expends substantial resources, time, and emotional labor to their nurturing and development. This ideology is linked to conceptions of the child as pure and in need of protection and works to individualize this responsibility as the private duty of mothers (Murphy 2000). Despite the considerable energy and expense demanded by intensive mothering, "good mothers" are framed as those who happily devote themselves to providing the highest quality socialization experiences. The ideal mother does not just fill her kids' bellies; she plans mealtimes so that children are able to appreciate "good food" and make healthy, quality food choices.

The idea that feeding children is a rewarding extension of mothers' care-work was a pervasive theme throughout the blogs and magazines we studied. One blogger introduced herself as a former magazine director who is now "a slave to her four-year-old Scarlett and is learning how to add kale to almost any recipe" (*Sweet Potato Chronicles*, "About"). This lighthearted introduction articulates the common association between maternal identities and foodwork. Also prevalent were earnest accounts of the personal fulfillment derived through mothers' intensive food labor, which is "worth every extra bit of effort for your kiddos" (*Peas and Thank You*, January 9, 2012). One woman described the newfound joys of foodwork after adopting the "Healthy Habits" advocated in *Cooking Light*, saying, "I spend more time cooking and going to the grocery store, *but I've never had so much fun*" (*Cooking Light*, January/February 2012: 62; emphasis ours). Threaded throughout these narratives is the understanding of foodwork as the individual responsibility of mothers— one that requires time and effort, but is an essential and rewarding component of women's care-work. As one blogger comments:

> Young children have to rely on their parents to make the right food choices for them. My daughters certainly can't go to the grocery store, pick out food, and make purchases without me leading the charge . . . So, as their mother, I am learning that it is my responsibility to buy and provide them with the right whole food choices even if it might require a little extra work on my part. (*100 Days of Real Food*, March 23, 2012)

While some women seem comfortable blogging about their success stories— sneaking kale into meat loaf, or keeping the family sugar-free for a month—the bar of "good mothering" is not always cleared in real life, and a fear of failure was palpable in our interviews. Here, the sociological concept of symbolic boundaries helps us understand what it means to be seen as a "good" mother, as well as the shame of feeling like an outsider. Boundaries refer to the "conceptual distinctions that we make to categorize objects, people and practices"; they help us understand who we are and significantly distinguish ourselves from others (Lamont 1992: 9, 233). The concept of symbolic boundaries has a long intellectual history (e.g., Becker 1963; Douglas 1966; Durkheim and Mauss 1963), and today it is strongly associated with Michèle Lamont's work (1992, 2000; see also Lamont and Fournier 2001), which convincingly demonstrates how boundaries reinforce and naturalize inequality. In Lamont's words, boundaries "potentially produce inequality because they are an essential medium through which individuals acquire status, monopolize resources, ward off threats, or legitimate their social advances, often in reference to superior lifestyle, habits, character, or competences" (1992: 12).

In terms of mothers' foodwork, boundaries are frequently drawn by observing foods eaten by other children or, to use postcolonial terminology, "the Other."[2] Carol's "judgmental eye" targeting other shopping carts was not an isolated comment, but was a theme recurring throughout mothers' narratives. Respondents admitted to sometimes judging others and were conscious of how their own feeding practices were scrutinized. Zahra, a South Asian writer with a nine-year-old daughter, said: "When you see younger kids who are a half a foot taller [than your daughter] you think, oh my god I'm doing something wrong. You think, maybe I should be force-feeding her or something. I think there is a general anxiety that their health is a marker of good parenting." From these comments and critical glances, it became clear that inclusion in the boundary of "good mother" depends on three interconnected elements: (1) providing healthy meals, (2) socializing children's developing palate, and (3) protecting children from food system risks. Carol's ability to mostly live up to these expectations was unusual; not every woman served quinoa-papaya pancakes on her child's birthday. However, many women expressed an awareness of these multifaceted mothering ideals. Carol's stellar example of health-conscious foodwork raises the question of how mothers with limited economic and cultural capital are marked as outside the boundary of the "good" mother (see Power 2005).

Critical race scholars like Patricia Hill Collins have persuasively argued that there is no universal motherhood experience, as mothering "occurs in specific historical contexts framed by interlocking structures of race, class, and gender" (1994: 56; also Skeggs 2002: 20). Similarly, third-wave feminists have insisted that studies of mothering should avoid extrapolating from the experiences of white, middle-class women (Arendell 2000; Baca Zin 1990; Collins 1994). The ideology of intensive mothering tends to legitimize white, upper-class mothering experiences as both universal and ideal (Glenn 1994; Scheper- Hughes 1993). Challenging these assumptions is vital, since not all mothers possess the privilege to facilitate individual mothering pursuits with such social approval. In terms of foodwork, the social and cultural specificity of privileged white mothering practices is often obscured, framed as universally desirable and attainable. However, we know from prior research that maternal food practices and ideals vary by race, class, and ethnicity. For example, in the study by Beagan and colleagues (2008) discussed earlier, many Punjabi-Canadians *did* describe cooking as women's work. The authors speculate that perhaps Punjabi-Canadian participants saw foodwork as a source of cultural preservation in the context of a dominant white society. These findings shed new light on DeVault's classic study and raise important questions: What happens when women are recruited into the project of intensive mothering, but do not share the means—or the desire—to fulfill these expectations? How are these expectations negotiated and experienced in the midst of multiple foodwork settings and identity projects?

We explore these issues below looking, first, at how mothers are positioned as guardians of children's health and taste and, next, how contemporary standards of responsible foodwork reflect the threats of an industrialized food system. Throughout, we highlight the emotional burden that these maternal foodwork expectations place on women.

2. Mothers as guardians of health and taste

When shopping and cooking for her family, Cindy seeks "nutritionally packed food that is flavourful." White, middle-class, married, and a part-time fitness instructor with two teenage kids, Cindy cooks mostly from scratch, save for the occasional frozen lasagna when things get hectic. "I don't trust a lot of packaged food," she explains. "I'd rather my kids eat homemade baked goods than store-bought cookies. 'Cause I know exactly how much sugar's gone in." While Cindy's foodwork is driven by a concern for her children's well-being, she says, "It's an expression of love for me as well." For Cindy, the notion of "food as love" is not a cliché; it is a meaningful expression of how she thinks about her labors in the kitchen. She recalls a failed baking project that she attempted one night while totally exhausted, in preparation for an event at her kids' school, and says, "It didn't work, because there was no love." Cindy laughs at the story, but her belief in its moral is sincere—even though an outsider might see a tired mother trying to pull off a late-night baking project as itself an act of love.

Even as Cindy takes seriously her commitment to healthy food, she laughs openly at the resistance she encounters from her kids. "They always question, 'Is this normal, or is this something you've played around with?'" Cindy laughs, but admits their concerns are not unfounded:

> I'll put vegetables in things, and they get really put off. Zucchini in macaroni and cheese. Once I filled the macaroni and cheese with quinoa. I got a little overzealous and I put too much. My daughter's eating it and she goes "Is there quinoa in here?" "No, there's no quinoa at all in there!" And then they're like "There's quinoa in here!" [laughs]

While such discoveries may fuel her kids' suspicion, Cindy takes pride in her many successes. These include a recipe for turkey meatloaf that incorporates finely chopped spinach. "My son loves it," she says with a grin. "He doesn't realize he's eating spinach."

We frequently heard tales of creative efforts to "trick" children into healthy eating, reflecting the expectation that mothers not only provide healthy food but go to great lengths to ensure that children enjoy it, or at least eat it voluntarily (Cook 2009a). Marissa, a black project management consultant who is married with two teenage sons, says that entry into motherhood fostered a new sense of "creativity and deception" in her cooking. In addition to sneaking vegetables into her kids' meals, Marisa also worked to foster her sons' adventurous appetites by "making things an occasion." She explains: "Instead of eating in the kitchen, we'd set the dining table, light a couple of candles and serve them their water in a wine glass." Marissa laughs and says, "You would not believe how gullible they are when it's presented that way." Now as teens, these habits have become second nature. "The kids actually insist on veggies," she says, adding "I think I bred them a little too well." Jokes aside, Marissa speaks with pride about these socialization efforts: "Of course it takes effort to do this but to me it was important."

In addition to socializing children into healthy habits, the good mother also cultivates the child's palate, fostering an appreciation for "good" food, as well as an openness to new things. "If you just feed children nothing but Wonderbread and marshmallow sauce then that's what they're going to grow up wanting to eat," says Nina, who is white, middle class, and works as an editor. Acknowledging that there may be a "snob factor" to her feeding practices, Nina declares, "I would rather [my children] eat a really good croissant than some yucky half-stale donut. It's a palate thing." Nina's allusion to the "snob factor" highlights the processes of class distinction within food socialization projects. Sociological research has shown how middle-class socialization involves raising children who embody "good taste" (Bourdieu 1984) and feel entitled to their privilege

(Lareau 2011). Nina's statement reinscribes classed food boundaries: between the refined middle-class taste for a really good croissant and the unrefined working-class tastes of "Wonderbread and marshmallow sauce" (see Bobrow-Strain 2012; Parsons 2014).

Eva, a white, middle-class mother who works in the nonprofit sector, says she is often surprised by the adventurous tastes of six-year-old Mackenzie. "I would say she's a foodie," she says, smiling at her daughter. "She was obsessed with snails for the longest time." While Eva expresses surprise at Mackenzie's sophisticated tastes, it is clear that these have been carefully cultivated. Reflecting on the various food-related activities they do as a family, Eva shares the memory of the container garden she and her husband planted when Mackenzie was a baby. "Her first words were like, chive and basil and she would take them and pop them in her mouth. Remember that?" Eva turns to her daughter, who nods her blonde head and says, "And the little tomatoes."

When it comes to children's diets, Eva believes that "parents shouldn't control what kids eat, they should provide healthy options so that kids make their own choices." To that end, she recently took Mackenzie for her first taste of McDonalds. "She's old enough now not to get addicted right? Old enough now to know how yucky it makes her feel." At her mother's mention of McDonalds, Mackenize scrunches up her nose and says, "Eghhhh!" conveying her distaste for the fast-food experience. When asked what she did not like about it, the six-year-old says, "I don't know, everything?" Eva laughs and adds, "It just doesn't feel good in our stomach." Instead, she says they would much rather enjoy a night out for sushi. Mackenzie grins. "My favourite food is sushi," she declares.

Socialization stories like Mackenzie's generate feelings of personal achievement for mothers. Yet, within these tales of success is the implicit understanding that mothers are personally responsible for children's eating. In this formulation, the child is a figurative extension of the self—their (un) healthy choices a direct reflection of mothering practices—leading to intense feelings of pride, guilt, and responsibility.

As a mixed-race single mother raising three kids on a tight budget, Theresa recounts the challenge of maternal foodwork. "I made a decision just after my third child was born that I was gonna be poor and be on welfare and raise my kids," she says. Theresa's story illustrates the struggles that women with limited resources may endure in an effort to adopt aspects of intensive mothering. In Theresa's case, this meant accepting the financial burden and social stigma of living on social assistance in order to carefully regulate her children's diets. "I was adamant that I'd be there when the kids came home for lunch,"

Theresa explains, "so I knew everything they were basically eating." Yet, despite her devoted feeding efforts, Theresa still encountered moments that left her feeling like a failure—such as the frozen waffles she served on "harried mornings." A break from the usual oatmeal, Theresa had thought of the waffles as a healthy alternative, especially when topped with fresh fruit. Years later she discovered "those waffles were one of the highest on the list of trans fat." Theresa winces as she relives the memory. "I felt so bad! Thinking that I was feeding my kids something healthy to start their day."

Theresa's guilt may seem unnecessary—how could she have known about the risks of trans fats before this became the subject of public scrutiny? Yet, serving a nutritious home-cooked breakfast is a powerful image in the cultural construction of the good mother. "The morning is your shot to make this day right," one blog encourages readers. "To put something hearty and nutritious, yet warm and comforting in your belly. To say, 'You, my loves, are precious to me'" (*Peas and Thank You*, August, 29, 2012). While women are invited to reap the rewards of expressing love through food, mothers' stories illustrate the emotional burden of performing the good mother, guardian of health and taste. For poor women like Theresa, the emotional burden of this maternal project is intensified by material constraints.

Still others lack the resources to even partially enact this maternal femininity and encounter mothering ideals from the position of the "failed" Other. Deb says that although she enjoys grocery shopping, "I'm not allowed to because I buy all the wrong things!" This comment generates a great deal of laughter in the focus group, and Deb goes on to confess the many ways she fails to fulfill dominant ideals of mothering. Forty-three years old and of First Nations descent, Deb describes how her Chinese-Canadian partner accuses her of teaching "bad habits" to their seven-year-old son. These range from buying expensive prepared items that "aren't on the list" (money has been especially tight since she was laid off six months ago) to eating fast-food. The other focus group participants chuckle at Deb's stories, which share a common theme of self-proclaimed food failures. "I try and set a good example for my son," she says, "but sometimes I fail miserably."

Despite Deb's apparent food "failures"—or perhaps because of them—she displays considerable commitment to teaching her son healthier practices than her own. "Because I'm overweight I've been really conscious of how I portray food to my son," she explains:

> I try to be very candid with him. He was like, "Why are you so fat, mommy?" And his dad was like, "Oh don't ask Mommy that!" And I said, no, it's okay.

I said, really, I worked a lot of hours for ten years and I ate at McDonalds, and I ate in a food court for ten years and didn't exercise. You can't do that, you end up like this. [laughs]

Deb reaffirms the boundaries surrounding the good mother to position herself as the failed Other of this maternal ideal. In doing so, she makes a lesson of her own food "failures" to ensure that they are not reproduced in her son—a confessional strategy that appears to offer a way of partially redeeming her mothering practices.

Amid these articulations of failure, the one aspect of foodwork where Deb feels successful is making her son's lunches. "I like making them in a bento box and they have to look a certain way," she says, drawing knowing glances from her friends. Originally motivated by a desire to provide her son with "healthy and balanced" meals that were also "visually appealing," this has evolved into an artistic project. Deb regularly posts pictures of the lunches on Facebook. When her friend Cynthia displays a photo of one of Deb's recent creations—a beautiful bento box featuring panda bears made of stuffed rice balls—the group erupts in praise. Deb accepts the compliments warmly, but admits that this masterpiece went uneaten. "Because it was for a field trip," she says, "and 'They had hotdogs, mommy.'" Her friends laugh and reassure Deb that no homemade bento box lunch could compete with hotdogs. While Deb maintains a lighthearted attitude, it is hard not to feel a pang of sympathy for this care-work gone uneaten and unappreciated.

While few of the mothers in our study spoke so openly of their "failures," Deb was not alone in expressing a sense of defeat in the face of mothering ideals. Manuela highlights feeding practices that are culturally valued in her home country, Cuba, but difficult to maintain in a Canadian context. For instance, she believes that children should have a warm, home-cooked midday meal and feels regretful as she sends her kids to school with a sandwich. "Every single day of the week, they come back and my husband and I, and everybody I guess knows that they had bad lunch. Little children having bad lunches," she says, with a weak smile. Because Manuela and her husband both work full time, bringing the kids home for lunch is not an option. Even though her children eat the same thing as their classmates, in conforming to the Canadian model of a packed lunch, she feels she has failed them. "Every single day. For five days a week, I feel bad," she says, her confession punctuated by short, awkward laughs. "So that's my eternal regret for a few more years, until they are independent."

Whether in promoting health or preserving ethnocultural traditions, women evaluate their own mothering practices according to a hegemonic maternal femininity—a standard that often seems impossible to achieve, but offers considerable emotional rewards for moments of success. While mothers have long been deemed primarily responsible for nurturing and socializing children through their foodwork, the requirements of this responsibility are historically specific. Amid contemporary debates about the risks of an industrial food system, North American mothers are recruited into a new maternal ideal: raising an organic child.

3. Raising an organic child

Studies show that women are more likely to buy organic foods (Bellows et al. 2010; Gonzalez 2009; Lea and Worsley 2005; Magnusson et al. 2001), and women with children in particular are high consumers of organics (Elliott 2013; Hill and Lynchehaun 2002). These trends are not surprising given the messages mothers receive about protecting children's bodies. In their "Ultimate guide to the grocery store," *Parents* magazine articulates a common caution that "kids are more vulnerable to harm from pesticides" and recommends buying "organic versions of fruits and vegetables that traditionally have the most pesticide residues" (August 2011: 114). The article also advocates spending extra money for "certified organic eggs," which are "produced without antibiotics and synthetic pesticides" (116), as well as "foods packed in glass or paper" since "canned foods may contain the chemical BPA" (118).[3] Presented as a series of helpful tips to "cut through the chaos" at the supermarket (113), the article reveals the challenges of feeding children in a moment marked by collective anxieties about industrial food. While food risks are the source of public concern, these fears intensify in the realm of feeding children, where they are bolstered by notions of childhood purity and potential (James et al. 1998). Given that mothers continue to be positioned as the "the moral as well as physical guardians of the next generation" (Burman and Stacey 2010: 229), maternal femininities are assigned the particular duties of protection and socialization deemed necessary within this historical context. In addition to acting as guardians of health and taste, the contemporary good mother carefully practices risk avoidance, monitoring food purchases to prevent harmful toxins or chemicals from entering children's bodies (MacKendrick 2011, 2013, 2014). This hegemonic maternal femininity also demonstrates environmental awareness and fosters ethical practices among tomorrow's consumers. The historical specificity of these pressures was not lost on our participants. In the words of Matilda, a white, middle-class woman with teenage children, "I don't think my mom sat there and thought, 'is it local, is it organic, is it ethical, am I supporting factory farms?' I mean, she just went and bought food."

Contemporary mothering discourses give rise to an idealized figure that we conceptualize as the "organic child" (Cairns, Johnston, and MacKendrick 2013). Mothers are increasingly encouraged to adopt feeding practices that not only promote children's well-being but also advance broad social and ecological objectives through conscientious consumption (Cairns et al. 2014). In this section, we explore the organic child ideal as it relates to: (1) the perception of children's bodies as pure and in need of protection, (2) the idea of socializing children to be ethical consumers, and (3) the class constraints that make the organic child difficult, if not impossible, for all mothers to attain.

Protecting purity: "I don't want that in my child's body"

Nearly all of the mothers we spoke with described a shift in their food practices with entry into motherhood. "I became a little bit more aware ever since I became a mother," says Agnes, a white, working-class mother with two children. Others in the focus group murmur in agreement as Agnes continues: "I do a lot of cooking now whereas before we'd do fast, takeout, not necessarily McDonald's. And then you have kids and then you're like, oh my god, wait a second, you know? You're more aware." This new food awareness was commonly linked to an understanding of children's bodies as fragile and in need of protection, which motivated many mothers (who were financially able) to increase their purchase of organic goods. Selena, who is white and training to be a midwife, describes how the birth of her daughter prompted her "to shell out a bit more because we think of a little growing body and how much more sensitive [she is] to pesticides." Similarly, Gail says that with the birth of her first child, "It really solidified some of those priorities around healthy food." She explains, "I didn't want to feed him non-organic fruit . . . I just wanted him to have the best really . . . So we do, even though we're making some sacrifices in other areas." Gail was not the only participant to suggest that protecting children's purity required sacrifice. Yin, who is Chinese-Canadian, middle-class, and does not have children, was struck by the shift in her friend's shopping practices after the birth of her first child. "She would go to [an upscale natural butcher] to buy meat for her daughter and then go to [a conventional supermarket] to buy meat for her and her husband," Yin recalls. The pattern left Yin baffled. "So we talked about it and she said there is no way we could afford getting all organic for the entire family." The experience raised questions for Yin about how she will balance these demands in the future. "It just stayed in my mind as one thing I need to consider if I want to have kids."

While raising an organic child was a pervasive theme throughout our research, several women spoke critically of the pressure on mothers to protect children through a carefully monitored diet. Paige, a white, low-income mother who works as a community food coordinator, recalls being bombarded with instructions about how to eat during pregnancy. Given the difficult combination of hunger and nausea that often accompanies pregnancy, Paige says, "if you're constantly desperately trying to put something in your mouth, you don't want to be like, is this the ideal, perfect food for my baby growing inside me?" Now that her daughter is a toddler, Paige says she has ended up just "trying to feed her what seems good and not stress about it."

Others described how they found their own expectations about good food-work to be unreasonable since having children. "What I imagined I would do as a parent, and what I'm *actually* doing are worlds apart," says Rosita (Chinese, Hispanic, Indigenous) who works part time at a food coop. Looking back, Rosita laughs at her plan to feed her son an exclusively organic diet. "Having a toddler things can get really intense," she says, chuckling. "If he's like 'BANANAAA!' and I can't get to an organic shop . . . and he's having a meltdown, then I'll go and get him a banana. And it won't be organic." Lisa, who is white and works in product development, recalls how her own shopping habits shifted when she had kids and suggests that this was prompted by "what we heard in the media . . . you know, no pesticides and the purity of when they're born and you should have the best quality foods to nourish." Now that her children are older, Lisa questions these demands. "You know what? The kids need to have milk and if it's not organic this week it's not gonna kill them. So I kind of just succumb. I kind of just compromise." Even as Lisa rejects the impossibilities of the organic child ideal, the suggestion that she has "succumb" to a less pure diet implies an element of failure on her part. Indeed, throughout our conversations with mothers, we were struck by this combination of critical reflexivity and emotional investment. Even as women discussed the organic child with critical distance, this ideal continued to generate powerful feelings in their foodwork as an internalized standard of good mothering.

This pressure to protect children's purity was the source of stress for many mothers, including those who reevaluated past practices in relation to the organic child ideal. "We eat a heck of a lot of chicken, and my daughter did go through puberty quite early," explains Cindy, sharing her worry that her daughter's physical maturation was accelerated by their family diet. The risks of industrial farming were not in the public spotlight when Cindy's children were young, yet she feels personally responsible for failing to shield her daughter from its harmful effects: "It's almost as though I became cognizant of it a little bit too late, you know?" While knowledge of these risks created stress for Cindy, it left some mothers feeling vindicated. When Vicky expresses concern that the hormones in meat can affect girls' development, Theresa responds, "Well my daughter started [menstruating] late, in grade 9. So I felt good about that." Theresa suggests that her daughter's relatively late start of menstruation is a sign that her development has not been altered by too much exposure to industrial foods. While Theresa's sense of accomplishment contrasts with Cindy's sense of concern, both women regard their daughter's physical development as a reflection of their feeding practices, embodying their *individual* choices and actions. What's more, the outcome of this evaluation is experienced emotionally, as a source of pride or regret.

Even as mothers invested significant emotion in raising an organic child, they were careful to calibrate this mothering project. Mothers distanced themselves from an "extreme" and controlling approach to protecting children's purity that was seen as overly restrictive. Mothers emphasized that while committed to a particular feeding regime, they allowed a degree of flexibility. In such instances, women were careful to distance themselves from the trope of the uncaring, uninformed mother (e.g., who feeds their kids Wonderbread), as well as from an overly perfect, overly disciplined approach. For instance, Carol comments that while "hormones and antibiotics" are a "huge concern," she is "not nuts about it." She explains: "If we're at a restaurant and they don't have organic milk, [my kids] are gonna have a glass." The fact that mothers feel compelled to demonstrate that they are not "nuts" sheds light on the difficult performance of raising an organic child. Enacting this maternal femininity requires that mothers devote immense time, thought, and concern to monitoring and regulating what enters their children's bodies. At the same time, they must calibrate this performance to distinguish themselves from the "obsessed," perfectionist mother—a pathologized femininity that evokes historical depictions of the female hysteric. "We do eat a lot of organic foods but not exclusively and certainly not sort of dogmatically," says Robin, a white graduate student who is married and has a toddler son. Robin clarifies that while she is concerned about her son's diet, she is determined to "not make myself crazy with it." She pauses, then adds, "I could totally drive myself crazy with it."

A common theme in mothers' narratives of protecting children through food choices is the idea of seeking *control* through foodwork (MacKendrick 2013, 2014). In the neoliberal context of individualized environmental risk management, it is striking that so many mothers believed profoundly in the power of foodwork to shape, nurture, and protect their children. For Fran, foodwork was explicitly linked to risk management. "That's the one thing I can exert control over in this environment," she said. "I can't control what's in the air that we breathe, I can't control what's in the water but I can control what I feed myself and my child." Aware of the many contaminants in her daughter's environment, Fran devotes her mental, emotional, and physical labor to those elements "that I can control, with what she consumes and what she eats." While raising an organic child provides Fran with a sense of agency, it also leaves her with the weight of this responsibility for the child she holds dear. "She's my daughter," she states matter-of-factly. "She's my number one priority."

Socializing ethical consumers: "I want to instill in her the sense of relationship with food"

Raising an organic child is not only about protecting children from risks but also socializing them to be ethical consumers. This child development project relates to a key food sociology theme explored in Chapter 2: the role of food as both a source of distinction and a tool for mobilizing social and environmental change. Many mothers in our study were committed to teaching children about where their food comes from, to foster a connection to their food source. "I want to instill in her the sense of relationship with food and where it comes from and how it's cultivated," states Fran. She laughs and adds, "that meat isn't something that's bought in a Styrofoam tray." Much like protecting purity, this socialization project is about counteracting the harmful effects of an industrial food system that alienates consumers from their food source. It is also about understanding children as emerging citizen-consumers who have the potential to build a more sustainable future through their food choices.

While fostering ethical practices among children was a goal for many mothers in our study, some reflected critically on this socialization project as a *gendered* responsibility. "I think that women are the ones that think about the food and their families," says Bronwyn, a white, middle-class community food activist with two young children. Bronwyn clarifies that this is not due to a natural maternal instinct, but rather because women are "trained to be the nurturers." Using her own family as an example, she says, "I'm the one that thinks about the family nutrition and how do we make sure we have balanced meals." This gendered responsibility extends to developing children's ethical orientation toward food production and consumption. "I want my children to grow up knowing how to grow food and have an appreciation for the amazingness of food and the amazingness of farmers," Bronwyn explains. While this socialization project was a source of pride for many mothers with young children, pursuing these same practices with teenagers held a different set of challenges. Often, these struggles centered on teens' desire to share "normal" food practices with their friends—going out for fast-food rather than eating the healthy, unusual, and/or environmentally conscious lunch their mothers packed for them. Deirdre recalls the day her daughter came home with a look of horror on her face and declared: "I can't be seen at school with quail eggs ever again, Mom."

Parenting struggles aside, the duty of socializing the next generation of ethical consumers was a frequent topic of discussion when we asked women about the changes they hoped to see in the food system. "Maybe it starts in prenatal classes," suggests Marissa. "Start talking to the mothers." While developing mothers' food literacy is surely a noble goal, this vision for change draws upon gendered—and neoliberal—conceptions of social reproduction that position individual mothers as personally accountable for addressing systemic food issues. These individualized conceptions of social change had strong support throughout our focus groups and interviews; in part, this speaks to the pervasiveness of neoliberal narratives of individual responsibility, but it also speaks to a pragmatic desire on the part of our participants to *do* something. In addition, it is important to note that we did encounter critical perspectives on this issue of maternal responsibility. For instance, Sarah, a Vietnamese-Canadian student, said, "The system has to change first. A single mom is not gonna care about getting an education about organic food. They're gonna just worry about feeding their kids period." As someone who grew up in poverty, Sarah is keenly aware of how individualistic accounts sustain structural inequities. "It's not fair that poor people suffer the most for the shit things that factory farming does, just 'cause they can't afford to go to farmers' markets," she says, adding, "It's really a privilege now to eat natural organic food."

We agree with Sarah's assessment: raising an organic child demands substantial resources that render this ideal inaccessible for many mothers. Nevertheless, we spoke with women living on severely limited budgets who strove toward protecting purity and fostering ethical consumers out of a desire to provide the best for their children. Thus, while the organic child ideal is most commonly adopted as a middle-class mothering practice, it remains emotionally binding for many poor and working-class mothers, generating intense guilt and frustration.

Class constraints: "I do what I can with what I've got"

"I am a 45-year-old single mom of a teenager daughter," writes Shannon, introducing herself over email. "I live on ODSP [Ontario Disability Support Program], so my money is limited but I try to do the best for my daughter that I can on a very fixed income." Articulating the significance of food to her identity, Shannon sheds light on how class exacerbates the emotional potency of maternal food-work. "I am disappointed and stressed that fresh food, good produce and non-processed food is pretty much out of reach for most people, especially those on a fixed lower income."

Sitting in a quiet corner of the public library, Shannon speaks passionately about the significance of food in her life. Her grey-blond hair pulled into a bun, Shannon's hoop earrings jiggle lightly as she speaks, her expressive face accented with blush and mascara. Like most of the mothers we interviewed, Shannon consistently returns to the topic of feeding her daughter. When asked how her shopping habits might change if money were not a concern, Shannon does not hesitate. "Ohhh, I would try to buy organic," she says, explaining that she worries about the environmental and health impacts of food additives and hormones. Despite these concerns, Shannon must focus on meeting her daughter's basic nutritional needs. "I try to make sure we have vegetables and that kind of stuff, fruit as much as I can," she explains, adding that she will sometimes "forgo those things first to make sure my daughter has them." While Shannon sees value in raising an organic child, this maternal project far exceeds her budget. This conflict—between maternal cultural ideals and lived material realities—creates tension on an emotional level. "It angers me," she says, "I tried to do organic for a little while and I just couldn't do it." Instead, Shannon must negotiate the pressures of maternal foodwork within these material constraints. "So I do what I can with what I've got."

Like Shannon, many of the poor and working-class mothers we spoke with were frustrated that they were unable to provide their children with what they understood to be the very best—the "pure," ethically sourced foods required to raise an organic child. Tara, a 36-year-old white woman who is also raising a teenager as a single mother, describes money as a key source of "tension" in her foodwork. "I love cooking and eating and feeding people, but I don't have a lot of money," she says. "In terms of priorities, that's the only tension that I feel." Imagining a world in which she did not have to think about money, Tara says, "It'd be all organic and all at farmers' markets, that kind of thing." But in real-ity, she says, "sometimes I'm looking at some fair trade and then I have to get something that's 99 cents."

It is clear that the organic child ideal created emotional strain for many poor and working-class mothers in our study. Yet, some of the more privileged women we spoke with also reflected upon the classed divisions perpetuated through this ideal. "There is a big class element about where you can get food and how much it costs," said Sue, a white, middle-class, family support worker. "If you're trying to feed a family, and you're not making very much money, are you going to go and buy a six dollar head of broccoli from the farmers' market?" Sue paused before answering her own question. "Probably not because that's not enough calories."

In addition to drawing attention to these material constraints, some of the mothers we spoke with also critiqued the elitism of the organic child ideal. Tammy, who describes herself as lower middle class and runs an in-home daycare, comments on how children's eating is scrutinized as a way of evaluating the "good mother." "The way you feed your child is almost like a status symbol. 'Oh, did you see these?'" she says, assuming an air of mock pretentiousness, "They're *organic*." Tammy notes how maternal foodwork is the site of potent symbolic boundaries. "When you are feeding your child out in public, you are advertising to people what kind of a parent you are," she says. Yet, even as Tammy voices skepticism toward these pressures, she is also committed to shielding her toddler's body from food additives and fostering his environmental consciousness. Thus, while mothers may critique the elitism underpinning the organic child, for many this remains an emotionally binding ideal that generates strong feelings in their foodwork.

The continued attachment to the organic child ideal is rooted, in part, in the way that mothers are held *individually* responsible for protecting children's purity and socializing ethical consumers. Thus, this maternal food femininity is sustained by neoliberal conceptions of personal responsibility that are embedded within contemporary consumer culture. Interestingly, Shannon, a single mother living on an extremely limited income, was among the few participants in our study who critiqued this fundamental assumption. Instead of viewing disease prevention as a personal responsibility achieved through precautionary consumption, Shannon calls for state regulation of industry practices: "That's absolutely crazy that we have to accept that these companies are allowed to do this and Health Canada is doing nothing about it," she said. Shannon provides a systemic assessment of what is predominantly imagined as a problem best tackled by individual consumers and articulates an important exception to the dominant neoliberal logic of individual responsibility and market solutions. It is noteworthy, but perhaps unsurprising, that her critique emerges from a position of class marginality. While Shannon is committed to providing the very best for her daughter, she is structurally prevented from pursuing the organic child ideal. This exclusion generates stress and frustration, but it also yields critical perspective on the structural dynamics shaping mothers' foodwork, which are so often masked by hegemonic maternal femininities.

4. Conclusion: The emotional potency of feeding children

In her bestselling book *The Barefoot Contessa Cookbook*, Ina Garten espouses a personal food philosophy that is enmeshed in maternal relations of caring through food. She writes that food is

> about more than dinner. It's about coming home and being taken care of. It's about Mom. I actually think that the food our mothers made may not be what we are nostalgic for. It's more an emotional picture of a mother who was always there, knew what we needed, loved us, let us run free when we wanted to explore. Food is about nurturing: not only physical but also emotional nurturing. (1999: 21)

This romanticized account depicts maternal foodwork as a feminine labor of love that is naturally suited to, and rewarding for, the nurturing mother. Critical as we may be of Garten's "emotional picture of a mother who was always there," this image figured prominently in our conversations with mothers. This is not to suggest that every woman embodied the performance of the good mother who joyfully serves her children delicious and healthy meals, using only organic ingredients. The women in our study did the best with what they had; daily meals were shaped by material constraints, ethnocultural traditions, nutritional needs and preferences, restricted schedules, and varying levels of skill. While food-work circumstances and practices varied, what *was* remarkably consistent in our conversations with mothers was an awareness of these mothering ideals, which served as a kind of gold standard that women used to evaluate their own feeding practices. Even those who were critical of these standards, and articulated an explicit effort not to get caught up in them, still made sense of their own feeding practices in relation to this ideal. For that reason, it appears unreasonable to expect that women will simply disengage from these practices, especially since they are enmeshed within cultural expectations, material practices, and deeply felt emotions.

Focusing on the intense feelings associated with feeding children, we have developed an analysis of maternal foodwork as emotionally binding, consti-tuted through the dialectic of positive and negative feelings. The pride and joy of successful feeding practices—Marissa's sons' love of vegetables, or Carol's children selecting produce at the farmers' market—must be understood along-side the worries and fears arising from apparent food "failures"—Cindy's regret over having fed her daughter industrially raised chicken. The emotional potency of these outcomes reflects not only women's attachment to their children but also cultural associations between mothering and foodwork. This leads to a cultural equation of children's choices as mothers' choices, such that picky eating or a love of fast-food signifies a failed socialization project and a lack of maternal effort. The price of such food "failures" is high, as children are figured as the promise of collective futures (James et al. 1998). Thus, mothers shoulder the burden of fostering the next generation of healthy, responsible food consumers, or risk being pushed outside the boundaries of good mothering. Today, this requires safeguarding children from dangerous pesticides and additives and developing their awareness of ethical food practices.

As mothers navigate these pressures, the balance of choice and control emerges as a central theme in their narratives. This is not the disciplinary, controlling mother of the past—the one who forbade children from leaving the table until every last brussel sprout had been eaten. Rather, it is a calibrated control based on the idea of socializing children to regulate their own appetites and make their own educated food choices. Reflecting the centrality of "choice" within neoliberal discourse, mothers work to develop their children's capacity for choosing wisely in a food system rife with unhealthy options. Think here of Eva and MacKenzie's instructive field trip to McDonald's, where a message of self-regulation and cultural capital accumulation was adopted; MacKenzie will undoubtedly not choose McDonald's for a special meal, but will instead gravitate toward things like sushi and fresh salads.

These foodwork stories resonate with sociologist Annette Lareau's (2002) research documenting a middle-class parenting style devoted to the "concerted cultivation" of children's tastes and talents. Lareau notes that while this parenting style expands children's experiences, it "creates a frenetic pace for parents" and affirms a "cult of individualism within the family" (2002: 748). In the case of maternal foodwork, we observe a clear synergy among middle-class parenting styles, intensive mothering ideologies, and a neoliberal discourse of responsibilization. The responsible mother takes firm control of food choices so she can raise the next generation of self-governing consumers, creating children who can one day be responsible for their own health and well-being. While these maternal practices appear congruent with neoliberal imperatives of individualism, as well as patriarchal tendencies of intensive mothering, this process is entrenched in everyday maternal emotions of love, care, and concern. Caring through food not only feels natural to many women, but to resist this work leaves mothers open to hurtful labels—as uncaring mothers, unconcerned about children's bodies and futures.

What's more, a maternal focus on food "choices" generates contradictory implications. For those raised on a steady diet of parental admonishments and directives (e.g., "finish your liver!"; "you're eating too much!"), these styles of foodwork can feel refreshing, even liberating. However, they leave open the possibility that children may *not* make the "right" choices, casting mothers in a poor light. MacKenzie loves to eat healthily, and this gives Eva great satisfaction, but other mothers worry about their children's food practices—worries that led to nervous laughter and even tears in our interviews and focus groups, such as when mothers wondered if their food choices contributed to or even caused their children's health problems. Such fears are accentuated for low-income mothers, who find it exceptionally challenging to raise a "pure" and self-regulating "organic child." The downloading of responsibility for health to individual mothers, thus, fosters endless opportunity for failure—a tendency reflected in the utterances of doubt, guilt, and self-criticism observed in our research. Additionally, as we explore next in the healthy eating discourse of the "do-diet," the discourse of "choice" can operate ideologically to obscure the continuity of food regulation and restraint in women's daily lives.

Notes

1. Karen Christopher (2012, 2013) points to the emergence of an "extensive mothering" ideology that involves managing and delegating care-work. Christopher's research explores how women articulate their caregiving decisions while managing mothering alongside employment. In this discursive context, she found that many mothers reject selfless narratives of intensive mothering and emphasize how their work is also mean- ingful to their identities. While we acknowledge these insights, our own interviews and focus groups show that in the domain of foodwork, intensive mothering remains a dominant ideological reference for the "good mother."

2. "Othering" is a process famously associated with the work of Edward Said, espe- cially his book *Orientalism* (1978). The process of creating a social Other allowed the colonial center to understand itself as superior to colonized people, thus naturalizing socioeconomic inequality and racism.

3. BPA refers to the chemical compound bisphenol-A, found in many canned foods and believed to have potentially harmful health effects. See MacKendrick (2010) for a discussion of the media framing of BPA in relation to individual responsibility for managing chemical body burdens.

Chapter 5

The "do-diet": Embodying healthy femininities

For Lisa, health is all about "balance." In addition to providing a nutritionally "balanced diet" when feeding herself and her family, Lisa also strives toward balance in her relationship to health ideals and does not fret over the occasional indulgence. "The health aspect is kind of weird," she says, sipping ice water as we sit chatting on her back deck. "I mean, it's been there since the beginning, but I'm not a fanatic." Lisa laughs, and adds, "I don't just drink smoothies and eat raw food or do anything that dramatic." This commitment to balance also informs Lisa's work life, where she spends four days a week as a product developer at a major food corporation. On the fifth day, she teaches yoga, a practice that she sees as critical to maintaining a healthy, "balanced" lifestyle in the context of a demanding professional life.

Sitting with the poise of a yoga instructor, Lisa explains that her eating is guided by embodied insights, rather than the latest diet fads. Instead of "getting caught up in the calories and how many I've had today," she believes it is healthier to "just listen to your body." Yet, even as Lisa rejects a regimented diet in favor of a more empowering model of healthy eating, body image pressures linger. "I always am thinking about being a little less weighty," she concedes. Noting that she lost eight pounds in recent months, she says "I don't really know why, but I feel better about it." Even as she acknowledges her desire for thinness, Lisa distances herself from a dieting femininity characterized by restriction. "I'm not one of those, you know, 'Can you put the dressing on the side?' or anything like that," she insists. Indeed, Lisa presents her healthy eating as a *choice*, rather than a response to external pressures. "If I feel like I want to eat healthy, I will pick up a healthier thing, but I don't always do that," she says. She pauses, as if searching for the right words, and remarks, "I've never had to eat and be concerned about [my weight] for my looks. I've been lucky that way."

Lisa's effort to achieve a "balanced" approach to health reveals the extensive calibration that surrounds healthy food femininities. In contemporary North American food culture, the ideal "healthy" woman must balance a complex constellation of factors. She should know what foods make her fat, but also avoid the appearance of "dieting." This woman is well versed on the latest research regarding health-promoting foods, and she has the skills to make nutritious food taste delicious. Perhaps most importantly, she understands how to control her body, but she also knows when to indulge. As the healthy eating magazine *Cooking Light* advises, "eating well isn't about depriving yourself of something. It's about finding balance and enjoying a variety of foods" (November 2011: 84). Instead of following a restrictive diet regime, today's healthy woman is encouraged to choose wisely and carefully to experience the pleasures of healthy eating—and the svelte physique that is an assumed embodiment of health. But does this new diet context allow women corporeal freedom? Is it enough that these women are avoiding the grapefruit diets of yesteryear?

This chapter charts the emergence of a contemporary food discourse that we call the *do-diet*—a healthy eating discourse that reframes dietary restrictions as positive choices while maintaining an emphasis on body discipline, expert knowledge, and self-control. The term "do diet" is drawn from a regular feature in one of our textual sources, the Canadian women's magazine, *Chatelaine*. The magazine asks: "Tired of living in a world of diet don'ts? So are we. That's why we developed the Do Diet, a radical new way to eat that's full of easy dos to get you on the right track" (March 2011: 78). Framed as an empowering discourse of choosing health, the do-diet has an explicit anti-diet message. At the same time, our analysis reveals how the pleasure of choosing health requires informed, disciplined, and carefully monitored food choices. This controlled vision of pleasurable eating is evidenced in the frequent advice to "indulge" in a single square of dark chocolate (but make sure it has at least 70 percent cocoa solids). While the specific language of the "do diet" was unique to *Chatelaine*, the do-diet discourse of healthy eating was pervasive throughout our data. The women we spoke with articulated a vision of healthy eating that emphasized choice over restriction while also describing how everyday eating involved considerable effort and control. More specifically, women engage in a balancing act to distance themselves from the two extremes of this tension; they work to avoid being seen as an out-of-control eater on the one hand or as a controlling "health nut" on the other. Through calibration, women actively manage their relationship to the extremes of self-control and consumer indulgence in an effort to perform acceptable middle-class food femininities.

In the next section, we outline how our argument builds upon two overlapping realms of scholarship: (1) embodied neoliberalism, with a focus on healthism and expert health knowledge and (2) feminist approaches to the body and post-feminism. We then document how the do-diet manifests in our interview, focus group, and textual data. The chapter ends with a discussion of the implications of the do-diet for feminist aims of social equality.

1. Embodied neoliberalism, fat-phobia, and "choosing" health

Drawing on the Foucauldian idea of bodies as sites of discipline and self-improvement (see Chapter 2), critical health scholars have demonstrated how a seemingly abstract ideology like neoliberalism can become embodied (Fusco 2006; King 2012; LeBesco 2011; Lupton 1999). Much of this work starts from the premise that health is socially constructed and builds upon Robert Crawford's (1980, 2006) writing on "healthism" as a moral discourse. Healthism suggests that achieving health is an individual's moral duty, a discourse that has clear implications for moralizing nutrition and food choices (see Bilktekoff 2013; Coveney 2000). Crawford suggests that "individual responsibility for health has become a model of and a model for the neoliberal restructuring of American society" (2006: 419). In this context, responsible citizens are those who seek out, assess, and act upon an endless stream of knowledge on the latest health threats. From a Foucauldian perspective, risk avoidance can be understood as a "technology of the self," wherein personal responsibility for illness prevention and health promotion "becomes viewed as a moral enterprise relating to issues of self-control, self-knowledge, and self-improvement" (Lupton 1999: 91).

This individualizing and moralizing approach to health can exacerbate social divides, at the same time that it idealizes personal responsibility. The logic of healthism obscures the privilege of advantaged populations that are most readily positioned to adopt "healthy lifestyle" practices (Crawford 2006; Guthman 2009) and are seen as superior to "unhealthy Others" with poor health, poor diets, or fat bodies (Biltekoff 2013: 9; Johnston, Szabo, and Rodney 2011: 306). Numerous scholars have connected embodied neoliberalism and fat-phobia, noting how thinness is idealized as an indicator of healthfulness, a corporeal expression of individual responsibility and self-control (Guthman 2009; LeBesco 2011; Metzl 2010). The stigmatization of fat bodies is certainly not new, but fat-phobia has gained new legitimacy through medicalized discourses of "obesity" that construct fatness as a health problem and fuel public panic about a so-called obesity epidemic (Guthman 2011; LeBesco 2011).[1] As food and embodiment scholar Kathleen LeBesco writes, "[t]he healthy body has come to signify the morally worthy citizen—one who exercises discipline over his or her own body, extends the reach of the state and shares the burden of governance" (2011: 154; see also Lavin 2013).

Even as thinness is equated with health and responsible citizenship, the embodiment of healthy femininities is complicated by the neoliberal imperative to consume. In a market-oriented culture that celebrates consumer choice as an expression of freedom, the good (and healthy) citizen cannot be marked solely by restraint. As food scholars Julie Guthman and Melanie Dupuis write, "we buy and eat to be good subjects" (2006: 443). Thus, they suggest that "the fetish of consumer choice" (2006: 442) exists in tension with "neoliberalism's hypervigilance about control and deservingness" (443). Exemplary citizens are expected to both consume and constrain themselves, yielding a discursive tension that is embodied in the neoliberal subject. As Guthman and Dupuis argue, "neoliberal governmentality produces contradictory impulses such that the neoliberal subject is emotionally compelled to participate in society as both out-of-control consumer and self-controlled subject" (2006: 444). This insight makes sense theoretically, but is not easy to resolve in everyday practice: How does one simultaneously embrace consumption and practice self-control? We take this tension as a key entry point for our analysis of the do-diet, as we examine how women manage this contradiction in their everyday food practices. Framed in positive terms of empowerment (as opposed to restriction), the do-diet mediates the logics of consumer choice and self-control through the practice of "choosing health." These logics appear to be in tension—one celebrating the empowering act of consumer choice, the other emphasizing the moral responsibilities of corporeal control—yet we demonstrate how they work together to facilitate the embodiment of neoliberalism and the expression of a postfeminist sensibility.

2. Feminist approaches to the body, health, and postfeminist empowerment

Feminist scholarship on the body provides crucial insight for understanding how neoliberal governance is embodied in the performance of femininity. In her foundational text *Unbearable Weight*, Susan Bordo (1993) demonstrates how Western consumer culture promotes the gendered beauty ideal of the slender female body, enacting cultural values of discipline, control, and heterosexual desirability. The slender ideal becomes a "project" to which the successful woman must aspire, curtailing her appetite in an effort to expel "excess" fat from her body (Spitzak 1990). Some have theorized this kind of feminine bodywork as a "third shift" of feminine labor, seeing it as work that the "successful" woman must squeeze into a busy day of paid employment and domestic responsibilities (Dworkin and Wachs 2009: 140). From a Foucauldian perspective, women's efforts to shape one's physical appearance (e.g., through diet or exercise) do not simply modify a preexisting female form, but actively *constitute* feminine embodiment (Bartky 1997). As Bordo writes, "[t]hrough the pursuit of an ever-changing, homogenizing, elusive ideal of femininity . . . female bodies become what Foucault calls 'docile bodies,'—bodies whose forces and energies are habituated to external regulation, subjection, transformation, and 'improvement'" (1989: 14). While research suggests that the slender ideal is associated with whiteness (e.g., Mears 2010; Milkie 1999), this hegemonic femininity generates corporeal aspirations among women from diverse ethnoracial and class backgrounds (Boyd et al. 2011; Kwan 2010; Reel et al. 2008).

The slender feminine body takes on new meaning amid contemporary discourses that equate the pursuit of health with good citizenship. While public rhetoric about health threats and the so-called obesity epidemic circulate widely, the work of protecting and embodying health remains closely linked to femininity (see Lupton 1996b: 11). This can be seen in the persistent gendering of "health as women's work" (Barnett 2006: 1), such that women—and particularly mothers—are tasked as familial "guardians of health" (Beagan et al. 2008; see our discussion of maternal foodwork in Chapter 4). Beyond the gendering of health-related care-work, recent feminist scholarship has highlighted the gendering of the healthy body itself. British sociologist Sarah Moore (2010) suggests that the contemporary "healthy body" is coded feminine.[2] Tracing historical shifts in the discursive construction of health (formerly associated with masculine traits of strength and utility), Moore forwards a feminist analysis of healthism:

> When we study contemporary health messages . . . and notice that they urge body-practices that have traditionally been associated with femininity, most notably the conscientious monitoring of the body and behavior that might cause bodily excess, we are also studying hegemonic gender norms. (2010: 106)

Building on Moore's analysis of the healthy body as an expression of femininity, we suggest that contemporary discourses of healthy eating must be understood within the context of postfeminism. A key postfeminist trait is the understanding of "femininity as a bodily property" (Gill 2007: 149) that one can and should freely develop, along with an associated "emphasis upon self-surveillance, monitoring and discipline" (Gill and Scharff 2011: 4). In a postfeminist context, beauty work is reframed as an expression of empowerment (Eskes et al. 1998)—a performance enacted on reality television shows celebrating the makeover of the female body (Banet-Weiser and Portwood-Stacer 2006; Ringrose and Walkerdine 2008). Within a postfeminist framing, even corporations can espouse the emancipatory goal to promote girls' and women's "self-esteem" through marketing strategies (e.g., the Dove Campaign for Real Beauty) that adapt a more expansive definition of beauty (Banet-Weiser 2012; Johnston and Taylor 2008). The postfeminist fetishization of "choice" reflects "emerging modes of regulation" that emphasize individual freedom and change—often at the expense of more significant discussions of structural gender inequality (McRobbie 2009: 51).

An analysis of postfeminist empowerment is critical to understanding how the do-diet engenders feminine embodiment. The do-dieter must invest in the body, but she must continually calibrate her position to avoid pathologized extremes. She needs to make healthy choices without becoming a health "fanatic." She must be in control without denying herself pleasure. She should be thin, but not on a diet. Our research demonstrates not only an aversion to the abject fat feminine body but also a distancing from a faultless or obsessive display of feminine control. Thus, negotiating do-diet discourse requires extensive *calibration*—the process of continually adjusting to approximate idealized and elusive feminine standards for good health and attractive bodies. Women in our study continually reference both ends of a pathologized dietary spectrum—the indulgent/ignorant overconsumer and the obsessive/controlling food restrictor—as they calibrate their own healthy femininities. As such, the calibration process reveals the challenge of negotiating feminine food standards in the context of a relatively narrow band of successful food behaviors. Calibration illuminates the unforgiving boundaries of successful food femininities and the gendered social pressures around "proper" healthy eating. All together, we gain a better understanding of why so many women feel like they are always striving toward but never fully achieving elusive standards of healthy eating and the closely associated goal of controlling and minimizing one's body fat.

While calibration is integral to women's food choices and body projects, we want to emphasize the simultaneous possibility of critique. Many of the women in our study were deeply critical of gender-based body inequalities perpetuated by the beauty and diet industry. We are wary of theorizing postfeminism in a way that overgeneralizes women's depoliticization or dismisses the empowerment women may experience through body projects (Arnot 2011; Jeleniewski Seidler 2011: 706; Taylor, Johnston, and Whitehead 2014; Walkerdine 2011). Yet, we demonstrate how the do-diet discourse makes use of women's critique in the service of neoliberalism, designating body image as another site where commodity solutions are idealized and feminism has been "taken into account" (McRobbie 2009: 15).

3. The do-diet: Calibrating choice and control

In this section, we document and analyze the do-diet in our empirical data, which includes our food media data sources as well as our interview and focus group research. The first half of our analysis focuses on *choice* and unpacks the idea of healthy eating as postfeminist empowerment. Second, we analyze a narrative of informed eating as an exercise in *control*, where women are encouraged to assume individual responsibility for their health.

A taste for choice

"Aren't you tired of nutritionists like me being a buzz kill? . . . It's time for a holiday eating column about the 'to dos' not the 'don't dos'" (*Globe and Mail*, November 7, 2011: L6). Like many of the texts we analyzed, this newspaper column frames healthy eating as a set of positive choices rather than "buzz kill" restrictions. In doing so, it adopts the language of *choosing health* that was pervasive throughout our data. Contrary to prohibition-based diets that render mealtime a regimented hardship, the do-diet reframes healthy eating as a "win-win" choice that need not sacrifice pleasure. Nevertheless, efforts to redefine restriction as *choice* are sometimes so blatant that they become comical—such as when the advice to *eliminate* evening snacking is reworded as "Do Eat smart after dark" (*Chatelaine*, March 2011: 78). Despite a consistent anti-diet message, the do-diet assumes weight loss as a universal goal, reproducing the slender feminine ideal. This conflation of health and thinness is evident in commonplace statements such as "your health—and your waistline—will thank you" (*Chatelaine*, March 2011: 167). With weight hovering in the background, the emphasis on "choice" in the do-diet is manifest through a consistent prioritization of health *over* body image and the framing of healthy eating as postfeminist empowerment.

Empowering, healthy choices

Women in our study commonly ranked health as their number one food priority—trumping issues like taste, cost, and ethics. For example, Eva (43, white, nonprofit sector) emphasized the need to facilitate healthy choices within her family: "Health first. We want to have as many healthy things in this house as possible so that *we can make healthy choices for all our meals*" (emphasis ours). Zahra (44, South Asian, writer) put it simply, "health actually wins out and trumps everything." Beyond simply prioritizing health, we were struck by the consistency with which women emphasized health *over* body image concerns. One focus group participant, Sadie (49, white, city employee), scoffed at our question of body image and turned the conversation immediately to healthy eating. Sadie's response was strong, but not atypical. Eva stated, "I've never done food stuff related to body image, really. It's more related to health." Like Eva, women in our study consistently articulated a discourse of *choosing health*—that is, framing healthy eating as a positive *choice*, rather than a response to body image pressures.

By adopting the discourse of choosing health, women distinguished themselves from a traditional dieting femininity. Gina (54, white, investment fund manager) stated, "I'm careful about what I eat, but I don't diet," adding "my philosophy is more moderation as opposed to abstinence." Through this process of calibration, Gina distances her own "careful" approach to healthy eating from an excessive level of corporeal concern. Similarly, Ingrid (46, white, unemployed) rejected the idea of a diet based in restriction, even as she acknowledged that certain choices are necessary to maintain her desired weight: "I don't restrict and count my calorie intake . . . I just sort of in general know how much I need a day and how much is okay for me to stay within my weight range." Statements like this were common in our focus groups and interviews, wherein women distanced their own body projects from the pathologized subject of a diet femininity—one who is shackled by food restrictions.

The do-diet ideal of choosing health was defined in relation to a past emphasis on diet restriction. Olive (27, black, fashion editor) framed this emphasis generationally, suggesting that her mother's generation felt that they had to "go on a diet," whereas her 20-something peers were more interested in maintaining corporeal discipline while embracing pleasurable, exciting, or challenging lifestyle choices:

> My generation, they're sort of taking their weight and their body image into their own hands, and they're doing extreme things like running marathons, swimming everyday . . . Ya, it's sort of the age of excess . . . So they'll eat and

drink and smoke and do recreational drugs, but then they'll run marathons and like, go rock climbing.

Olive's impressions of her peer group suggest that while food restrictions are shunned as old-fashioned, women today are still expected to maintain an acceptable body weight and have the personal responsibility to take body projects "into their own hands." Olive identifies with a contemporary discourse of healthy eating that portrays this lifestyle as enjoyable and fulfilling, as opposed to a past era of restrictive, unpleasant diets.

In keeping with the do-diet emphasis upon choosing health, the idea of restricting consumption was not only deemed disempowering but was also gendered as an expression of pathologized femininity. Tiffany (28, white, university student) lamented situations where "there'll be a room full of girls and we're having tea and then somehow the conversation will go to food and everyone's talking about their current restrictions." By contrast, she said, "I never have those conversations with any guys that I know." Tiffany draws upon a gendered construction of health in which diet concerns are coded feminine (Gough 2007; Richardson 2010). After sharing her frustration with femininities linked to food restrictions, Tiffany said, "I find it really refreshing when people discuss it in a positive way, like, I'm deliberately going and finding these organic [foods]. But I find that it can also be framed very negatively, like, 'I'm not doing this, and I'm not doing this, and you shouldn't do this.'" Tiffany identifies with a distinction at the heart of the do-diet—the idea of framing healthy eating as a choice, rather than a restriction—and aligns herself with the "positive," agentic feminine consumer who embraces healthy options.

While many women, like Tiffany, embraced the do-diet's emphasis on healthy eating as an empowering choice, not all of the women in our study felt empowered by this discourse. When we asked a group of 20- and 30-somethings about health and body image, Carmen (33, Chinese-Canadian, librarian) laughingly remarked, "don't look at me!" Carmen lamented her recent efforts to "eat smaller portions" and monitor the nutritional value of her meals, exclaiming, "That's too much thinking!" Such expressions of exasperation were rare in comparison to the pervasive narrative of empowerment through choosing health. Nevertheless, it is crucial to recognize "cracks" within do-diet discourse. While Carmen challenged the win-win framing of pleasure and health, Joanne (60, white, retired) critiqued the persistent emphasis on weight loss, even as dietary restrictions are reframed as health-promoting empowerment. In her words: "now they're trying to kind of counter [dieting] with trying to eat healthy and all that sort of stuff. But there is still a whole lot of discussion about weight." As Joanne points out, the do-diet does not free women from feminine body ideals. Rather, it repackages these expectations through the language of postfeminist empowerment and consumer choice. In this way, the do-diet places women in a double bind. Those who openly restrict their diet are viewed as disempowered and image-obsessed, but those who do not monitor and control their eating may fail to embody the healthy (read: thin) ideal. Staking out desirable femininities between these two extremes requires active calibration efforts.

A postfeminist approach to bodies: "I'm not a vegetarian because I think it makes you skinny"

In keeping with the do-diet discourse of empowering healthy choices, many women explicitly distinguished their approach from one motivated by social expectations about thinness. For example, Alejandra (42, Hispanic, journalist) emphasized that her healthy eating choices were "self-motivated" and involved more "than simple vanity and thinking 'Oh my god, that's cellulite.'" Alejandra makes clear that to the degree that she regulates her eating "to fit into her clothes," she does so as a personal choice, rather than as a response to beauty ideals. Similarly, Joanne stated: "I'm not a vegetarian because I think it makes you skinny. I know that some women might adopt a veggie lifestyle or a vegan lifestyle thinking that they will lose weight, but I never adopted it for that reason."

As Alejandra's and Joanne's comments suggest, the do-diet inscribes boundaries between the empowering pursuit of health and the superficial pursuit of physical beauty. Put differently, dieting becomes stigmatized not only as a gendered site of restriction but also through its feminine associations with vanity. The negative associations—and the need to distance oneself from them—became particularly apparent during one focus group hosted by Kerri, a white occupational therapist in her mid-thirties. When Kerri retrieved a dog-eared book from her coffee table to espouse its health insights, she then became embarrassed that it was titled *Eating for Beauty*. "I'm vain," she said, laughing sheepishly. "But I'll admit it, there's an element of, it's health, but it's also," As Kerri fumbled to find words, her friend Christine jumped in: "It's a win-win. It's just that, the main factor is still health." Kerri appeared relieved to receive this justification. "Yes! Exactly. It goes hand in hand. When you eat better, you feel better, when you feel better, you look better." Recovering from this embarrassing disclosure, Kerri reframed the book's title to position beauty as a positive effect of healthy eating, rather than a goal in itself. In highlighting this dynamic, we do not mean to question the validity of women's claims—that is, to imply that they are masking body image concerns with health discourse. Rather, our aim is to unpack the process of calibration required to perform healthy food femininities.

The imperative to distance healthy eating choices from feminine beauty ideals is shaped by postfeminist critiques of punishing body standards for women. As noted in Chapter 2, postfeminism draws selectively from feminist ideals (McRobbie 2004: 256), and the do-diet draws from feminist critiques of patriarchal body image standards (e.g., Greer 1970; Orbach 1978; Wolf 1990). The women we spoke with were often critical of media representations of the female body, which they deemed unrealistic and unhealthy. "I am not going to starve myself because of some perceived image of what I should look like," said Donna (46, black, entrepreneur), adding "because half of those people are airbrushed anyway." While voicing these critiques, women suggested that such feminist ideas had reached the level of commonsense. "Women are pressured beyond belief, certainly, but I think there's also an awareness of that," said Martha (47, white, baker). Another member of this focus group, Olive, supported Martha's assessment from her perspective in the fashion industry: "I feel like the public knows this now. Before they were so mesmerized by celebrities, by models and these unattainable images. Now I think people are wise enough to know that that's photo-shopped, that the model does starve herself to get that thin." Women brought a critical gaze to the slender feminine ideal and believed this critique had widespread acceptance among postfeminist consumers who are "wise enough" not to starve themselves in the name of beauty.

Paradoxically, this postfeminist perspective on gendered body ideals did not mean that women felt free of such pressures. Carol (42, white, film producer) put the issue in simple terms: "as women, you can't get away from body image." Carol's matter-of-fact assessment illuminates the complexities of postfeminist empowerment. The women we spoke with did not deny that body pressures exist; rather, they were resigned to these pressures as an inevitable burden of femininity, albeit one that they critiqued. Asking about body image in one group of close friends produced knowing glances and chuckles, as these young women shared stories about how their mothers and grandmothers judged them to be too "fat." They insisted that these comments did not influence their eating choices, but also described various high-fat foods as their "downfall," suggesting that body image pressures may be internalized even when they are critically assessed. Similarly, Maria made clear that health was her priority, but admitted, "I still struggle with body image. It's something I hope will subside at some point, but yeah, it's definitely present." Some women alluded to the emotional reward of losing weight, which carries social benefits in a fat-phobic culture. For example, Wei (40, Korean Canadian, communications) described the positive feelings she experienced when people remarked that she looked thinner after becoming vegetarian. In addition, Cindy (44, white, fitness instructor) described how she had enjoyed the feeling of being extremely thin in the past, even when she reached an unhealthy body weight to the point that she had stopped menstruating. Women may be deeply critical of body image pressures and explicitly align themselves with a discourse of choosing health, yet simultaneously internalize fat-phobic ideals on an emotional level.

Part of the reason such pressures persist, of course, is due to the continued surveillance of women's bodies. Many women described how their food choices were judged by family, friends, and co-workers. "My boss will be like, 'why aren't you eating a donut?'" said Sarah (26 Vietnamese Canadian, student). "And I'll be like, I'm actually just not hungry right now. But you kind of face all these questions where you can tell they're like, okay, she's dieting." Shannon (45, white, unemployed) noted that dietary choices carry high stakes, as women's body practices are held to standards seldom applied to men (Wright et al. 2006):

> Men just seem to be able to do whatever they want to do. There's not much criticism that goes with that [laughing]. Women are always criticized. Did you buy the wrong thing? Did you wear the right thing? You're wearing the wrong color, you're eating too much fat, you're putting on too much weight—we're always criticized for stuff.

Shannon's and Sarah's words highlight the difficulty of managing gendered corporeal pressures and suggest the inadequacy of a postfeminist response that urges women to individually negotiate body pressures to achieve maximum empowerment. Collectively, there remains considerable social attention given to women's bodies and their relative conformity to idealized beauty standards. No matter how empowered women feel in their individual choices, they may still face gendered judgment for their bodily (mis)management. This constellation of surveillance and judgment produces an ironic outcome: even when women frame their food choices as health-motivated, others may perceive them as dieting for weight-loss purposes. For instance, Gina said that she was "very skeptical of people who say they're gluten intolerant," describing this as "an easy way of saying 'I'm not gonna have a cookie.'" Regardless of whether these suspicions were well founded, our point is that, collectively, women's eating practices are under surveillance, despite the discursive emphasis on "choosing health." Sarah describes the challenging terrain between healthy eating and dietary restriction:

> It's easier to say I'm detoxing than I'm dieting. Or "I'm only eating organic" . . . because diet's kind of become a taboo word, especially among young women who are educated. Like, everyone is too educated to admit that they're worried about the way they look. It's seen as being shallow. So people choose more of the, "I'm on a raw food diet" or "I'm on a juice cleanse." Which, you know, I'm sure has its benefits, and I believe that people are trying to be more health conscious. But I think a lot of times in young women "health conscious" just means that they're watching their weight.

Sarah's perceptive observations touch upon many elements of the do-diet: an emphasis on health over body image and positive choice over restriction, and the paradoxical (and patriarchal) demand that women actively manage their bodies while giving the impression that this work is effortless.

Restricted membership in the do-diet club

While our qualitative sample does not allow for statistical generalization, our research suggests that the framing of choosing health over body image is not equally accessible to all women. We found that women possessing various kinds of social privilege, including the privilege of embodying the slender feminine ideal, more readily articulated do-diet discourse. In one focus group, two young women who were both quite thin insisted that they enjoyed food too much to care about body image. Their friend Syd (26, white, part-time actor) responded:

> Body image is an interesting one for me because I was sort of along the same lines as these guys for a long time where I sort of thought I would never care because I love eating and blah, blah, blah. And then I gained a bunch of weight [laughs]. And then I realized how much it upset, like, I actually became really uncomfortable with my own body. And so, and I do make [pauses as if she's trying to decide how to express herself] my eating choices, there are a lot of things that are involved in that, and you know, I'm vegan and health is a huge part of it, too, but I am aware now of like, calories and not adding to my weight, and ideally losing some weight.

Following Syd's disclosure that body image matters to her, the fourth member of this group, Tara (36, white, social assistance), said she had felt similarly when she gained weight. The discussion revealed how the dismissal of body image (through the discourse of choosing health) is more easily taken up by those whose bodies resemble hegemonic ideals of thinness.

This kind of embodied privilege also facilitates a socially acceptable embrace of food's pleasures, a point that was brought to our attention by Jackie (30, Middle Eastern, student), who was involved in fat activism. Jackie noted how ordering a rich or fatty dish is a choice that is viewed differently depending on embodiment: "for the thin person it would be almost like, 'wow how do you do it?' And for the fat person it's like, 'why can't you have a bit of self-control?'" Jackie's critique reveals how the do-diet's pairing of choice and control is embodied within the slender feminine ideal, reproducing fat-phobia and privileging thinness. While thin femininities are celebrated for choosing pleasurable indulgences, the same consumption practices are read onto the fat body as a sign of poor health and lack of control. This suggests that the do-diet's logic celebrating individual choice is not equally accessible, particularly in a context where fatness is dominantly perceived as a moral fail-ure to fulfill the responsibilities of healthy eating (Guthman 2003; Lavin 2013; LeBesco 2011).

In addition to body privilege, the logic of choosing health (versus dieting) was more commonly subscribed to by the most economically privileged women in our sample. Many low-income participants discussed health and body issues through the lens of economic constraint, as this was the dominant factor shap-ing their everyday food choices. Harsha (28, South Asian), who was living on social assistance, said "it's almost good that I don't have that much money to indulge on food because that keeps me happy with my body." Upon reflection, she added "maybe I'm trying to placate myself by saying it's okay that I don't have that much money for food." Shannon (45, white), who was not working due to a disability, described how budget restrictions prevented her and her daughter from eating as healthily as she would like. "I almost find that the junk that fits in our budget doesn't help with weight," she said, adding, "I'm eating what I can afford." She described "being restricted in my budget and then feel-ing kind of shitty about life so I pick up junk. Like, I like my Coca Cola and I'll drink it, I love it and I crave it and then I sit and I go oh god why did I drink that again?" Shannon's emphasis on economic necessity, and the emotional difficulty of experiencing poverty alongside an extremely limited food budget, challenges the universality of an empowering middle-class discourse of "choos-ing health." Shannon does not have the privileged resources required to enact the empowered, choice-centered consumer femininity celebrated in the do-diet and experiences her distance from this figure on an emotional level, as a source of guilt and disappointment.

In this section, we have demonstrated how contemporary ideals of healthism and postfeminism intersect within the do-diet to render healthy eating a site of empowerment through the exercise of consumer choice. However, this empowered healthy femininity must be well informed and carefully monitored. This means that the do-diet simultaneously involves elements of corporeal control.

Embodying control

The control side of the do-diet equation emphasizes the hard work, discipline, and education that are the assumed precursor to good food choices. Guthman and Dupuis note that the neoliberal ideal of control involves an element of "deservingness" and rewards the individual "who is expected to exercise choice and to become responsible for his or her risks" (2006: 443). To "deserve" good health, women must take control of their food choices. As one of our interviewees, Judy (56, white, legal publisher), said, "I feel it's my obligation to do anything that I can do to make sure that I stay healthy." Below, we document the control aspects of the do-diet; we chart the relationship to expert knowledge and corporeal restraint and discuss implications for class inequalities and food anxieties.

Expert knowledge: "Think you know your nutrients?"

Expert knowledge is a central feature of healthy eating discourse (Moore 2010; Ristovski-Slijepcevic et al. 2010; Warin 2011) and constitutes a core logic for dietary control. Informed consumers are encouraged to incorporate such knowledge into everyday food decisions to protect their bodies from the ravages of disease, age, and excess weight. While the dietary knowledge covered in this discourse is extensive, the advice for healthy eating is typically framed as easy. "Great news," declares *Chatelaine*: "When researchers looked at the effects of choline (a B vitamin in eggs and milk) on brain aging, they were amazed . . . Do it now: Add eggs, milk, fish, chicken and kidney beans to your plate to help improve your memory" (March 2012: 118). Three pages later, we encounter more important health findings: "Here's an extra reason to reach for a warm cup of tea: It could help prevent lung cancer . . . DO IT TODAY: Drink black tea regularly to help protect yourself" (121). The translation of research into individual action is seductively simple and empowering: simply drink tea and eat eggs for optimal health.

While individual prescriptions are framed as simple, the overall do-diet project is one of continual education and self-improvement. Readers are often invited to test their health knowledge: "Think you know your nutrients? Take my quiz"

(*The Globe and Mail*, January 12, 2011: L.4). "Food Labels: Decoded," reads one health column, with the caution that "'nutrition facts' aren't as straightforward as they seem" (*The Oprah Magazine*, November 2011: 124). The do-diet frames this stream of expert knowledge as a source of empowerment for the healthy woman who skillfully controls her food choices and keeps abreast of the latest nutrition research.

During focus groups and interviews, many women described their interest in accumulating expert food knowledge (especially in comparison to male partners) and integrating this knowledge into their own eating practices. Christine (36, white, nurse) described how this lengthens her trips to the grocery store: "You're incorporating what you've read about, or what you see on TV, you're incorporating it into your shopping as you're reading the labels. Like, at least I am. I'm actively thinking about things I've learned." As women integrate health and nutritional information into everyday food choices, healthy femininities become a site for ongoing improvement. Women frequently spoke of efforts to expand their own food knowledge in order to achieve maximum control over their health. "I always feel like there's something I can improve," said Petra, adding, "maybe all the reading I do." Gail described her ongoing efforts to optimize the nutritional benefits of her diet: "I feel I'm doing some of that just by eating organic . . . but I would like to shift and eat a little bit more fermented food or some of the superfoods." Gail's reference to "superfoods" echoes the do-diet language of scientific knowledge and nutritionism (Scrinis 2013). The media sources we studied were rife with advice on "health-promoting nutrients" that "help purge the body of potential carcinogens" or contain "neuroprotective properties that may fight diseases like Alzheimers" (*Whole Living*, March 2012: 88–95). This sophisticated nutritional knowledge was presented as key to controlling one's health and one's body.

Incorporating expert knowledge and controlling food intake is framed as a health objective, but one that delivers thinness as a natural reward for self-discipline. Kelsey (27, white, marketer) emphasized how she channels knowledge toward controlling the effects of food on her body: "I read a lot of health research . . . [and] I find that once you really get a perspective of what things are doing to your body . . . you realize that the more healthy food you eat, the more fulfilled you're gonna feel and *you'll just look better*" (emphasis ours). Similarly, in a post titled "healthy is the new skinny," blogger Meghan Telpner points toward the beauty payback of healthy eating, noting that "when we feel great, *looking great is a by-product*" (*Making Love in the Kitchen*, October 25, 2012). Beauty benefits are part of the "deservingness" framed as owing to women who engage in controlled, educated, healthy eating. As health is read onto thinness as a reflection of corporeal control, fatness is stigmatized as an indicator of an individual's poor health, rather than an issue of aesthetics (Burgard 2009; Guthman 2003; LeBesco 2011). In this way, weight loss is normalized as the deserved outcome of healthy (normatively thin) femininities, and health replaces "skinny" as the paradigm of control.

While we look critically at the challenge of negotiating do-diet discourse, it is important to acknowledge that some women described positive associations with the availability of health knowledge. This was true for Nadine (48, white, social assistance), who shared a story of personal transformation through increased self-awareness about her diet. After being diagnosed with a hernia, Nadine was told that she needed to lose weight. She met with a dietitian who helped her develop a food plan and began to do her own research on health and nutrition. Nadine framed this shift as a process of informing herself in order to take control of her health and described her shock when she learned how much sugar she had been consuming through seemingly healthy items like fruit juice. At the time of our interview in her tiny studio apartment, Nadine had lost 55 pounds and felt quite proud of this achievement. Wearing black tights and a loose-fitting grey shirt, she apologized for not having any cookies or treats to offer, since she avoids keeping these kinds of things on hand. Nadine spoke in a lively voice with animated facial expressions and hand gestures, swinging her black-framed glasses in her hand as she shared her story. Retrieving the small scale that she uses to weigh food for her meals, she explained that corporeal control was closely linked to her sense of self-worth, as it was for many of the women we spoke with: "I don't want to be skin and bones," Nadine clarified, calibrating her performance of this healthy femininity, "but I want to be the best person I can be." From a feminist perspective, it is important not to dismiss the sense of agency that Nadine derives from control over her diet. Thus, even as we analyze the disciplining tendencies of the do-diet, we are conscious of the fact that many women experience the controlled, knowledge-seeking polarity of this discourse as pleasurable and affirming. Using expert knowledge to guide her food choices allowed Nadine to feel in control of her health and also gave her access to a gendered and classed marker of idealized femininity—a thin body (Bordo 1993).

Control and class: "Poor people . . . should know better"

Sociological scholarship shows that food has immense cultural significance as a marker of status (e.g., Bourdieu 1984; Warde and Martens 2000; see Chapter 2, this volume). Critical food scholars have demonstrated how the "good," controlled, educated eating practices of reputable middle-class consumers are often defined in opposition to "the knowledge poverty of the working class" (Hollows and Jones 2010: 309; see also Guthman 2003; Johnston, Szabo, and Rodney 2011). During focus groups and interviews, class boundaries were often articulated in relation to the uninformed consumer who eats unhealthy processed food. "I have a hard time when poor people, like, they should know better not to eat Dominoes [Pizza], you know, go to the corner store and have Cocoa Puffs or something," said Cassandra (31, white, film industry). "Come on, chocolate milk on your cereal is not good," she continued with a laugh. "But when it's all you have and when it's all you're raised on, I guess you, how do you determine, like if your mom came home with KFC every night." Cassandra criticizes the unhealthy food choices she associates with a classed upbringing characterized by a lack of food knowledge required to practice appropriate self-control. Her explicit naming of class was less common than statements in which class was coded through particular food choices. Alyssa lamented "people who have eaten Beefaroni for dinner and wonder why they get," she paused, considering her words. "I was going to say cancer, but that's a really bad thing. Really intense. But we wonder why all these diseases are all over the place." Although Alyssa did not name class outright, her reference to Beefaroni invokes inexpensive, processed foods commonly associated with an unhealthy working-class consumer (Guthman 2003). As Alyssa continued, she emphasized the individual responsibility of making informed food choices in order to control one's health:

> People are like, oh I am so tired. Well, what did you eat for breakfast? . . . I am not a judgmental person, but when people are like, they've got a shopping cart full of meat, like hotdogs, whatever, it's just like, if you want to have this conversation, I will have it. Let's sit down and watch a documentary, or let's google with me. I will do it with you. But the choice is yours.

Once again, class is signaled through the reference to a particular food product (hotdogs) that symbolizes an uninformed consumer who is unable to control themself in a food system filled with tempting but unhealthy foods. Alyssa offers to educate this unhealthy Other, implying that individual ignorance and lack of control are the key obstacles to healthy living.

These examples demonstrate how the do-diet narrative of personal empowerment through individual self-control supports a classed and neoliberal conception of health as the deserved outcome of individuals' educated food decisions. "We have to make better choices, and not let the environment control our decisions," said Li (47, Chinese Canadian, life coach). Even as Li argued for expanding health education throughout the population, she articulated health as the moral duty of informed individuals: "I'm not going to use these coupons as enticing as it is . . . When you buy cheap foods you get cheaper quality and it's not as fresh. And you don't know where it's coming from or what they put into it." Li understands "cheap food" as a temptation that holds health risks and demands personal willpower to resist. While understandable, her critique suggests that healthy eating is simply a matter of individual decisions and that every woman has equal ability to resist the allure of low-priced food. This individualized narrative resonates with neoliberal discourses of personal responsibility and self-improvement and obscures the structural inequities that powerfully shape classed health disparities (e.g., Mikkonen and Raphael 2010).

It is important to note that some participants—particularly those living with limited resources—called into question the do-diet's individualized, meritocratic vision of corporeal control. For example, Deb (43, First Nations, unemployed) made clear that avoiding cheap, processed food was a class privilege and one that was not readily available to her: "if you have a lower income you shouldn't have to eat processed food that's crap. You should be able to eat healthy like everybody else." Even those with privileged access to cultural and economic resources may find this performance of controlled eating difficult to achieve. While the do-diet presents informed consumption as the key to dietary control, these extensive knowledge demands can leave women feeling anxious about their *lack* of control over their diet.

Control and anxiety: "We all know what happens when you don't eat well. You get sick or die."

As critical health scholar Robert Crawford notes, health warnings can have the ironic tendency to "aggravate the very insecurities they are designed to quell" (2006: 415). For example, Ingrid, like many middle-class women we spoke with, expressed considerable worry about being exposed to bisphenol-A (BPA) through canned foods: "Anything that's canned food I know there's always the risk of BPA from the lining of cans and some manufacturers are now looking at that and changing it. But you just don't always know if that's taken place yet." Indeed, in our interviews and focus groups, soaking your own beans (as opposed to buying canned beans potentially contaminated with BPA) appeared as a consistent marker for showcasing one's heightened food knowledge and control over food decisions.

In addition to concerns about specific health risks like BPA contamination, participants expressed a generalized anxiety about whether they had adequate knowledge to inform food decisions. For example, Li said, "I am wondering whether the food I'm eating is really providing enough for my well being." Li described the sometimes agonizing challenge of decoding food labels and factoring in food's long-term bodily impact: "Sometimes I want to buy something, like yogurt, and I want to know that I am going to be okay eating it . . . You have to be really aware of what you're eating and how you're feeling, especially two or three days after you eat it. Like, it's still going through your body." This kind of heightened corporeal self-awareness is celebrated within the do-diet, as women are encouraged to incorporate new knowledge into their food choices and to closely monitor their body's response. While such informed consumption is promoted as a source of control, it can have the paradoxical effect of engendering insecurity, even for highly informed consumers like Li. Thus, the empowerment promised through the do-diet brings great responsibility, as women are rendered personally accountable to control food intake and generate their own healthy futures. Li saw these informed food choices as a key strategy for protecting oneself against health risks: "Your food is your, I guess, medicine so to speak. It is your health prevention," she said, adding, "We all know what happens when you don't eat well. You get sick or die." In this individualizing narrative, women must control their food decisions carefully, since these decisions are conceptualized as the key determinant of their health—even to the point of life and death.

While many women embraced this personal responsibility with the same determinism as Li, some were skeptical of the message of corporeal control and expressed frustration with the tide of health information on offer. "I can't STAND those wellness magazines at health food stores," said Hilary (28, white, barista). She explained:

> "10 power foods you absolutely must eat!" Or, you know, "you absolutely, absolutely CANNOT eat this food," or too much of that, or "Did you know that this food gives you cancer in 20 years?" . . . It is just consumerism because these wellness magazines are just selling an image that makes you want to buy stuff at those certain stores.

While Hilary criticized the consumerist message within health food discourse, Zahra described a personal "backlash against too much information coming from women's magazines." While she enjoys reading the recipes, she said she "can't read anything more about superfoods and fighter chemicals." Olive (27, black, fashion editor) reflected critically on the seductive dual-promise of choice and control and linked this to corporate marketing campaigns. "Companies that offer you the option are also banking on people's desire to control what they eat," she said during a focus group. "I had a Starbucks coffee today and I got a non-fat, sugarless syrup, green-tea latte." Olive laughed as she recalled her order. "Starbucks is totally playing on the idea that when I buy a coffee I'm gonna make it as low-fat as possible. And that's stupid on my part because it's like, a sugary coffee . . . but they distract you, right? And they also play on that whole idea of, you're trying to control what you eat." At this point, Heather (28, white, chef) jumped in: "They're giving you artificial choices." Olive agreed: "For sure. I made several artificial choices this morning, but I sort of delighted in it. I was like, see, I got a non-fat, green tea latte, aren't I smart? I didn't get the regular one [laughter]. Ya. But you're not really in control." Even as Olive engages reflexively with the do-diet promise of empowerment through corporeal control, she acknowledges how she is emotionally drawn into this discourse and delights in the sense of control that comes with making her "artificial" choice. This interaction highlights how the do-diet sutures the seemingly contradictory logics of choice and control and delivers the promise of health, beauty, and thinness.

4. A do-diet discussion

This chapter has charted the contours of the do-diet, a discourse that promotes healthy eating as a positive choice, rather than a restriction, while linking food choices to self-control and individual responsibility. Our analysis has shown how gendered body ideals associating femininity with thinness persist, but are obscured by a discourse of choosing health. Women position healthy eating as an empowering act of informed choice, distinguished from outdated techniques of calorie counting and the vanity of dieting. At the same time, do-diet discourse valorizes expert knowledge and promotes an ethos of perpetual improvement and risk management. In this way, the do-diet discourse successfully combines the seemingly contradictory neoliberal logics of continual consumption and corporeal control (cf. Guthman and Dupuis 2006).

We have shown how this dietary shift can engender positive emotions associated with the experience of choice and feeling in control of one's health; however, we feel it is crucial to simultaneously recognize how the do-diet reproduces and legitimizes fat-phobia and undermines feminist aims for social justice. Despite its anti-diet message, this discourse repeatedly equates health with thinness and naturalizes weight loss as an automatic and positive benefit of healthy food choices. The food femininity idealized within the do-diet appreciates the pleasure of healthy foods and distances herself from restrictive diets of yesteryear, but also maintains a controlled, closely monitored relationship to food that is implicitly body-focused. In keeping with previous scholarship on the moral regulation of fatness within neoliberalism (Guthman 2003; Lavin 2013; LeBesco 2011; Saguy 2013), the do-diet constructs boundaries around the categories of fat and thin bodies, good and bad food choices, and knowledgeable and uninformed consumers. Women navigate these boundaries as they calibrate healthy femininities and work to avoid extremes—that is, the anxious health "nut" addicted to green juices or the uneducated consumer eating Beefaroni. While many women were critical of unrealistic bodily expectations, these expectations were accepted as a cross they must bear. Women might defend their nonconforming bodies against hegemonic feminine ideals, but the do-diet associations of health, thinness, and moral duty were firmly entrenched at the level of subjectivity and entangled with the intense emotions that accompany food decisions and body image. In short, the feminine body remains a site of surveillance, evaluation, judgment, and regulation, with the fear of fatness appearing as a backdrop in most of our data.

A second and closely related implication of the do-diet is the way this discourse co-opts and repurposes feminist claims. In her book *Fat Is a Feminist Issue*, Susie Orbach (1978) put forward a psychotherapeutic context for dealing with women's painful embodiment issues, but insisted that individual psychotherapy be joined with feminism as a collective movement. Orbach's feminist approach insisted that "those painful personal experiences derive from the *social context* into which female babies are born, and within which they develop to become adult women" (1978: 5; emphasis ours). The contemporary postfeminist moment looks quite different. In a context where a "critique of dieting has become common sense for many women and girls" (Beagan et al. 2015: 126), the do-diet presents a deeply individualized response to unhealthy beauty standards. This discourse suggests women are now beyond a culture of restrictive dieting, even as it emphasizes strategies of corporeal control associated with thinness. This healthy food femininity *chooses wisely* in the interest of *health*, and it is assumed that thinness will follow.

Because of the do-diet's model of postfeminist empowerment, contemporary diet discourse is inhospitable to a sustained critique of gendered body ideals—a critique that foregrounds questions of power, privilege, and structural inequalities. A postfeminist ethos emphasizes individuals making healthy and empowering food choices and assumes thin bodies as the feminine gold standard. Yes, this postfeminist approach offers some critique of calorie restriction, but it also takes women's body pressures for granted. In this context, calling for a more collectivist critique of feminine food and body projects can sound hopelessly old-fashioned, even though we believe that this kind of critique is precisely what our data calls for.

Our conversations with women suggest that not all critical capacity has been lost. As we have shown throughout the chapter, women voiced various forms of skepticism, frustration, and reflexive critique when it came to health and body ideals, double-standards that penalize women, and the virtues of superfoods. This frustration seemed most profoundly felt by the women most disadvantaged—women who lacked resources to fully invest in the do-diet or whose bodies did not easily conform to normative standards of thinness. Our claim is not that women today are dupes of do-diet discourse. Rather we argue that women must negotiate body projects in the context of a dominant discourse of "choosing health" that replaces feminist critique with a postfeminist narrative of empowerment through informed consumption. This discourse engages immense amounts of women's energies, appealing to individual pleasures, consumer choice, and a feminist imperative of self-care while drawing attention away from the structures that generate and naturalize fat-phobia, class-stratified health outcomes, and gender inequality.

Notes

1. The equation of fat bodies with poor health has been widely critiqued. See LeBesco (2011), Guthman (2011), Campos et al. (2006), and Burgard's (2009) account of "health at every size." For a critical realist analysis of the obesity "epidemic," see Patterson and Johnston (2012).
2. While our focus is on the links among health, diet, and femininity, we acknowledge that masculinities are also governed through health discourses that include a concern for physical appearance (e.g., Beagan et al. 2015: 129–33; Crawshaw 2007; Dworkin and Wachs 2009).

Chapter 6

Food politics: The gendered work of caring through food

"I really felt like I REALLY wanted to be interviewed for this," Deirdre says excitedly as she pours a fresh pot of tea. A white woman in her fifties, Deirdre wears a floral blouse and jean shorts with an apron tied around her waist. Among the many items hanging on the yellow walls of her kitchen is a framed certificate recognizing the farmers' market where she acts as manager. Gesturing toward the slow cooker on the counter, Deirdre explains that dinner tonight will include beef cheeks from one of the market vendors. Laughing, she adds, "nose to tail, as they say."

When asked about her food priorities, Deirdre is unequivocal: "Real food. The first thing would be REAL food." For Deirdre, "real food" means eating locally, seasonally, and ethically. Beyond feeding herself and her family this way, she also emphasizes the importance of eating "communally." Deirdre is passionate about building collective initiatives through which to support farmers and nourish communities. "As we move towards a more organically-based society we will just naturally be moving away from oil, eat better, live better, exist cleaner, *take care of each other better*," she explains. "When your neighbour is the person who's growing your food you're gonna take better care of them."

These shifts in Deirdre's food priorities have inspired changes at home. "In the past two years I have focused EVERYTHING how we eat here in this house on eating ethically and seasonally," she explains. "And we live like kings. And the health and the taste stuff are like the tail of a kite." Having transformed her family's diet, she now finds it difficult to eat in settings where she does not know the story behind her plate. "I cannot go to a Christmas dinner where the turkey is a Butterball that I know has been frozen for what, three years?" she says with exasperation. "And that every person who handled that turkey and who was involved in the processing was *maybe* paid a fair wage? Maybe not. That the turkey itself suffered?" For Deirdre, these questions are a matter of "thoughtful" eating, where "you are making a choice with every bite you eat."

Even as Deirdre embraces the win-win narrative of eating for change—that is, ethical eating is better for the world, healthier *and* more delicious (Johnston and Cairns 2012)—she admits that her food life is not tension-free. Describing her husband as a "meat and potatoes kind of guy," Deirdre says her family got tired of her always talking about food issues. When out for dinner at a restaurant, her teenage daughters would groan when she asked where meat was sourced, and she quotes her husband saying "Deirdre, please for god's sake just don't do that here." As Deirdre's political commitments came into conflict with her family foodwork, the only way she could see to resolve this tension was to assume complete responsibility for food provisioning in their home. She explains:

> I had to stop talking the talk and start walking the walk. And cooking things here [at home] a lot more often than I was. I was very much a convert. Only ate the good stuff myself. My husband was eating from the different restaurants. He now packs a lunch every day. He's able to do that because he has me here cooking . . . I just kind of resigned myself to it, but it's better that I do.

While she loves providing her family with the "real" food she believes in, Deirdre admits this "wasn't a terribly easy journey." She says, "I have resented winding up as a real, you know, 'homemaker,'" shifting to a mock cutesy tone. While this gendered division of foodwork is clearly a source of tension for Deirdre, she emphasizes the rewards of her ethical food labor: "It is more at home work but I'm learning how to enjoy that again. And the pay-off is massive."

In this chapter, we turn our attention to food politics—a hot topic at a time when citizens are urged to consider the social and environmental implications of what they eat. With the proliferation of farmers' markets, community gardens, and blockbuster documentaries like *Food Inc.*, growing attention is directed toward the story behind our food—where, how, and by whom it was grown or raised, harvested, packaged, transported, and sold. While environmental issues feature prominently in this discourse, what is often missing from these conversations is attention to the *labor* required to eat in politically mindful ways—for example, researching ethical options, traveling to organic butchers, cooking from scratch—as well as the question of *who* is shouldering this burden. Deirdre's story is instructive here: as she describes it, enacting her food values required that she devote significantly more time, resources, and effort to domestic foodwork, not to mention the emotional work of managing these changes within her family. Given that women continue to be the primary food planners, shoppers, and cooks within the home, shedding light on the *work* of food politics is a feminist issue.

Probing this oft overlooked dimension of food politics, this chapter explores how ethical consumption operates as an extension of women's care-work. The first section of the chapter reviews key debates in the study of food politics, including the ways ethical eating can reproduce race and class inequalities. We draw upon feminist scholarship on care-work in order to shed light on the gender dynamics nested within these issues. Second, we use our interviews and focus groups to examine the gendering of ethical consumption as a performance of femininity and consider the implications of this pattern for both food and gender politics. The third section of the chapter examines how women engage with food politics *beyond* the realm of individual consumer choice. Drawing upon our interviews with food activists, we highlight creative ways women engage with food as a civic practice. At the same time, we argue that it is crucial to recognize how a shift from the individualized practice of ethical consumption to a food politics based in collective action does not, in itself, guarantee gender equality.

1. Eating for change?

Invitations to "eat for change" abound within contemporary food media. Consumers are increasingly informed about problems in the food system and presented with advice about "voting with your fork." As one blogger notes, "More and more of us are realizing that industrial farming is bad news for our planet and for our health" (*Making Love in the Kitchen*, September 13, 2012). What to do in the face of food-related risks to individual, collective, and environmental well-being? "If all of us make the right choices together then we can make a big impact," writes another blogger, "which will help change our country's food system for the better" (*100 Days of Real Food*, "About"). Despite the gravity of these issues, the realm of food politics is not all doom and gloom; our analysis of food media supports our previous finding that ethical consumption is discursively constructed as a "win-win" endeavor that yields personal rewards of health and taste while advancing social and ecological justice (Johnston and Cairns 2012). In the words of one holistic nutritionist, "food that is local and in season is always the freshest and most flavorful" (*Whole Living*, November 2011: 2).

Media narratives of eating for change reflect a discourse of ethical eating that connects personal food practices to social and ecological issues (Johnston and Cairns 2012; Johnston et al. 2011). Although it is clear that food politics has reached an unprecedented level of interest, scholars and activists continue to debate whether ethical eating drives meaningful social change. Can shopping ethically act as a political "stepping stone" by encouraging individuals to reflect upon the broader implications of their everyday food practices (Seyfang

2005)? Or does this individualization of responsibility stymie collective action, giving the false assurance that one can create change simply by shopping (Maniates 2002)?

In addition to debating the transformative potential of ethical consumption, food scholars have also questioned the inclusivity of mainstream food politics. Who is welcomed into the food movement? Who sees themselves reflected in its values, spaces, and practices? Who has the resources required to participate? Financial resources are perhaps the most obvious barriers to ethical consumption, given the expense of things like organic beef or locally grown heirloom tomatoes. However, exclusionary dynamics are not limited to price and may be embedded within the very culture and structure of the ethical foodscape. As food scholar Julie Guthman writes, "many of the practices of alternative food hail a white subject and thereby code the practices and spaces of alternative food as white" (2011: 264). This critique has support from research demonstrating a link between ethical consumption and whiteness (Alkon and McCullen 2011; Slocum 2007, 2008), as well as class privilege (Carfagna et al. 2014; Guthman 2003; Goodman et al. 2012; Hinrichs 2000; Johnston and Szabo 2011; Johnston et al. 2011; Lockie 2009). Drawing upon research in farmers' markets in California, sociologists Allison Alkon and Christie McCullen reveal the existence of a "white farm imaginary" that "romanticizes and universalizes an agrarian narrative specific to whites while masking the contributions and struggles of people of color in food production" (2011: 945). This is a particularly notable omission given the critical role played by racialized workers in American and Canadian farm labor (Holmes 2013). Other studies have found that many farmers' market shoppers believe the mostly white vendors harvested the food themselves and articulate this sense of connection as fundamental to the market's appeal (Smithers et al. 2008). The erasure of racialized and low-wage labor within this exchange is just one of the ways alternative food spaces can unwittingly reproduce the ethical consumer as white and middle class.

While critical scholars have fought to expand the scope of food politics to include questions of race and class, the gendering of these processes has received less attention. Only recently have scholars begun to raise questions about the gendered expectations and responsibilities associated with food politics (Allen and Sachs 2007; Cairns, Johnston, and MacKendrick 2013; Cairns et al. 2014; Isenhour and Ardenfors 2009; Kimura 2011; MacGregor 2006). Writing in a German context, Vinz draws attention to "the feminization of responsibility for the environment" (2009: 163). She asks: "Will it be women who must bear the burden of solving our ecological problems through ecologically oriented household management when those problems are caused by factors well beyond their control?" (163). This gender dimension has been largely overlooked within critiques of ethical consumption as a neoliberal transfer of responsibility. Critiques of neoliberalism often assume a gender-neutral consumer, when in fact ethical consumption is closely linked to femininity. Thus, the argument that narratives of "eating for change" individualize social and ecological problems can be deepened by attending to the *gendered* nature of this discourse.

Below we use our interviews, focus groups, and textual sources to unpack the gendered dimension of ethical consumption. We strive to develop a feminist analysis that takes seriously the problem of a neoliberal individualization of responsibility *and* the political potential of caring through food. By attending to women's food stories, we hope to contribute to this debate without reproducing simplistic analytic binaries that obscure the complex ways food and consumer politics are negotiated in everyday life (Banet-Weiser and Mukherjee 2012; Johnston and Cairns 2012).[1]

2. Ethical consumption as care-work

Seated cross-legged on her living room floor, Hilary's skinny jeans are tucked into wool socks, and her auburn hair hangs halfway down the back of her oversized wool sweater. Enlarged landscape photos hang on the wall, and an old-fashioned typewriter is artfully displayed next to a deer antler in the corner of the room. When asked about the significance of food to her identity, Hilary says, "I'm extremely passionate about the politics of food." She notes that when she and her partner began dating, he was skeptical of the organic movement. "He'll tell you about the arguments that we've had about it," she says, laughing. But thanks to Hilary's impassioned defense, he has come around. Reflecting on the evolution of her own food identity, Hilary describes a shift from caring for herself and others through food to an expanded sphere of care in the realm of food politics: "So instead of just caring about, you know . . . healthy eating and caring about the social aspects of a meal together, the whole organic part just really became a big, big, big focus in my food and in my food choices." For Hilary, food politics comes down to the need for a collective change in values, from a food system that is motivated by profit to one oriented toward "thinking about sustainability, and thinking about the health of people, animals, and the ground."

While Hilary focuses on the "values" that underpin her commitment to organic farming, this caring disposition is expressed in material, embodied practices. Working as a coffee barista, money is a major constraint when putting these politics into practice. Nevertheless, she says, "I will do as much as I can in my limited income to support [the organic] industry." In addition to financial resources, Hilary's food ideals require visiting multiple food vendors (including a meat CSA share, bulk store, two organic produce shops, and a grocery store) and devoting the time and effort to cooking a meal from scratch at the end of a long work day. Despite this highly conscientious food routine, Hilary suggests "there should probably be more." She gives the example of fair trade as something that is "just not actually a deciding factor for me right now . . . I hope someday I will be educated enough to care again." The fact that Hilary feels she is not "educated enough" to care about fair trade highlights another form of invisible labor in her ethical food practices: the ongoing research required to inform politically motivated food choices.

Like Hilary, many of the women we spoke with described their ethical eating as an expression of care, whether for animals, workers, farmers, or ecological sustainability. These women understood their food choices to be impacting others and wanted to ensure that impact was positive. It was this sense of responsibility that compelled Judy to shop at a particular farmers' market that was struggling for business. "I felt an obligation to show up and be supportive even if I didn't really need to go there," she says. Judy admits that her ethically minded food shopping can "make myself a bit crazy sometimes," but says that "supporting those kinds of businesses in the market is really important to me." Judy suggests that as a single woman with no children, she can pursue her own food ideals without having to satisfy the needs and preferences of others. However, if we expand our understanding of care-work beyond the domestic sphere, Judy's commitment to supporting small, local food producers also constitutes a form of caring food labor. Thus, when we say that ethical consumption extends the gendered labor women have historically performed through domestic foodwork, we do not mean that this care-work is inherently familial. Our research indicates that the care-work of ethical consumption can be readily embraced by single women who are not feeding others within their home but who think deeply about the well-being of those affected by their food choices. Our principal argument is that ethical eating discourse includes familial care, but *extends* the sphere of care beyond immediate others while building on a history of gendered care-work.

Caring about animals

The care-work of ethical eating was frequently expressed through participants' concern for animal welfare. "It sounds cheesy to say, but I just feel like I have a certain connection with animals," said Syd. "And it just feels weird for me to eat them." Sometimes women expressed their care for animals in lighthearted ways that self-consciously referenced gendered discourses of feminine empathy. "We joke that I only eat things that don't have eyelashes 'cause they're not cute," Cindy says, laughing. Others, like Rose, spoke earnestly about the responsibility that comes with taking the life of another: "I think if I eat it, I should be able to kill it."

The link between food choices and animal welfare was an emotional topic for some women in our study. For instance, multiple women described the stressful experience of choosing between "conventional" and more expensive free-run eggs. Sally said: "I sometimes spend four embarrassing minutes just standing in front of the egg display, like, I gotta make a decision!" Kim and Roy described this as an ongoing negotiation in their shopping routine. "Every time we go to the grocery store together we have an ethical conversation in front of the eggs," says Roy. Kim jumps in: "Yeah, I am like, these ones are really, really, really cheap, but these chickens probably suffer a lot." Roy adds, "she'll well up. Literally, I can see her eyes." It is noteworthy that although Roy and Kim are shopping together in this story, the emotional dilemma is experienced by Kim alone. This distinction fits with a broader pattern in our research, in which caring for animals through one's food choices was gendered as an expression of femininity. In contrast to Kim's and Sally's stories of tearing up in front of the egg display, a group of four men spoke at length about their egg shopping decisions without ever mentioning animal welfare. Instead, they emphasized issues of taste and quality, and not wanting to eat a low-priced, "crazy weird factory egg."

While ethical food femininities were enacted through expressions of care, some men actively distanced their own ethical eating from this narrative. For example, Ryan states that he is "vegetarian because of environmental reasons" and jokes, "I could care less about animals. I actually would like less of them to be born." As the conversation continues, Ryan emphasizes this distinction: "I usually have to make that caveat where I'm like, I don't actually care about animals. Because most people are like, oh, you're a vegetarian, eh? So you like cows a lot or something? Ya, there's a lot of people who are like, oh, so you're gay too, right? [laughter] No actually, I just don't eat meat." Ryan's reflection on how his vegetarianism shapes the way others perceive him (including his sexual orientation) highlights the deeply gendered meanings ascribed to food practices—a fact that was not lost on this group. Eric commented, "there's something emasculating about being a vegetarian . . . there's a perception that it's somehow feminine." The cultural association between meat and masculinity is widely documented in feminist scholarship (e.g., Adams 1990; Sobal 2005). We want to draw attention to the way that such gendered meanings can inform articulations of food politics—such that expressing care through ethical eating is understood as a performance of femininity.

To be clear, not every female vegetarian in our study framed their decision not to eat meat in terms of caring for animals. Gina explicitly prioritized environmental issues over animal welfare concerns, stating: "It's not so much the argument against the mistreatment, although that's part of it, but it's more that I'm trying to reduce my reliance on the industrialized food chain." Similarly, the caring ethical consumer is not exclusive to women. Rosita described how her raw-food-vegan partner showed his affection early in their relationship by respecting her food preferences. "I remember the first time he actually made me an omelet with happy eggs and cheese and stuff like that. And he had a green juice or a smoothie and sprouted quinoa bread," she said, laughing. Thus, to say that foodwork and care is connected to femininity does not mean that only women care about animals or that only women are vegetarians. Our data challenges this kind of essentialist thinking, but also makes clear the gendered ways food politics are understood and enacted.

The food*work* involved with caring

The gendering of ethical consumption also emerged in household food negotiations among family members. Women shared stories of coaxing male partners and children to appreciate, or at least tolerate, their politicized food commitments. This narrative of feminine responsibility (and masculine tolerance, or passive support) was repeated frequently in our conversations with women. Sitara comments that her husband is "conscious about what he eats and where it comes from," but notes that "he doesn't make the grocery decisions and the menu decisions. I end up doing that." She pinpoints a crucial distinction within the care-work of food politics—while *interest* may be widely shared among environmentally and socially conscious individuals, the *work* of implementing these concerns into everyday food practices tends to be performed by women.

An interesting perspective on the gendered labor of food politics was voiced by Cassia, a writer and food activist. Cassia explains that she and her husband are both invested in "providing" for their family, but they pursue this in different realms. While he works in a high-paying technology job, she works as a freelancer and assumes the role of "grounding us in terms of how we live as a family culture." Given their investment in different spheres, Cassia says her husband will sometimes "want to take the shortcut" when it comes to ethics and gives the example of buying dishwasher soap at the convenience store rather than waiting until she can purchase an eco-friendly version. Despite these tensions, Cassia says "more often than not, he will stop himself and allow me to run that, to provide that, what I consider to be a necessity in order to stick to these values." Cassia is conscious of how the gendered organization of her family life might be negatively perceived: "If people are looking in, do they look at us and say, 'Wow that's really . . . there's real gender stereotyping there in that house'? Maybe. Do I care? Not at all. I don't give a shit because it actually isn't." Cassia clarifies that her household division of labor is a conscious choice, rather than an outcome of gender roles, and emphasizes how this choice allows her to enact food values that are central to her identity.

Family decisions are deeply personal, and we do not want to replicate the judgmental gaze that Cassia alludes to when she defends herself against "gender stereotyping." However, the fact that women may *choose* to perform ethical food labor, and that it may be important to their identities, does not negate the persistent gendered *relationship* at play at a structural level. Women's ethical foodwork may not always result from sexist beliefs about the responsibilities of men and women; nevertheless, the fact that a pattern of gendered inequity persists in the social division of this care-work is itself a feminist issue.

Calibrating care-work: "I'm not fanatical . . ."

While many women in our study embraced the care-work of ethical consumption, this performance required active calibration. Women were quick to point out that, while committed to the politics of food, they are not dogmatic in their approach. Thus, even as politically minded participants distanced themselves from an uncaring, unethical approach to food, they also rejected an overly perfect or righteous model of ethical eating, especially if it inconvenienced others. Regarding her vegetarianism, Gina said, "If a potato has been baked in a pan with the chicken, I'll eat the potato. I'm not that fanatical." Gina makes clear that her politically conscious food choices remain within reason and do not require significant accommodation from others.

Calibration was also used to get family members on board with ethical eating. Much like mothers hide vegetables in their children's meals, women may minimize ethical decisions when feeding others. For instance, Maria suggests that her partner accepts their weekday vegetarian diet because she is not too "extreme" about it:

> I try not to make it explicit. I try to just kind of slip it under the radar. [laughs]
> I'll cook what I cook. And he always thinks it's delicious whatever I make. And

I don't bring attention to the fact that there's no meat in it . . . And I think he's more on board because I'm not really extreme about it.

Maria recounts how she calibrates her ethical commitments in order to ease certain practices into family foodwork. Not all women described this process in such explicit terms, but many positioned their food ethics as reasonable, and not requiring excessive accommodation. This narrative also emerged in our analysis of food media. For example, in one magazine article, a former vegetarian described how she returned to meat-eating because she felt like a pain (*Whole Living*, November 2011: 50). Although her "sympathies went out to all those cows, pigs and chickens," ultimately she decided that "it seemed wrong to inconvenience anyone with my 'special' diet." Here, we see the penalty of the positive extreme, as the author's ethical food femininity is deemed excessive and a nuisance to others. Her reflection also illustrates how the calibration process involves a balancing of care-work between distant beings and those closer to home. Idealized feminine subjects must care for distant people, animals, and ecosystems, but these feminine subjects become pathological if their political commitments inconvenience, overshadow, or marginalize their immediate care relationships.

Politics via food consumption: "I can be political with the choices I make"

The gendering of ethical consumption must be understood in relation to women's structural position as primary food shoppers, as well as their historical marginalization from the public sphere. Given that patriarchal conceptions of politics have tended to devalue the contributions of women, it is not surprising that some women may look to care-work for political efficacy. For instance, Carol says, "I don't find I'm a terribly political person, per se. But I feel I can be political with the choices I make . . . I can vote with my pocketbook." Similarly, Fran says, "I do view my food shopping as [political] because it's something I can control." Fran extends this sense of control to the collective impact of her personal food choices. "There are people I want to give my money to. There are a lot of other people I don't want to give my money to . . . That's something that I do have control over. And that's the one way I can exercise it." For women like Carol and Fran, deciding what to buy and where to buy it is a political act with the potential to create social change. From a feminist perspective, it is important not to dismiss this gendered articulation of political agency. Stacey says that believing her shopping is political helps to counter feelings of powerlessness in the food system. "It's really in the interest of the companies that I feel powerless and helpless because that's when you're sort of apathetic," she says. "Whereas if I feel like I am taking action and can do things, that feels like it can make some change."

At the same time that we recognize the political significance of women's food labor, it is important to consider the limitations of "eating for change." Constructing food system concerns as the private burden of consumers can generate material and emotional costs for women who feel responsible for addressing systemic problems in everyday food practices—a responsibility that is costly, time-consuming, and full of contradictions. For example, Yin expresses concern about industrial meat production and describes the struggle to ensure that her meat purchases are ethical, given the pressures of both money and information: "It's so hard to understand what happened in the farm and how the meat was produced, especially when meat from the high end places is so expensive." Svetlana feels similarly confused about how to most effectively target her food dollars and describes how she was motivated to join a Community Supported Agriculture (CSA) program in order to avoid the stress and uncertainty of ethical shopping decisions. "I was always struggling," she says. "There were just so many considerations in choosing your food, that it would just take me forever . . . which is why I like these [CSA] boxes. It makes the choice for me." Highlighting the mental and emotional demands of ethical consumption, Svetlana challenges a choice-centered conception of food politics and opts for a more collectivist alternative that involves less individual choice.

In addition to the strain of addressing food system problems through targeted shopping choices, some participants questioned whether individual consumer actions could bring about meaningful change. After hosting a focus group, Carmen emailed us to follow up on the idea of "voting with your dollar," noting that she is "skeptical of that kind of consumer/capitalist-based activity enacting any kind of real social change." Instead, Carmen suggests, "the role of government in shaping food policy is paramount." A similar critique came from food activist Vanessa, who believes that the "voting with your dollar" mantra has "opened the door to these neoliberal approaches to quote-on-quote change." In fact, Vanessa suggests, "it's not change because the structures are very much maintained." To illustrate this point, Vanessa raises the issue of migrant worker justice and asks "how come we're not using that dollar for planning that actually affords living wages in the food system?" Even as Vanessa critiques the limits of shopping for change, she acknowledges that discourses of ethical consumption can have the positive effect of "making food sexy" to a broader public. She gave the example of a friend who "doesn't give a shit about the do-gooder piece" and instead is "buying the commodity and the prestige" of ethical consumption. Vanessa said if that is what it takes to get her friend to buy an organic apple, then so be it.

Distinction practices: "People walking around very high and mighty that they eat organic"

Vanessa's reference to the "prestige" of ethical consumption brings our attention to issues of status and distinction within consumer food politics. As someone who can barely afford her weekly groceries, Harsha critiqued the elitistism she perceives among ethical consumers. She described "people walking around very high and mighty that they eat organic," who then "find it necessary to push it onto other people." Another low-income participant, Sarah, highlights the tension between the political potential of ethical purchases and the reproduction of status hierarchies: "We can say to a certain extent at least people are trying, but at the same time, a lot of it is just a class thing. Like, if this food is better than that kind of food you can find at No Frills, then I'm going to buy it because I can and it makes me feel good."

Clearly ethical consumption can operate as a form of distinction, enabling a kind of boundary work that allows privileged consumers to feel good about themselves, their peer group, and even their neighborhood (Johnston, Szabo, and Rodney 2012; but see Brown 2009). These boundaries can be racialized as well as classed. The association between "alternative" food spaces and whiteness was evident in one focus group of three white vegans. When discussing the ethical shopping venues in their neighborhood, Alyssa expressed disappointment that a local vegan store ("Oasis") had closed and attributed the closure to a larger store ("Green Goods") moving into the neighborhood. Attempting to articulate her feelings about these shopping spaces, she says, "it's hard to say this without sounding racist." Alyssa then contrasts the "passionate" approach of Dan at Oasis (a white man whom she knows by name) and the "Asian family" who run Green Goods in a way that "feels like a business." While she had felt a connection to Dan, Alyssa says that at Green Goods she "can't really talk to them." Alyssa articulates this distinction as a felt experience, but her concern that these comments might "sound racist" is a clear indicator of how race shapes her relationship to these shopping spaces—a form of boundary work that we explored in Chapter 3.

In addition to symbolic exclusions, the political potential of ethical consumption is also constrained by material barriers. Put simply, the appeal to "vote with your dollar" only works if you have enough money to "vote." Financial access was a frequent concern during focus group and interview conversations about food politics and was raised by participants from a range of class backgrounds. Wei describes how other shoppers laugh under their breath at the contents of her grocery cart because "almost everything I'm buying is organic, and it's like twice what somebody's bill will be." Wei recognizes that she is "privileged" to shop this way, whereas "a family of four who barely have housing, they are not going to be able to make those kind of food choices." While Wei reflects on these barriers from a position of privilege, women who were financially prevented from practicing this kind of politicized consumption described feelings of guilt and frustration. Harsha says that while she would like to "make more political statements with my foods," at this point food shopping is not political, "it's a necessity." She explains, "I don't have a lot of money so just surviving sometimes you have to let go of any political ideologies." Enacting an ethical consumer femininity is not simply a *choice*, as the "eat for change" mantra suggests, but rather a hegemonic performance that is facilitated by class privilege.

Political agency, markets, and the role of the state

Many of the food activists we interviewed were critical of individual choice-based models of food politics. Neela works at a community health center in a low-income neighborhood with a large population of recent immigrants. She notes that "it isn't an accident that convenience stores and higher priced grocers are strategically placed in these communities because community members don't have choice or access to travel for lower prices." Bronwyn, a community food activist, makes a similar point, highlighting how the ideal of "choice" is structured by class. She notes that while "we get to talk about organic and local food as a middle-class, upper-class . . . Everyone wants that across the board. People who are low-income want it and people who are rich want it and those of us who can afford it just have the privilege of choice."

This kind of systemic critique was not limited to our interviews with food activists. Some economically marginalized women expressed frustration with their exclusion from consumer food politics. For those who lack choice in the market, the invitation to "vote with your fork" affords little political agency. Nadine, who lives on social assistance, suggests "it would be nice if almost there was no choice . . . That everything was ethically grown and raised." In the context of poverty, consumer choice is not a source of agency for Nadine, but a reminder of the political agency she lacks. When asked who is responsible for creating change in the food system, Nadine looks to the state. "I would say government. Because in industry, capitalism rules here, so it's going to be the bottom line in money, right?" Not wanting to deny herself any degree of personal responsibility, Nadine notes that she does make choices, but says that ultimately "it's hard when you're struggling to put decent food in your mouth."

Significantly, Nadine's call for government-led change in the food system was uncommon in our focus groups and interviews. More often, participants regarded the state as a relatively ineffectual force in the face of powerful corporations. These participants tended to see the market as a more effective channel for political action, which often led to the conclusion that responsibility lies with consumers. For instance, Donna, who is middle class, believes that change *should* come from the government, but recognizes that "big business is also very powerful." Emphasizing the need to "be realistic" in our efforts, Donna suggests that the greatest impact will come from raising awareness, so that consumers know "they do have the power to make a choice."

Disillusionment with government clearly reflects a neoliberal emphasis on the market over state regulation and redistribution, but also holds important gender implications. Ethical consumption occurs within patriarchal structures where women experience less public authority and more expectations in the domestic realm. In this context, women may see greater potential for political change in the market as opposed to the state; thus, the gendering of ethical consumption draws upon, and can in turn *reproduce*, a gendered division of domestic labor and gendered realms of authority. Many women explicitly located their food politics within individual consumer practices, as opposed to social movements. For instance, Alejandra says she sees food as political, but clarifies this is "not because I go in there with a placard and you know, sisters in solidarity colors or anything. But I know that I vote with my wallet. So I choose to vote wisely." Alejandra distances herself from a collective approach to food politics that she deems ineffective and, instead, adopts the pragmatic performance of the ethical consumer.

While some participants explicitly aligned themselves with consumer-driven change in the food system, ethical consumption was not always neatly separated from collective food politics. This point was brought to our attention by longtime food activist and coordinator of the Toronto Food Policy Council, Lauren, who suggests that the "voting with your dollar" model can provide a "pathway into political action." She believes many concerned citizens "hit a wall" when trying to create change through private consumption and will then look for other forms of involvement, such as organizing to oppose GMOs. Thus, Lauren suggests that a key challenge for food activists is "making those pathways clear" and available to a broader public, so that when consumers do feel politically motivated they can find collective projects to support.

While individual consumption decisions may be the most common way women connect food and politics, it is not the only way that politicized food femininities are enacted. In the next section, we focus on women who identify more strongly with "citizen" end of the citizen–consumer spectrum and engage with collectivist strategies to transform the food system.

3. When foodwork becomes a civic practice

As the executive director of FoodShare, Canada's largest food security organization, Debbie is a well-known figure in Canadian food politics. We meet in the FoodShare greenhouse, sitting among planters labeled "beets and horseradish." Carrying a thick binder in one hand and a cup of tea in the other, Debbie moves swiftly from her last meeting straight into our interview. Despite her clear enthusiasm for our research, she is a somewhat intimidating figure to interview, as any list of questions seems woefully inadequate to capture the depth of her wisdom and experience. Rather than attempt to follow our preset interview schedule, the conversation follows Debbie's points as they arise—from her childhood in a poor family with an immigrant mother to her past experiences in feminist activism, to her work at FoodShare, and her relationship to food as a wife and mother.

It was as a parent that Debbie first became involved in food activism, initiating a lunch program at her son's school. From her own childhood, she knew how a subsidized lunch program had "mitigated the impact of poverty" on her life. Drawing upon lessons she had learned in the women's movement, she began to explore "the collective solutions, not the personal solutions" in the realm of school nutrition. Her involvement quickly expanded beyond schools to a broader mandate of food security as she joined forces with FoodShare, becoming executive director in 1992. Now, 20 years later, Debbie continues working "to build a better food system." In a context where "there's so, so much that needs to change," she says, "what a little group like FoodShare and a bunch of feminist food activists do is try our best to create a new system within the belly of the old system."

Debbie's food activism is deeply informed by her experiences with feminist organizing. "What we learned in the women's movement is that the personal is political and in changing myself I change society," she declares. "That's the vision I brought to FoodShare which is change ourselves, change our communities, and then be ready to say to government that we want you to participate in change with us." Debbie distinguishes this grassroots approach from a top-down model of food system change and strives to achieve the right balance between community mobilization and state support. Despite persistent challenges, Debbie remains optimistic and says she is "very happy that women all over the world are carrying this burden and making these changes at the local level."

When we asked participants about sources of optimism in the food system, it was often the kind of work that happens in FoodShare offices that they found most inspiring. Across a range of political perspectives, food priorities, and socioeconomic backgrounds, participants consistently pointed toward community gardens, food co-ops, and other local initiatives that represented a glimmer of hope in a troubled food system. In this section, we shift our focus away from consumer-centered food politics to profile women who locate their political pursuits in collective food initiatives.

Creating a collective food politics

The first time she saw a community garden, Maria says it was "like a door opened in my mind." This discovery inspired years of work in food security, which culminated in a recent transition into policy. Describing food as both a "personal passion and a professional calling," Maria clearly locates her food politics at the collective level, adamant that people cannot achieve "a healthier and more sustainable way of feeding themselves on an individual basis." Similarly, Lauren is committed toward mobilizing state support for change in the food system. As the staff coordinator of the Toronto Food Policy Council, she is active in various projects advocating food security, both proactive (as seen in a recent urban agriculture report) and reactive (e.g., responding to issues related to food security raised in City Council). Reflecting on many years of food activism, Lauren notes that she has always approached food through an interest in the "collective angle" of community organizing and policy, rather than the angle of "individual consumer choice."

While Maria and Lauren focus their food activism within community and government initiatives, others target their energies toward supporting sustainable food ventures. As a food lawyer, Carly works with "small food entrepreneurs and producers, and others seeking to build more sustainable food systems." In addition to "brass tacks legal support" (e.g., advising a woman who is starting her own preserves business), Carly pursues "policy and advocacy" work driven by the question of "how to create food justice." She has recently joined a web project that is working toward "demystifying food laws," so that people who want to start their own food projects are not discouraged by legal hoops. Carly notes that while this kind of support *should* come from government, hopefully she and others can lay the groundwork for broader, systemic change.

The goal of moving beyond individualism to a collective food politics was a common theme in our activist interviews. In these conversations, issues that had arisen throughout our interviews and focus groups were reconfigured through a collective lens. When Cecilia, a Brazilian-Canadian food activist and scholar was asked about her primary goals, she paused and then said "social justice." Cecilia said this focus "guides me in terms of the work that I do," including a recognition of how the inequalities underlying food security work "against women." Similarly, when community food activist Bronwyn discusses the importance of control, she focuses not on individual consumption but on communities "being able to make decisions together." Bronwyn describes the goal of food sovereignty as "being able to control your food, your food system and where you get your food, how safe your food is and whether it's culturally appropriate." This commitment to community building also informs Bronwyn's family foodwork, where meals are shared with two other families through collective cooking and childcare. Bronwyn notes the political possibilities of communal living. "We want to be able to effect change in ourselves and in our neighbourhood and in the city," she says, "and that happens so much better when you're doing it as a group."

Even as we highlight the transformative potential of collective food politics articulated in activists' own words, it is important not to romanticize civic practices. Many of these activists expressed frustration with the leviathan that is the modern food system. The fact that they remained committed in the face of this challenge is admirable and makes their stories all the more inspiring, but it does not erase these structural challenges. Bronwyn suggested that many food activists have both a "doomsday approach, like what happens if our world falls apart . . . and also this really hope-filled, isn't food amazing, kind of thing." Indeed, throughout the interviews, activists described food as both a site of terrible injustice—corporate exploitation, ecological degradation, class and race inequality—and hopeful possibility as a vessel for culture, connection, and political agency. Many activists saw this dialectic of hope and despair as a generative tension within struggles for social change.

The gendering of collective food politics

In addition to the immense challenge of working to counteract the inequitable and unsustainable features of the modern food system, our interviews with activists also revealed how collective food politics are deeply gendered. "I think it's true that food is still primarily the realm of women and social reproduction," says Lauren, "and women are often drawn into this work from that angle and from a community organizing and food provisioning angle." While she believes that "there are more women doing this work," Lauren suggests there is need for a careful gender analysis within different realms of food politics. While community-level foodwork tends to be dominated by women, she says, "in the policy realm, especially on the agriculture side, the discussion is dominated by men," a pattern documented in previous research (Sachs 1996). Lauren points to her own experiences in food policy and says, "I go to a lot of meetings where I am the only woman under fifty and it's all men in suits." Lauren relates this "gender gap" to the areas of food access and food production, which are largely divided along gender lines, and suggests these divisions have significant consequences. She points toward agricultural policy that prioritizes exports, market competition and economic prosperity, and health policy that largely overlooks the link between food and health, discounting the value of wellness and preventative care. Similarly, Cecilia notes that the field of food security is dominated by women, not only because food is traditionally considered to be women's realm, but also because the two professions most heavily involved with food security are the female-dominated fields of social work and nutrition. Yet, she notes that as you move up into the "higher decision levels," the representation of women decreases—a pattern that she finds "disturbing." Debbie puts this issue in more provocative terms and declares that "one of the reasons we have global hunger is that women are not yet actually running the world politically."

Many activists supported Lauren's assessment, highlighting the greater participation of women in community food projects, and men in food policy—a pattern that connects to women's historical responsibility for care-work, as well as patriarchal structures that perpetuate a gendered division of labor. Chandra notes that food is still regarded as "women's work" and highlights a gender divide in keeping with Lauren's comments about food access versus food production: "If you look at food and innovation conferences or food and technology conferences, there's a lot of men who are attending those things. So it's not that they're not in food. They're just not in food in the kind of ways that [women] are in food." Vanessa relates this pattern to women's historical responsibility for care-work and asks whether the predominance of women in community food-work is rooted in "the social helper role, or is it the very gendered things about food and helping together?" In contrast to this feminized realm of community foodwork, several activists noted that the "heroes" of the contemporary food movement are mostly white men—figures like Michael Pollan and Mark Bittman, who have come to represent the public face of a more sustainable food future. Significantly, one of the few areas of food politics that is publically led by women is fat activism. Jackie says "it's nice that [fat activism is] lead by women because it's like, one thing to be led by women in the world." Yet, Jackie recognizes how this pattern reflects a gendered devaluing of body politics. "It's kind of sad that this is the thing, because who else is going to do it? Nobody else really cares about it." Jackie's astute observation makes a key sociological point: spheres with high prestige tend to be dominated by men (Allen and Sachs 2007).

This striking disjuncture—between the feminized sphere of community foodwork and body politics and the masculinized realms of policy and leadership—suggests that a collective approach to food politics does not, in itself, create gender equality. This raises the difficult question of how to value and draw upon women's knowledge and commitment, without reproducing an inequitable gender order. Lauren is well aware of this tension:

> If women are still the ones doing most of the cooking and shopping, and then most of the community food organizing, why is that? When we create community food spaces, new community centers, new kitchens in communities, are we perpetuating that gender divide? We need to ask ourselves that question.

Lauren proposes that the critical question is how to "interrupt" these patterns, especially when "it's easier to say, 'I'm going to take responsibility for that because I care about it' than it is to find men to be engaged or drawn into this work." Lauren's words resonate with our previous discussion of the gendering of ethical consumption as an extension of women's care-work, suggesting that these gendered dynamics also operate in collective food politics. In keeping with this question of how to disrupt gender patterns of community food labor, Neela describes how her community health center specifically targets male participation. She gives the example of a boys' cooking club in which young men mentor adolescent boys, communicating the message that "cooking is important." Similarly, in the context of community gardens, Neela describes how they capitalize upon the food knowledge of immigrant men who were involved in farming in their previous country. In each of these programs, the effort to involve men in community foodwork reflects a targeted effort to address gendered inequities.

While gendered divisions in collective food politics was a central theme in our activist interviews, not everyone saw these issues in the same light. Within the Slow Food movement, Cassia believes that "individuals are compelled by their values, and not by their gender." She suggests that if gender patterns do emerge, this is because people gravitate toward work they are comfortable with, not because they feel pressured. Carly and Chandra make a different but related suggestion: women may be drawn to food politics in order to *escape* the sexism they encounter in other realms—in their cases, law, and academia. While such analyses are insightful, it seems politically important to interrogate the collective impact of these individual choices, whether based on the "pull" of finding a comfortable space or the "push" of escaping sexism. As noted above by Neela's work with young men cooking, and echoed by seminal research on gender hierarchies (Hochschild 2003), sometimes disrupting gender relations requires an uncomfortable process whereby women take on more responsibility for public realms and men address a historical neglect of social reproduction.

The activists we interviewed drew attention to exclusionary dynamics within food politics that were not limited to gender, but intersected with race, class, and body politics. Debbie describes a new FoodShare initiative focused on "food justice and dismantling racism," that begins from the understanding that "the dominant food movement globally is primarily white and excludes people of colour." Debbie suggests that, in part, this is an issue of who is seen to be driving change in the food system and whose food labor is ignored or degraded. She points toward food documentaries where "it's all about white people going shopping at organic farmers markets and that's the food revolution that we hear about." In this dominant cultural imaginary, Debbie notes that groups who are outside this white, middle-class ideal are mostly represented as "eating the wrong foods. You don't see a community kitchen of really fit beautiful immigrants cooking healthy food from scratch."

While Debbie critiques the racism operating within representations of the food movement, Vanessa speaks to her experience of these racial exclusions as a woman of color. As founder of the food justice consultancy FoodSpokes, Vanessa believes that working toward food justice requires first working "internally" to address racism *within* community food organizations, which are very much shaped by whiteness. She notes the challenge of working within a Canadian context, where racial inequality is obscured through a discourse of "multiculturalism," and emphasizes the need to move "beyond just representation" to a more substantive engagement with food justice. Vanessa explains that many food organizations in Toronto now know not to take her picture, since she long ago learned the "value of having my face on their pamphlet" and is tired of being used as a token of "diversity." As a result of these experiences, Vanessa is skeptical of the recent focus on "food justice" within community food organizations, even as she believes these organizations are doing important work.

4. Conclusion

When asked about the kind of changes she hopes for in the food system, Gail says she "would like to see everything a bit kinder." She paints a vision of food politics that centers on relations of care, as both the driver and outcome of food system change: "the idea of caring for ourselves and caring for our families and caring for our health and caring for our environment, it all stems from the kitchen." Gail is sympathetic to grassroots struggles for food system change, but personally feels she can make the greatest impact through everyday food practices. She contrasts the experience of shopping at a corporate supermarket to shopping at her local organic grocer and says, "I feel TOTALLY different about it." For Gail, the latter is "a place for community . . . It's not just about the bottom line. I pay more when I go there for something because *I think that they care*. Yeah, I don't know how to say more about that. It just feels good."

In this chapter, we have examined the gendering of ethical consumption as an extension of women's care-work. Many of the women we spoke with approached politicized food shopping as an expression of care—not only for those whom they were feeding but also for the people, animals, and ecosystems that were impacted by their purchases. Some reflected openly on how their faith in consumer food politics helped ward off feelings of powerlessness in a corporate-dominated food system. The way these women channel desires for social transformation into food shopping challenges a vision of politics restricted to formal institutions or deliberations in the public sphere. At the same time, we have seen how ethical consumption may add to women's social reproductive labor. This is particularly evident among women like Deirdre who self-identify as feminists, but find themselves assuming traditional gender roles in order to uphold ethical principles. We understand this pattern as a new phase in the rationalizing of gendered foodwork (Beagan et al. 2008). In this way, the chapter extends classic feminist scholarship on the reproduction of women's oppression through domestic care-work, as it sheds light on the contradictory ways gender inequalities are reformulated according to neoliberal ideals of choice and individual responsibility.

Taking stock of the gendered workings of consumer food politics, we encounter a tension between two prominent theoretical frameworks. On the one hand, our analysis draws insight from theories of neoliberal governmentality that critique the way in which structural problems are individualized as personal responsibilities to be addressed by consumers in the market. As others have noted, the "vote with your dollar" narrative obscures dynamics of power, suggesting that we are all equally affected by food system problems and equally responsible for addressing them (Maniates 2002). Many of the economically marginalized and activist women in our study were critical of the way in which "eating for change" fails to address systemic issues and can actually reinforce race and class inequalities. Yet, from a feminist perspective, we do not want to dismiss the political agency women may experience through their food choices. These expressions of food politics resonate with the seminal feminist idea that the personal is political—a challenge to masculinist conceptions of politics that have historically devalued women's political contributions and positioned them with less political authority.

Rather than align ourselves wholly with critiques of neoliberal individualism or feminist perspectives on the personal-as-political, we have strived to incorporate insights from each, even when they appear in tension. We approach this tension as a generative one which pushes scholars and food activists to move beyond dismissing consumer politics as simply "yuppie yoga moms" shopping for organic baby food (e.g., Strauss 2011). While committed to critiquing the individualizing, consumerist tendencies of neoliberalism, we are wary of the way this critique can dismiss key feminist insights about the politics of social reproduction and reinforce gendered inequalities. That is, critiquing the performance of an ethical consumer femininity can have the effect of blaming women for carrying the torch of neoliberalism, ignoring how the gendering of ethical consumption is structured by women's social reproductive labor in a patriarchal system. What's more, even as these modes of theorizing appear in tension, we must attend to the ways patriarchy and neoliberalism work together in the formation of ethical consumer femininities. The gendered care-work of ethical consumption is produced, in part, through the definition of food system problems in a neoliberal context, namely, as private issues to be addressed by conscientious consumers making responsible choices. Thus, in addition to women's historical responsibility for domestic care-work, the gendering of ethical foodwork is further entrenched through the individualization of food system transformation as a matter of consumer choice and household practices. Here, we see how cultural discourses of femininity and structural divisions of gendered labor intersect with neoliberal discourses of individual responsibility and market-driven change in order to produce the gendered figure—and *labor*—of the ethical food consumer.

Finally, this generative tension between feminist politics and critiques of neoliberalism also helps unsettle analytic binaries that too often package food politics into bounded categories of citizen versus consumer. We have organized our analysis around the citizen–consumer spectrum and believe that it can be useful analytically to unpack the meaning of these terms in specific empirical contexts (Johnston 2008). Our interview and focus groups highlight how the boundaries of citizen and consumer are blurred in the lived experience and expression of consumer politics. By calling these categories into question, we are not suggesting that most ethical consumers are also heavily engaged in collective food politics; our data do not support such a claim. However, many of the women we spoke with who strove toward shopping for change *also* pointed toward community gardens or food co-ops as sites that made them feel optimistic about change in the food system. What's more, many of these interviewees believe that the state *should* play a role in creating food system change, though they lack confidence that it will. These blurry boundaries are politically and analytically significant, for they reveal what may be lost through a binary conception of food politics. In particular, our research suggests that many ethical consumers are *sympathetic* to collective initiatives, even as they may see their shopping choices as the central way that they can personally "have an impact." This finding brings us back to Lauren's argument that activists must work to make collective "pathways" visible and accessible to those who become frustrated with the limits of consumer food politics.

In addition to shedding light on the gendered complexities of "eating for change," our research also shows how, despite good intentions, structural inequalities can be reproduced within collective food projects. The activists we interviewed shared their experiences with the gendering of foodwork in the public sphere, describing how community-oriented food security work tends to be coded feminine, while the realms of policy and food production remain male-dominated. This troubling pattern raises the question of how to disrupt historical gender divisions within community food politics—a question that highlights the thorny relationship between feminism and foodwork that we explore in the final chapter. Food activists and scholars face the challenge of developing an antiessentialist approach to gender that recognizes and values women's food knowledge and care-work while also working to disrupt gender inequality. Our analysis has shown how gender divides are deeply embedded within systems of race and class and thus foregrounds the need for an intersectional feminist food politics—one that draws insight from Bronwyn's dialectic approach to food as both oppressive and transformative, a site of injustice and a vessel for people's hopes for change. The poles of this dialectic are intertwined; food's hopeful possibilities rely upon a sustained, systemic engagement with its injustices. In Bronwyn's words, we must recognize not only how food is used "to act out people's oppression" but also "that we can use food, then, to act out people's power and choice and strength."

Note

1. For more on how we conceptualize the agency of food politics, see Chapter 2, section 3.

Chapter 7

Food pleasures in the postfeminist kitchen

Judy proudly identifies as a "food-obsessed, cheese-addicted locavore." A white woman with curly grey hair and diamond earrings, she colorfully narrates her 56 years according to significant shifts in her "food style." Judy laughs remembering her "low-fat eating" days in the 1980s, which were phased out as she "kindled an intense love of anything Italian" in the 1990s. In the past decade Judy has come to appreciate "the seasons of food"—a discovery she describes as "life-changing." Explaining that she shops almost exclusively at farmers' markets, Judy shares photos of her favorite market vendors. When we arrive at a picture of fresh peaches, she gasps. "I do live for peaches," Judy exclaims. "Of all of the things in the whole cycle of the year, Ontario peaches are probably the thing I get most excited about. And I always hold back with that kind of exquisite pain until the Red Havens." Judy pokes fun at herself for taking her food passion to the extreme, but speaks earnestly about its significance to her identity. "People who know me invariably say they've never seen anybody who gets as excited about their food as I do," she says. "And who is as animated and passionate. And I think that's really true. But that's just what I've come to be. It's my kind of thing."

Judy acknowledges that this food-centered lifestyle is not for everyone. In her efforts to share the joys of local, seasonal eating with others, she has faced skepticism from friends who have kids and are "all about convenience, economy, being able to make something to feed a lot of people quickly," Judy laughs. "They see the ridiculous extent that I run to this market and that market . . . And I'm spending a ton of money for it and they think I'm nuts." When Judy hosted a "locavore potluck" and asked guests to contribute a dish made with local ingredients, one friend was shocked at the prices she encountered at farmers' markets. "She was just pissed off that I forced her to do something that she thought was so wasteful and ridiculous," Judy explains. "So yeah, I think a lot of that divide is when you have a family to feed. And there are issues of time and cost and different people having different tastes." Judy contrasts the balancing act of feeding a family with her own lifestyle as a single person. "I have only myself to worry about. I do worry about the money and I have a busy life and a limited amount to go to all these different sources to get stuff, but yeah, a lot of my friends think I'm nuts."

Judy highlights the tensions that may arise among pleasure, cost, convenience, and familial care-work in the performance of food femininities. While some might interpret her passion as excessive, there is no denying that Judy displays deep care and concern for food. Of course, sociological research reveals how this kind of food-centered lifestyle can serve as a source of status. We live in a cultural context where "foodies" have risen to prominence as icons of informed, pleasurable eating (Johnston and Baumann 2010). Nevertheless, the fact that Judy is regarded as "nuts" reveals the contradictions that underpin the figure of the *feminine* foodie. The precise meaning of "foodie" remains fluid and contested (e.g., Naccarato and LeBesco 2012: 76), but the term is associated with people who understand food—eating it and learning about it—as central to their identity, leisure, and lifestyle (Johnston and Baumann 2010: 59–60; de Solier 2013). As Judy articulates, and as we have explored elsewhere (Cairns et al. 2010), the self-oriented aspects of pleasurable eating and foodie passions can come into conflict with hegemonic femininities that involve caring *for others* through food. Judy is mostly able to avoid this tension, but she suggests it would be difficult to maintain her current food practices if she were responsible for feeding others. We heard a similar assessment from Cassandra, a white woman in her early thirties, who said "I know I am fanatically neurotic [about food], which is why I do not have children or a partner. And I know all my choices will change when those things, if or when they happen."

In this chapter, we explore the sometimes-fraught relationship between femininity and food pleasure. Having explored the pleasures of food shopping in Chapter 3, here we focus on the pleasures of eating and cooking. Even as women in our study embraced the joys of cooking and eating delicious food, many articulated an ambivalent relationship to food's pleasures. We suggest that these ambivalences yield important insight into contemporary food femininities. The very culinary pleasures that are celebrated in foodie culture often come into conflict with hegemonic femininities characterized by care-work and corporeal restraint. These contradictions are elided in media representations of the female foodie who blissfully eats everything. Here, think of the television persona of food celebrity Giada De Laurentiis; she stands at her stove savoring a rich chocolate dessert, all while maintaining her glamorous appearance *and* her domestic responsibilities as a gracious host. Not only do such celebrity food depictions solidify a sense of women as responsible for domestic foodwork, but they make culinary bliss look easy to achieve (Johnston, Rodney, and Chong, 2014; Naccarato and LeBesco 2012: 55). In our conversations with women, the pursuit of delicious, home-cooked meals was much more fraught, and we documented key tensions among pleasure, bodily projects, care-work, and feminist politics. These tensions extended beyond the realm of eating and into practices of preparing and cooking food, raising their own specific set of questions. What transformative possibilities lie in women's everyday food pleasures? How do women negotiate the pleasures of cooking in a broader context where women continue to perform an inequitable share of food labor?

We explore these questions throughout the chapter. First, we review key texts that help us understand the acute—but often underestimated—tensions between food pleasures and femininity in a postfeminist climate. Second, we examine the pleasures of eating and outline key features in the performance of foodie femininities, which center on the development of a discerning, omnivorous palate, often articulated through a search for exotic and authentic food experiences. While profiling the feminine foodie, we demonstrate how this performance is inflected with race and class and also consider the gendered penalties of prioritizing pleasure.

In the final section of the chapter, we discuss the pleasures of cooking and examine the construction of domestic foodwork as a site of care and leisure. Our focus groups and interviews reveal a gendered distinction in the "everyday cooking" that is an assumed component of women's domestic foodwork and the "leisure cooking" enjoyed by a privileged male foodie who *chooses* to spend his free time experimenting in the kitchen. We juxtapose these pleasurable cooking experiences with the daily struggle to put food on the table when money and time are tight and consider how cooking pleasures emerge at the intersection of gender and class privilege.

1. Ambivalent appetites: Food, pleasure, and postfeminism

While there is a long-standing cultural association between food and femininity, this pairing has not historically emphasized the *pleasurable* aspects of food. On the contrary, gendered conceptions of food as a site of devotion, sacrifice, and corporeal control have traditionally emphasized a repression of women's desires and a commitment to care-work, distancing femininity from food pleasure (Charles and Kerr 1998; DeVault 1991; Lupton 1996; Murcott 1983). In light of this historical denial, the "politics of pleasure" emerged as a significant theme within third-wave feminism (Zeisler 2008), inviting women to openly pursue their desires as an expression of empowerment. Yet, even as new pleasurable femininities are enacted in the realms of sexuality (Castañeda 2012) and beauty (Lazar 2009), tensions persist. In our previous research with foodies, we examined how foodie women navigate competing discourses of pleasure and care (Cairns, Johnston, and Baumann 2010). We found that women foodies challenged aspects of hegemonic femininity by embracing, and sometimes prioritizing, pleasurable food experiences. Although this culinary emphasis had transgressive gender elements, it was clearly facilitated by class privilege and was not straightforward. Our interviews with foodie women revealed how a self-oriented commitment to food pleasure rubbed up against gendered ideals of caring through food.[1] This suggests that the relationship between femininity and food pleasure is an ambivalent one that transcends a binary conception of *either* reproducing *or* resisting an oppressive gender regime.

The pursuit of food pleasure holds clear feminist potential in terms of challenging hegemonic femininities defined by self-sacrifice in the service of others. Still, we must consider how contemporary food pleasures are constituted within a postfeminist climate in which gender equality is commonly framed around "individualism, choice and empowerment" (Gill and Scharf 2011: 4). British feminist Angela McRobbie suggests that a core postfeminist theme is the valuing of an individualized, ironic performance of hyperfemininity as the collective roots of feminism as a social movement fade into the background. In keeping with this analysis, Lazar highlights the postfeminist theme of "celebrating femininity," which "reclaims and rejoices in feminine stereotypes" (2009: 371). In this context, it becomes difficult, yet important, to ask feminist questions that move beyond individual choice to consider how domestic foodwork continues to be shaped by patriarchal power relations and may inadvertently perpetuate harmful feminine stereotypes.

Critical scholars have examined how these postfeminist tensions manifest, and are obscured, in popular culture (McRobbie 2004, 2009; Tasker and Negra 2007), including food media (Hollows 2000, 2003, 2007; Naccarato and LeBesco 2012: 41–66). British communications scholar Joanne Hollows's seminal work examines how food writer and television cook Nigella Lawson navigates the identities of "feminist" and "housewife," which have historically been defined in oppositional terms. Her work shows how "Nigella's cookery attempts to negotiate the demands of both pleasing the self and pleasing and caring for others" (2003: 186). Hollows argues that class mediates Lawson's culinary performance, as her emphasis on cooking pleasures fits within "the aesthetic dispositions of the new middle classes" (187). Yet, even as Lawson popularizes the pursuit of food pleasures for middle-class women, her portrayal of domestic foodwork is not tension-free, as her cooking remains enmeshed in gendered conceptions of domestic foodwork as morally respectable and recognizably feminine (Hollows 2003: 187). Nigella Lawson is known, after all, for her sexually suggestive performances, which connect her own culinary pleasure with the pleasures of the male gaze (Andrews 2003). While the tensions surrounding domestic foodwork are rooted in patriarchal relations of power, in a postfeminist context they are reframed as individualized choices (Hollows 2003: 197). As a result, the costs borne by women who reject these choices, or who do not have the resources to "choose" a Lawson-esque domestic balancing act, are obscured from view.

Hollows' analysis raises important questions to explore in our focus groups and interviews, as we attempt to unravel the ambivalent connections among food, pleasure, and femininity. These ambivalences relate not only to competing constructions of foodwork as oppressive or empowering but also to the judgmental gaze that may be cast in the name of feminist struggles. As Hollows points out, the performance of domestic femininity is "bound up within a series of moral 'rules'—feminist and otherwise" (2003: 198). While often unstated, such "rules" serve as reference points as women articulate their own relationship to food pleasures and determine what food "choices" they are comfortable making (e.g., make cupcakes from scratch and feel like a feminist sell-out, or buy cupcakes at the grocery store and feel like a failed woman?).

Our discourse analysis of food blogs and magazines revealed few instances of food pleasures conflicting with other food femininities. Instead, we found overwhelming evidence of a "win-win" discourse that connects food pleasures with hegemonic feminine ideals, like maternal domesticity, or conventional beauty and thinness.[2] In this win-win representation, culinary pleasure is aligned with ideals of care, ethics, and health. This is not altogether surprising, given that pleasure represents a key theme in alternative food discourse, which continually asserts that ethical food choices—like local, organic, and home-made—are inherently more pleasurable than industrial, factory-farmed options (Biltekoff 2013: 86–8). As such, popular recommendations for making "good" food choices tend to emphasize the pleasures they involve. These range from advice on how to "Raise a Foodie" who can indulge alongside of you (*Parents*, March 2012: 23) to the taste and nutritional benefits of the Mediterranean diet: "health habits won't stick if they're a burden. Food has to be a pleasure, not an obligation" (*Bon Appetit*, March 2012: 38–41). Sometimes the win-win performance of a foodie femininity is celebrated outright, such as the profile of a blogger who "creates dishes that are so luscious, you'll forget they include no meat, refined sugar or other nefarious ingredients" (*Bon Appetit*, March 2012: 74). In bringing a critical eye to this win-win portrayal, we do not want to disparage the joy felt when feeding loved ones or deny that healthy eating can be pleasurable. Yet, it seems analytically and politically important to ask how women experience the dominant win-win discourse. If food pleasure is presented as seamless and simple, how do women negotiate the tensions that may arise among their food pleasures, domestic responsibilities, and physical embodiment? In the next section we explore these tensions as they relate to the performance of foodie femininities.

2. Eating pleasures

"Just an absolute passion for food and flavor": Performing foodie femininities

"It's never just been about fuel," declares Alejandra as she scoops a spoonful of oatmeal into her daughter's mouth. Originally from Columbia and now a Toronto writer, Alejandra's dark hair is starting to grey, but her youthful personality is signaled through the frilly shoulders on her blouse. "I've never understood people that just live to fuel up and go," she continues. "For them food has no meaning other than just human fuel. They're not my friends." Alejandra laughs, then continues. "I just don't understand that mentality. It means so much more."

Alejandra was not the only woman in our study to distinguish her own relationship to food from those who simply eat to live. "The way I approach food is not just for sustenance," says Wei, a 40-year-old Korean-Canadian who works in telecommunications. "It's really something I look forward to every day. Every meal when I can actually devote the time to sit down and enjoy it, that's a key priority of mine." Wei's commitment to savoring every meal and Alejandra's evaluation of food as "so much more" than fuel speak to their food-focused identities. Given the import of pleasure in foodie culture (Cairns et al. 2010: 598), the female foodie can be regarded as a kind of gold standard of pleasurable food femininities. As we show below, performing foodie femininities involves cultivating a discerning palate, prioritizing omnivorous food consumption, and seeking out "authentic" and "exotic" food experiences.

Of course, an interest in food pleasure is not exclusive to foodies—many people enjoy eating, and not all coveted foods are gourmet fare (Naccarato and LeBesco 2012: 85–112). Here, we extend sociological research on people who approach food pleasure as a major life priority and identity project—whether they call themselves foodies or not (Johnston and Baumann 2010). This literature documents the class-specific nature of *prioritizing* food's pleasure, as well as the social construction of good taste, and reveals how "taste" itself is shaped by economic and cultural privilege. Historically, it has been relatively privileged people who have seen food as a source of leisure, a site for the application of an "aesthetic disposition." Sociologist Pierre Bourdieu coined this term to describe a way of seeing the world that involves aesthetic distinction and appreciation—not only of art but also banal objects like food (1984: 5, 28). From a Bourdieusian perspective, rejecting the notion of food as fuel is not merely an embrace of pleasure but also an expression of privilege. The foodie derives pleasure not simply from the act of eating but from articulating and satisfying standards for *good* food, cultivating an aesthetic disposition associated with privileged modes of consumption and a distance from economic necessity (Bourdieu 1984: 5).

How do these foodie traits relate to femininity? Our prior research—supported here—demonstrates that the foodie ideal contains important linkages to gender, class, and racial privilege (Cairns et al. 2010; Johnston et al. 2010). Viewed positively, foodie femininity involves a reworking of hegemonic femininity, challenging the idea of feminine self-sacrifice and denial. At the same time, foodie femininity rests on and reproduces class privilege, even as it rejects outright snobbery. The performance of the feminine foodie involves a classed performance of cultural consumption that designates *particular* foods and cuisines as pleasurable. As we show below, this has important race and class implications.

Central to the classed performance of foodie virtue is the accumulation and display of culinary knowledge, or what Naccarato and Lebesco call "culinary capital" (2012). The cultivation of an aesthetic disposition toward food requires extensive self-education. One cannot simply eat, but must spend time researching culinary techniques and restaurant trends, gathering diverse food experiences (often through travel), and developing individual preferences and proclivities that make up modern projects of selfhood (de Solier 2013; Giddens 1991; Gill and Scharff 2011: 8). For example, when asked how and when she became interested in food, Donna remarks that this is a strange question and responds, "How I became *discerning* about food I think is probably a better question." A 46-year-old entrepreneur of Caribbean descent, Donna prides herself on her extensive food knowledge. She shares a photo of the pistachio ice cream she and a friend made from scratch and launches into a detailed review of various gelato shops throughout Toronto. Eager to share her extensive food knowledge with others, Donna passionately recounts the exact composition of specific meals that were significant in the development of her discerning palate—even those that happened 20 years ago.

> If you're saying that you're going to San Francisco then I will tell you to go to La Fringale, which in French means hunger, like you're absolutely ravenous. They have an incredible duck confit with lentils. And they also do scallops with bacon. People do that all the time but I went there in the early 90s and they were serving the scallops with the bacon as an appetizer. It was good. I went three times in 24 hours to eat.

While Donna happily indulged in French cuisine three times in a 24-hour period, she is not willing to feast on just anything. "Nothing makes me more hostile than bad food," she declares. Donna draws a clear boundary between the kind of food experiences that she enjoys and those that she avoids—a boundary she attributes to her extensive food knowledge. "People know that food's important to me," she explains. "So if we're in a group to choose a restaurant they'll usually defer to me." She takes pride in cultivating this discerning appetite in others and remarks with a laugh, "I could say I've created food snobs." Donna is quick to clarify that this is not about "high class shee-shee-poo-poo restaurants. When I say snob, it's more of a being picky about what we eat, but just an absolute passion for food and flavour." Thus, Donna presents the educated palate as legitimate grounds for distinction, as opposed to the elitism of expensive dining, where food's legitimacy is connected more directly to price.

Like Donna expresses here, a foodie femininity typically rejects the outright snootiness of classic gourmet cuisine. Celebrated blogger Deb Perelman writes in the "About" section of her hit-blog, *Smitten Kitchen*:

> What I'm wary of is: Excessively fussy foods and/or pretentious ingredients. I don't do truffle oil, Himalayan pink salt at $10 per quarter-ounce or single-origin chocolate that can only be found through Posh Nosh-approved purveyors. I think food should be accessible, and am certain that you don't need any of these things to cook fantastically.

Statements like this reflect a larger omnivorous cultural context where the explicit connection between high-status consumption and high-status people has broken down (Peterson 2005; Peterson and Kern 1996; Warde and Martens 2000). Foodies are known in sociology of culture circles as "omnivores," a cultural type that eschews high-brow snobbery (e.g., opera and caviar) and instead consumes across high-brow and low-brow boundaries. This pattern was widely embraced by foodies in our study. "I'm a food snob but I don't like snobby ostentatious restaurants," Donna explains, adding, "I like good food but I've gone to some DIVES." Similarly, Arielle (25, white) lists a wide range of food establishments that she frequents, including "everywhere from a little dim sum place in Chinatown to a hole-in-the-wall pub, to fine dining restaurants." While these diverse tastes appeal to democratic values of inclusivity, critical analysis reveals how omnivorousness can constitute a new and more complex kind of status hierarchy. Even as foodies eat across high-brow and low-brow cuisine, they still draw boundaries to distinguish worthy and unworthy food; chain restaurants are often used to draw these boundaries (Johnston and Baumann 2010: 198). For instance, Judy expresses horror at a coworker's suggestion that they eat lunch at the Pickle Barrel (a chain restaurant often located in shopping malls). She makes a gagging sound and exclaims, "I did not want to go to the Pickle Barrel at all! I mean, had they even suggested some greasy spoon diner or something like that I would have been thrilled."

Given this omnivorous appetite and thirst for culinary knowledge, the feminine foodie must continually expand her food experiences by trying new dishes and cuisines. This culinary openness is also a site for drawing social boundaries, as seen in Donna's recounting of a failed blind date: "When the menu came, he was picky. He doesn't like this, he doesn't like that. I knew right there, it would NEVER work." Similarly, Wei suggests that "it can be a real reflection of someone's character if you are willing to eat anything." For women to embrace an adventurous foodie appetite is significant, given, first, the venerable association between femininity and restricted eating (Lupton 1996) and, second, the long-standing association between food adventuring and masculinity (Heldke 2003: xxiii). Consider the words of Gina, who is white, 54, and manages a private investment fund. She says, "We try to find less conventional sources for where to eat . . . we try not to eat on the beaten path." This interest in dining "off-the-beaten path" speaks to a desire for cross-cultural, and often cross-class, food experiences. Gina says she and her husband occasionally go for "very fine dining," but otherwise "eat a lot of 'ethnic' food." She explains that when her kids are home from university, "they're always on the prowl for the best, you know, down and dirty." Gina's interest in diverse "ethnic" dining experiences was a common sentiment in our research—one that was clearly articulated in a focus group with young, white participants as a desire to go beyond "boring white people food."

While the desire for extreme or norm-breaking culinary experiences has been linked to masculinity (Cairns et al. 2010), these examples show that the valuation of novelty and exoticism are not exclusively masculine traits and may also be linked to the performance of foodie femininities. Yet, a taste for the "exotic" is not only gendered but also has racial underpinnings. As theorized in Edward Said's seminal work, *Orientalism* (1978), exoticism can be understood as a form of cultural appropriation constituted through Western fantasies of the "ethnic" or colonial Other. The appeal of the exotic derives from a desire for the unknown as simultaneously enticing and threatening (Huggan 2001), such that ethnic diversity becomes "spice, seasoning that can liven up the dull dish that is mainstream white culture" (hooks 1992: 21). bell hooks (1992) suggests that the experience of "Eating the Other" is fundamentally related to the production of adventurous eaters, a process which tends to privilege the white subject as the ultimate arbiter of a food's cultural legitimacy (see also Heldke 2003).

Ideals of culinary adventure were clearly present in our conversations with women, along with some of the troubling, exoticizing tendencies noted by scholars like Said and hooks. However, our findings suggest two noteworthy complexities. First, we found that a desire for deeply norm-breaking foods (e.g., eating unusual animals or body parts, like testicles) was relatively rare among women in our sample. Foodie women expressed interest in culinary novelty and openness, but performing foodie femininities did not require positioning oneself as an exceptionally daring eater. Instead, having extensive food knowledge was sufficient to indicate one's culinary capital. Thus, our research supports the previous finding that food adventuring (especially when linked to eating unusual animals or cuts of meat) is culturally constructed as a masculine trait (Cairns et al. 2010). Of course, this does not mean that a desire for the exotic cannot be incorporated into foodie femininities. Consider the case of Arielle, who says, "when I think about traveling in the future, the thing I'm most excited about is food. And eating really obscure things that I might be repulsed by at first. And just having that experience of trying them." Arielle's commitment to appreciating foods she is initially repulsed by displays a deliberate process of developing taste. This involves actively cultivating an aesthetic disposition so that one's capacity for food pleasure is broadened and deepened. While Arielle's dialectic of repulsion and desire may seem contradictory, it fits within a broader logic of exoticism that is central to foodie culture (Johnston and Baumann 2010).

The second complexity in our findings involves unsettling the binary of the white, colonizing food consumer and the passive "ethnic" Other (who is consumed). At the same time that we critique the idealized white eater within foodie discourse (Johnston et al. 2010), we must also attend to the ways in which foodie ideals are embraced and reworked by women who do not embody this privileged vantage point. For example, Donna, who is Jamaican-Canadian, described bravely eating "mystery meat" in Hong Kong. "Around the table I was the non-Asian and some of the American-Asians wouldn't eat it. They wouldn't eat it. But I had seconds!" Donna laughs. "And to this day I don't know what the hell it was." Donna's words—although relatively exceptional—suggest that although the desire for norm-breaking food experiences is a dominantly masculine foodie feature, it is one that women foodies can enact and gain symbolic capital from.

The complex relationship among foodie femininities, pleasures, and race can be further unpacked when we consider the foodie value of "authenticity."[3] A desire for "authentic" food was commonly referenced in our interviews and focus groups, often denoted by culinary experiences that were "true" to a particular ethnocultural tradition. Critical race scholars have shown how the notion of "authentic" cuisine relies upon an essentialist and romanticized conception of nonwhite cultures (Molz 2004). Thus, like exoticism, authenticity has problematic connections to whiteness, as a form of cultural appropriation that decontextualizes and reifies the food practices of ethnoracial groups (Abarca 2004).

While foodie magazines tend to construct authenticity from the vantage point of a privileged white eater (Johnston and Baumann 2010: 94), our interviews reveal complex gender and race dynamics at play in the pleasures of culinary authenticity. For the foodie women we spoke to, an interest in authenticity was not *simply* a marker of whiteness. On the contrary, some immigrant women of color conceptualized authentic food experiences as an extension of respect for their own ethnocultural practices and gendered culinary traditions—the food of home, family, mothers, and grandmothers. For instance, Yin expresses an intense love of "authentic" food, ranging from the Chinese cooking techniques she learned growing up to the food she experiences while traveling. Noting the important role women play in preserving culinary traditions, Yin relates culinary authenticity to the performance of food femininities. "Being the oldest girl in a Chinese family, I'd have to learn to cook," she explains. "I just spent a lot of time with my mom in the kitchen and just chatting with her." For Yin, these culinary lessons from her mother are an important way of "keeping the culture and making all the traditional recipes"; these experiences were foundational to her conception of authentic Chinese cuisine, as well as her gendered identity. In addition to valuing the role of women's food knowledge in her own socialization, Yin also seeks out this gendered knowledge through travel. Describing a recent trip to a small town in Sicily, she notes that "women play a really important role in food culture there." Similarly, when sharing photos of a Brazilian market, she explains "we always try to find the best markets and just look at how women there do their daily things." Thus, while Yin relates her desire for authentic food experiences to her own Chinese heritage and respect for traditional foodways, she locates the production and preservation of authentic cuisine within the *gendered* histories of women's foodwork.

Yin's account of culinary authenticity suggests that this foodie value can be more fully understood by unpacking its connections to gender and ethnicity. But class is also central to the performance of foodie femininities. Performing a foodie femininity—a woman who appreciates culinary authenticity, eats in "dives," but also knows about new high-end restaurant openings—is clearly linked to class. Low incomes and hunger tend to breed culinary conservatism, since an unpalatable new food choice cannot be casually discarded or left uneaten (Tannahill 1973: 393). Cultivating an aesthetic disposition toward food represents a privileged (but not exclusively white) food femininity. Taste habits were a common way that women drew symbolic boundaries that reinforced class distinctions. Nowhere was this clearer than in discussions of fast-food or an understanding of food as "fuel." As mentioned above, many middle- and upper-middle-class women demarcated good food from bad food using criteria of mass production versus authenticity—that is, chain restaurants and fast-food versus artisanal, hand-made, or local specialties. This hierarchy makes sense from a foodie perspective, since fast-food falls short on criteria of both authenticity and exoticism (Johnston and Baumann 2010: 198). However, our conversations with low-income women provide a contrast to the privileged rejection of chain restaurants and the delegitimized notion of food as "fuel." Consider Harsha (28, South Asian), who self-identifies as a foodie but describes how her ability to pursue food pleasure is limited by her low income. "I don't want to eat fast food, but that's what I can afford," she says, as we sit chatting in her small basement apartment. "So then you just have to go grab that $2 burger from McDonald's just to fill yourself so you can get through the day." Harsha goes on to describe how her desire for culinary adventure is constrained by resources. "I love trying different foods of different ethnicities, however right now, given the position I am in with my income level, it's quite hard to experience new foods," she says. "At this point in my life even though I love the taste of food, it's more used as a fuel to get me through the day." Seeing food as a source of pleasure and adventure is not exclusively a middle-class ideal, but Harsha's words make clear that *fulfilling* feminine foodie ideals requires economic resources.

This section has shown that foodie femininities create significant space for food pleasure centered around culinary exoticism and authenticity. However, class remains a significant stumbling block for enacting foodie femininities, even for women like Harsha who espouse many of the same foodie ideals but cannot fulfill these ideals in their daily food practices. Beyond these class tensions, prioritizing pleasure can also create tensions for women who attempt to navigate competing feminine ideals of care, ethics, and corporeal restraint.

"You can't have it all": The penalties of "choosing" pleasure

"I've always been a very indulgent person," says Arielle. "I'm a hedonist." White and 25 years old, Arielle works in fashion marketing. Her black v-neck and tights are accented by dangly earrings and gold bangles. A long braid hangs over her shoulder, leaving wisps of hair around the edges of her face. Flipping through photos on her laptop, she stops at an artfully composed shot of a wedge of cheese. "I used this interview as an excuse to go buy food," she says, laughing. "That was my dinner last night. The cheese." Arielle embraces indulgence as fundamental to her identity, but also regards it as a personal weakness. "I've always had this kind of battle between just over-consumption and not wanting to over-consume, wanting to be smart with my choices . . . so fighting those two sides of me."

This narrative of the indulgent, conflicted eater provides Arielle with a framework through which to make sense of the apparent contradictions in her food practices. "I value my health but my eating behaviour doesn't align with that," she says, describing a pattern of "giving in to cravings, not having any self-restraint." Similar tensions arise in the realm of ethics. "When I was in school, I took an environmental ethics class and my final research paper was on vegetarianism," she explains. 'And I was arguing that we should all be vegetarians," Arielle giggles. "I almost convinced myself. I was that close to becoming a vegetarian because of my wonderful argument," she says, laughing openly now. "But it didn't happen. It's too pleasurable to eat meat."

Arielle's candid account of her own seemingly contradictory food practices reveals the tensions that may arise between competing food femininities—particularly between those oriented around pleasure, feminine ideals of care, and physical as well as financial restraint. While Arielle was especially forthcoming about how her desire for delicious eating trumped values of health and ethics, other participants voiced similar tensions. Many of the women in our study who valued pleasurable eating spoke about having to compensate through body work, to maintain an appearance in line with hegemonic femininity. "I'll joke about having to exercise more so that I can keep up with the way I normally would want to eat," says Wei. She notes that food is "such a huge part of enjoying life" that she does not want to miss out on its pleasures. Yet, even as Wei challenges restrictive conceptions of the feminine appetite, she accepts vigorous exercise as a responsibility that accompanies this diet. In her words, "I'm really active so that I can eat that way." Judy articulates a similar commitment to body work as a corollary to her foodie lifestyle. When sharing her food photographs, she laughs, recalling a friend's comment that "I should have a picture of my gym because of all the time I have to spend at the gym to offset all of the eating that I'm doing!" Even those who explicitly prioritize pleasure over body image acknowledge the tension between these ideals. The most adamant critique of the corporeal-pleasure tension came from Claudette, a white, French Canadian chef. On the topic of body image, Claudette says, "I try not to get too caught up in that stuff because I think women spend too much time on that crap." She rejects moralizing conceptions of controlled eating and says "the table is really about pleasure."

While Claudette refuses to allow body image pressures to dampen her pleasure at the table, the tension between pleasure and feminine embodiment was salient for many foodie participants who felt pulled between competing food ideals. Mediating this tension through narratives of moderation, women calibrated their foodie femininities in relation to those associated with overindulgence and excess. "It's all about moderation," says Alejandra. "You can have that cheese from France, you can have those three star Michelin meals. But you don't want to eat yourself sick either." For Alejandra, the pursuit of pleasure requires an element of control (echoing the choice/control dialectic explored in Chapter 5). "You're a food lover and you love croissants, you're gonna get the best," she continues. "It's butter you're eating so one will do. Two maybe. But not five." Lisa (42, white) also emphasizes moderation as a component of her foodie identity. "I'm a foodie and I love French food," she says. "If I was in France and there was foie gras or something in front of me I'd eat it. But do I eat it every day? Of course not."

While expectations about controlled, responsible eating were the most common source of tension for foodie femininities, the desire for delicious food experiences sometimes conflicted with ethical ideals. "One thing I feel really bad about is tuna, blue fin tuna," says Yin. "Tuna is one thing I really, really love, but I also know how that is to the environment." She recounts the enticing selection of seafood on offer at her favorite sushi restaurant and confesses, "I haven't been able to say no to the shark fin when [the chef] put it in front of me." Reflecting further on these tensions, Yin also notes how her foodie emphasis on diverse culinary experiences has been facilitated by postponing motherhood. "We make choices," she says. "There are people who chose to start the family earlier and buy a house or a car earlier in life, but we chose to spend our money traveling and eating." While Yin finds satisfaction in prioritizing food over other aspects of her life, she notes that weighing such commitments is "always a struggle": "You realize that you have to give up all these things in order to live a certain way and you can't have it all. So right now I'm trying to find that balance."

Resigned to the fact that she "can't have it all," Yin narrates her foodie femininity as someone who has "chosen" pleasure over a feminine vision of good mothering and food ethics. Yet, in "trying to find that balance," she alludes to the hope of reconciling these seemingly incommensurable food femininities. Analyzing the tensions articulated by foodie women, we have shown how enacting pleasurable foodie femininities can mean ceding to a *failed* femininity in the domains of health and body, mothering, or food ethics. These tensions are embedded within hegemonic articulations of femininity and food pleasure, but become personalized through a discourse of choice that positions individual women as failing to live up to feminine ideals.

Having explored the ideals and tensions involved in performing foodie femininities, we now turn to the topic of cooking and the pleasures and ambiguities it generated for women in our study.

3. Cooking pleasures

Despite her passion for food, Judy did not always find cooking pleasurable, particularly after her separation. "When I was first living on my own, I felt like I wasn't worth going through the effort to make something special," she explains. Judy's experience resonates with research indicating that many women feel unmotivated to cook for themselves (Bugge and Almas 2006; Charles and Kerr 1988), an idea repeated in our interviews and focus groups with surprising persistence. Judy describes how she cultivated a love of cooking for herself over the years, but notes that, ultimately, "food is a way of showing love." For this reason, she says, "I probably get more pleasure out of cooking for other people than I do out of cooking for myself."

Judy's struggle to cultivate a pleasurable relationship to cooking speaks to the historical construction of women's domestic foodwork as a site of labor rather than leisure. In this hegemonic configuration of feminine cooking, pleasure is derived through care-work—that is cooking *for others*. In order to understand the long-standing finding that women derive less pleasure cooking for themselves, we must situate cooking pleasures in relation to feminine ideals of care and selflessness, as well as historically oppressive gender relations in which cooking has been a component of women's domestic burden. These cultural discourses and structural relations continue to shape the performance of food femininities. However, with the rise of foodie culture and postfeminist claims of feminine empowerment, many women are reclaiming cooking as a site of personal pleasure, choice, and agency. In this section, we map out some of the continuities, ruptures, and ambivalences in the relationship between femininity and cooking pleasure.

"If I like you, I'll cook for you"

"There's a huge satisfaction in feeding people," says Gina. "I don't know if that's maternal or if it's cultural, but to have people eat your food is always to me a huge satisfaction." Gina's comment that perhaps this satisfaction is "maternal" alludes to the enduring association between femininity and caring through food. The theme of deriving pleasure through cooking for others was nearly universal among women in our study, cutting across age, class, race, sexuality, and relationship status. Alejandra puts it simply: "If I like you, I'll cook for you. And that's my way of showing I care."

Throughout our focus groups and interviews, women consistently emphasized the social and emotional significance of cooking as a source of joy, articulating a form of cooking pleasure that is in keeping with hegemonic constructions of feminine relationality (Lupton 1996: 40). Wei also emphasized the pleasures of cooking *with* others, noting that "the act of sharing food and preparing everything with someone, that's like a fun event. And in being able to share food with people I'm close to, it's really like an act of love." Wei relates the emotional rewards of cooking to the performance of caring femininities. "When you're sharing food with other people, there is a nurturing quality about that," she says. "And it makes a lot of sense to me that women would identify so strongly with food because of that sitting together and socializing." Wei contrasts this relational approach to cooking to one that is "just utilitarian, you know, finish your meal and back to, okay this is totally stereotyping, but like, back to watching the game or something." Wei laughs, signaling her own critical reflexivity toward this essentialist gender binary—the woman who cooks and the man who wants to get "back to the game." In doing so, she simultaneously references and undermines historically dominant femininities and masculinities—a discursive maneuver that speaks to the ambivalent role such gendered figures play in contemporary food femininities. Even as women critique what they view as old-fashioned images of women's foodwork, such cultural constructions of femininity provide powerful reference points with which to make sense of pleasures derived in the postfeminist kitchen.

As emblematic of cooking as care-work, many women in our study describe an absence of pleasure when cooking for themselves alone. Kalise (26, black, retail) states this directly: "I enjoy cooking for others. I don't enjoy cooking for myself." Similarly, Hilary (28, white, coffee barista) says that while cooking for others brings her "joy," she feels a "lack of inspiration for cooking just for myself." Somewhat paradoxically, Hilary attributes this lack of motivation to her own high standards. "When I cook a meal I feel very unsatisfied with it just being kind of like, not amazing in some way," she explains. "It is something that I need to feel proud about." This commitment to taking pride in her cooking means that each meal requires considerable effort—effort that Hilary is not willing to expend for herself alone. Hilary contrasts her current life in Toronto to the previous year, when she lived in Northern Ontario with her partner and roommate. With two hungry dogsledders to feed, she found no shortage of culinary inspiration. "I was cooking all the time . . . I was just really inspired and really wanted to just feed these boys well and like, make it as beautiful as I could for myself," she says. "To compare then versus now, time is an issue, money is an issue, and the lack of time creates a sort of lack of inspiration." While Hilary's story is unique—no other participant had fed dogsledders in Northern Canada—her experiences speak to a larger theme in our data, namely, that the pleasures of cooking are care-focused but also *contextual*. Most women said they enjoy cooking at least some of the time—but only if they have sufficient time and resources, are making something they enjoy, and, most importantly, have someone to share it with.

Everyday cooking and leisure cooking

The pleasures of cooking are also shaped by family context and the extent to which cooking is a required component of domestic labor. As the primary cook for her husband and daughter, Eva views a night alone as a break from cooking. "I won't cook for myself," she says. "I think if my life was different maybe I would, but given the way my life is right now, with the rigour and the business of it, I feel like I have a day off." Eva situates cooking pleasures in the context of a gendered division of food labor wherein the "business" of everyday cooking is clearly a form of work. Eva's husband considers her comment and responds, "Which is funny because when I'm here alone I do cook for myself. I do, but I don't cook most of the time, right?" Their dialogue illuminates how cooking pleasures are structured by the gendered division of foodwork. For Eva, a night alone is a "night off" from cooking; for her husband, a night without Eva is inspiration to cook.

Eva and her husband's musings were echoed throughout our focus groups and interviews in the distinction between "everyday" cooking and "leisure" cooking. While our data reveal a clear departure from rigid gender roles designating foodwork as women's work, there remain gendered patterns in the frequency and form of domestic cooking. In keeping with previous research (Cairns et al. 2010; Short 2006), participants described cooking femininities enacted through the "everyday cooking" of domestic care-work and cooking masculinities performed through "leisure cooking." Cynthia (55, Chinese-Canadian, retail) says that while her husband is the better cook, she is primarily responsible for daily meals. "Sometimes he'll cook because he does it as a break," she says, "and he finds that really relaxing. Whereas me, it's more like, okay, this is yet another meal I have to serve." Kerri (36, white, occupational therapist) articulates this distinction as the difference between "weekday" and "weekend" cooking. Her friend Brenda (46, white) builds on this assessment from her perspective as a stay-at-home mom: "I've been cooking everyday for twenty years. There are times I don't even want to cook. Last summer it hit me for two weeks. I could hardly do it." While Kerri murmurs in agreement, her partner Brad (36, white, investment banker) chimes in with his vision of pleasurable cooking. "One of the greatest pleasures for me in the world is having a Saturday where I know I can just, whatever I want to make for dinner, go out, shop for it . . . bottle of wine, you know, just sit in the kitchen, cook stuff. It's actually therapeutic for me." Describing the restorative joys of "weekend cooking," Brad acknowledges he would feel differently if cooking were an obligation. "I like cooking enough that I thought that I'd like to be a chef," he says, "but I realized having talked to chefs . . . it becomes a job, probably very similar to when you're a mom, and it's forced upon you." Brenda says, "ya," and it is clear this is a feeling she knows all too well. Brad concludes: "So I don't ever wanna lose that." Brad's decision to keep cooking as a leisure activity is a privileged "choice" not available to those who must feed others as an assumed component of care-work.[4]

In their cooking narratives, participants noted not only the relative amount of domestic foodwork performed by men and women but also the relative significance attributed to their cooking labor. "I will make a lot of the weekday meals and I will be fast," says Sophie, a white, 32-year-old teacher. She contrasts her own style of cooking with her husband's: "his meals are always thick and they're always like, something is happening with this meal! I am mastering the brisket!" Sophie's friends laugh, and she continues: "I am a good cook . . . but I feel like he gets more cred for his cooking." Sophie points out how men's *specialty* cooking may receive greater recognition in a context where women's *everyday* cooking is taken for granted. This gendered dynamic evokes the historical figures of the masculine professional chef and the feminine domestic cook (Hollows 2003b; Ketchum 2005; Swenson 2009). Such gendered performances were by no means universal in our research—for instance, Derek, a white construction worker, spoke fondly of caring for his family through daily cooking. Nevertheless, these contrasting depictions of cooking femininities and masculinities were a consistent pattern in our focus groups and interviews—one centering on care and everyday foodwork, the other associated with leisure and the preparation of special meals.

Some men in our study reflected critically on the special recognition they receive for their culinary contributions. "I definitely get a pat on the back for being a dude who cooks," says Roy, a white, 32-year-old teacher. "I can stand near the oven and people will hug me, like, 'fantastic meal!'" Gesturing toward his partner, Roy says, "Kim will bake something, she is a really good baker, and they will be like, 'oh, I don't really care for this. It's a bit dry, the fruit is sour.' Whereas, it's, 'Roy! You are majestic! You are a chef!'" Kim and their friends laugh at what they know is all too true. Another couple in the group weighs in with further evidence of how gendered assumptions can diminish women's culinary expertise—in this case, the association between meat and masculinity (Adams 1990; Inness 2001; Neuhaus 2003). "I remember when I bought the Weber grill," says Carmen, who is 33, Chinese-Canadian, and works as a librarian. "Peter's dad came over . . . I think he said something like, 'Is this your new toy?'" Carmen's partner, Peter, chimes in, "And I was like, *me*?" Peter's incredulity makes it clear that the grill is Carmen's territory. This particular focus group of young, educated foodies was highly critical of the persistent gendering of cooking—a pattern that they sought to challenge in their daily food practices but that they saw reinforced regularly in the evaluations and perceptions of others.

Embodied (and classed) cooking pleasures

Interestingly, when women in our study described cooking as pleasurable in its own right (rather than primarily a way of nourishing others), they tended to emphasize the *embodied* practice of making food. These embodied narratives ranged from the "meditative" pleasures of chopping to the "therapeutic" experience of kneading dough and the sensory joys of home canning. "I like breaking a piece of fruit or a vegetable into other shapes. I just find that really pleasant," says, Camilla, a white, 54-year-old writer who is an avid preserver. Camilla relishes the aromatic process as her kitchen fills with steam. "You're absorbing something wonderful and good and it makes you feel good." Similarly, Deirdre (51, white) delights in the sensations of jam-making. "I had no idea what it was to make strawberry jam," she confides. Deirdre describes the "thrill" when "the lids do that 'pop' kind of noise," and says, "I thought you could only get that from sex!" Even as Deirdre exaggerates for comedic effect, there is no question that her enthusiasm for jam-making is genuine. She and others recount the embodied pleasures of cooking—the repetitive movements, distinct textures, aromas, and colors—pleasures derived through the *practice* of making food, rather than through the exchange of feeding others.

Crucially, though, the pleasures of cooking are facilitated by various forms of privilege. Viewing cooking as hobby rather than necessity suggests that one is not only unburdened by the responsibilities of daily foodwork but also has ample time and resources to devote to culinary pursuits (Cairns et al. 2010; Hollows 2003b). "I don't enjoy cooking that much," says Lucia, a 42-year-old social worker, originally from Cuba. As a single mom, Lucia's time is at a premium. "I don't have the time to learn and prepare and sort of to enjoy it. I do it as a chore." For Lucia, cooking is yet another task she must squeeze into an already hectic day, although she wishes she had "more time to learn to cook, and to *enjoy* the cooking." Of course, time is not the only resource required for leisure cooking, as noted by Sarah, a Vietnamese-Canadian university student. Sarah highlights the considerable resources required to foster an aesthetic approach to cooking: "I can't risk making a bad meal," she says. "If I had a lot of money I could try a bunch of things without the risk of having to throw food away." As Sarah points out, the culinary experimentation that is central to foodie culture requires a degree of financial and temporal flexibility that relies upon class privilege.

Narratives of cooking in the context of poverty bring to light the stark inequities that structure cooking pleasures. For Kendra, these constraints mean lack of access to a private kitchen. Forty-eight years old and originally from Trinidad and Tobago, Kendra is currently living in a women's shelter. "I do enjoy cooking," she says. "When I had my own place, I was cooking every day." Kendra says the biggest tension in her current food practices is that she "cannot get up in the morning as I used to and go in the kitchen. It's not my kitchen, it's their kitchen." Kendra refuses to eat the food provided at the shelter, which she finds stale and unappealing. Instead, she purchases her own food and prepares sandwiches in the communal kitchen. Kendra describes how the experience of living in a shelter deprives women of "your self-respect, your dignity, your decision-making process." Her story of struggling to maintain control over her diet, and to make her own limited choices about what she eats, brings into sharp relief the privilege of cooking for leisure and culinary experimentation.

4. Conclusion

In this chapter, we have explored the increasingly celebrated, yet often fraught relationship between femininity and food pleasure. We intentionally reserved this topic for our final empirical chapter, for pleasure occupies a unique position relative to the other food femininities examined throughout the book. While previous chapters have shown food femininities to be contradictory and contested, the realms of shopping, mothering, health, and ethics afford ample opportunities for enacting food practices that align with hegemonic feminine ideals of care-work, morality, and bodily restraint. In contrast, food pleasure and femininity are not so easily reconciled—despite the win-win portrayal in contemporary food media. One the one hand, the prioritization of food pleasure is an encouraging sign of everyday feminine resistance. Unlike so many of our maternal ancestors, the feminine foodie prioritizes her own pleasure and does not deny herself the joys of eating delicious, extravagant meals, especially when she can share them with others.

At the same time, our research reveals the performance of foodie femininities to be the source of significant ambivalence. In prioritizing the *self-oriented* pleasures of eating experiences that are carefully selected, delicious, and often expensive, foodie femininities challenge other long-standing feminine goals of health promotion, ethical responsibility, and caring for others—goals that are deeply interwoven within cultural renderings of food and femininity. Some of the women we spoke with accepted this tradeoff—recall Arielle's identification as an "indulgent" eater, or Yin's assessment that "you can't have it all." But even these committed foodies struggled with tensions in their everyday food practices and alluded to the lingering sense of "failing" on these hegemonic dimensions of food femininity. While such tensions speak to the gendered relations of power that structure foodie culture, they also reflect significant forms of privilege. Foodie women may struggle to reconcile their refined taste for authentic and exotic cuisine with ideals of feminine selflessness, but the pursuit of these tastes relies upon economic and cultural resources that are out of reach for many women. As Harsha made so clear when describing her "survival mode" approach to shopping and eating, a foodie femininity is, itself, a form of privilege.

Of course, food's pleasures are not limited to the act of eating, and in the second half of the chapter we examined the pleasures that can be found through cooking. While many participants described cooking as a rewarding pursuit, they were clear that not all cooking is equally pleasing. While "everyday cooking" is a taken-for-granted component of women's daily foodwork, "leisure cooking" is more readily pursued by those who are free of everyday domestic responsibilities. Recall Brad's declaration that he loved cooking too much to let it become a routinized "job," followed by Brenda's knowing sigh as someone who feeds a family every night. Significantly, gender was not only implicit within these conversations but was also the topic of explicit reflection, dialogue, and critique. We are reminded here of Roy and Kim's comical account of his near-saintly status as a "guy who cooks," or Eva and her husband's contrasting perspectives on a night alone—she takes a break from cooking, whereas he is inspired to cook a wonderful meal. Yet, as we have seen consistently throughout the book, this reflexive awareness of gendered inequities did not mean that participants were free of gendered patterns in their daily food lives or had discovered simple strategies for avoiding the resulting tensions.

These reflexive discussions of femininity and food pleasure reveal the complex ways that women draw upon entrenched gender ideals as they calibrate the performance of pleasurable food femininities. This is not a straightforward embrace of hegemonic femininity—on the contrary, many women openly critique and even laugh at old-fashioned, essentialist conceptions of the dutiful housewife. At the same time, such gendered figures serve as important reference points in the performance of contemporary food femininities. Think here of Wei's playful contrast of the woman who cooks to express her love, and the man who just wants to "get back to the game." Wei laughs at this stereotypical portrayal, distancing herself from such outdated notions. Laughter here signals a reflexive understanding of gender scripts, as well as the prevalence of postfeminist sensibilities. Often, we laugh at old gender hierarchies because we think (and hope) that we are now free of them. We further unpack these ambivalences in the concluding chapter as we delve into the difficult question of what constitutes a feminist food politics and whether cooking can constitute a feminist act.

Notes

1. In De Solier's recent study (2013), she argues that foodies disrupt normative gender roles, given that both men and women embrace the idea of cooking as leisure.

2. Sometimes, feminine bodies are displayed among the delicious offerings available to readers. For example, a *Bon Appétit* article titled "Columbia Brewing" features a picture of a young woman titled "local beauty" (January 2012: 48).

3. Johnston and Baumann argue that "authenticity is a key element of how foodies evaluate and legitimate food choices" and demonstrate how authentic foods are socially constructed through appeals to geographic specificity, "simplicity," personal connection, or historical and "ethnic" traditions (2010: 69–70).

4. The gendering of cooking as labor or leisure was a strong theme in our data, but participants noted the ethnocultural specificity of cooking femininities and masculinities. Drawing upon her own socialization in the Caribbean, Donna said, "West Indian

men are raised to be able to cook, iron, do their own groceries or whatever. So most West Indian men can probably cook better than the women." The gendered signifi-cance of ethnocultural tradition also arose in our youth discussion groups. One young woman from China noted that her dad does most of the daily meal preparation. She added: "Mom says look for a guy who can cook!" drawing laughter from her friends.

Chapter 8

Conclusion: Cooking as a feminist act?

The red walls and blue cupboards of Camilla's kitchen are visible from her tiny living room. In this colorful space, she and her partner share cooking equally. Yet, in her 54 years, Camilla has seen how things could be otherwise. "I have also had a stint at being the wife and mom who cooks every day," she says, recalling ten years as the sole food provider for her previous husband and his daughter. "I did daily lunches and all that kind of thing. And of course that's an interesting little dance of duty and subservience." When asked to explain further, Camilla looks pensive. "Well, I have a couple of thoughts about that," she says, shifting her long grey hair behind her shoulders.

> When I was a kid, every single morning, my mom got up earlier than my dad . . . And every day she would put out the same tray. She would put a plate and cutlery, a glass with juice in it and she would take an orange, cut it in half and section it so it could be eaten. And I remember when I was sort of 15, 16, 17, around those ages, I kept thinking, how could she bear that? How could she stand to do that? Now, living with [my partner], he's coffee maker-challenged. And when he's working, he wants a cup of coffee at home in the morning. So every single night I set up the coffee maker so that he can push the button and have coffee in the morning. And I realize now that it was not a harsh duty for my mother. She liked doing it. It was a pleasant routine and it was a little expression of love. It was ultimately a pleasure and one of the things that kind of makes life real and good.

Camilla smiles at the memory of her mother lovingly preparing her father's breakfast. Although her teenage self had questioned what she perceived as the "harsh duty" of a housewife, this is now a form of pleasure that she can relate to. She contrasts this kind of caring through food—a relationship of love and mutual appreciation—to the dynamics surrounding foodwork in her previous marriage. As Camilla speaks, it becomes clear that this was an emotionally abusive relationship. Her husband was often "offended" by something about the dinners she made each evening and would angrily leave the table. Upon reflection, Camilla now sees that food was often "used in an oppressive way" within their marriage: "the question of who was cooking and what was being cooked and who was eating it became like battle rounds in a war."

Camilla's two memories present a powerful juxtaposition: her mother's cooking as an expression of love; her own cooking as a form of oppression. Both memories are evoked from the context of her current relationship, in which she and her partner share foodwork equally. The contrast reveals how the gendered pleasures of cooking are embedded within relations of care, love, and responsibility, but also relations of power. Camilla's memories highlight the ambivalent place of cooking pleasures within dynamics of gender inequality, as well as the ways in which the figure of the domestic housewife haunts the performance of contemporary food femininities.

As the previous chapters have shown, the question of who makes dinner (and lunches and breakfasts) has deep emotional resonance and feminist significance. Behind this question lie many others: Who does the food shopping? Who thinks about the health and environmental impacts of items in the cart? Who develops creative strategies to get kids to eat vegetables? The preceding chapters have shown that while rigid gender roles are widely regarded as a thing of the past, food and femininity remain deeply connected. We see this connection through the way women view their bodies, search for culinary pleasures, care for others, and strive for change. This connection is evident in magazine articles advising women to monitor their family's sodium intake, but it is also deeply embedded in women's everyday lives and emotional attachments.

In this final chapter, we draw upon our participants' experiences to think through the interconnections between feminist ideals and foodwork routines. We examine competing discourses of choice, responsibility, and (in)equality that give meaning to ambivalent food pleasures and pressures; we end with suggestions for how to develop a more explicitly feminist food studies (Avakian and Haber 2005). A few caveats are in order: like the rest of this book, our arguments here draw on the specific North American context where we carried out our research and are not intended as universally applicable. Additionally, because the majority of our participants were heterosexual, the following discussion on foodwork routines focuses on the challenges of distributing household labor between women and men. That said, we are encouraged by evidence of more equitable partnerships forged in nonheteronormative couples and see this as a site of possibility to build from in feminist struggles (Dunn 2000; Kurdek 2007; Mundy 2013).[1]

Before staking a claim about a feminist politics of foodwork, we want to review some of the book's core contributions, as these empirical findings and theoretical insights provide the backdrop for our feminist claims making. First, our study of food and femininity has revealed significant continuities with past generations of feminist research while also identifying important ways that today's food femininities are shaped by contemporary postfeminist sensibilities. In highlighting these empirical continuities, we want to pay tribute to the feminist scholars who have laid the foundation for this research. Important pieces of feminist scholarship have documented a long-standing link between food and femininity (e.g., Bordo 1993; DeVault 1991; Lupton 1996b; Schenone 2003), and we see our work as affirming the contemporary salience of this connection. Like previous feminist research (e.g., Avakian and Haber 2005; Beagan et al. 2008; DeVault 1991), we have found food to be powerfully connected to women's identities—to their sense of self as women, mothers, caregivers, consumers, and citizens. This connection was powerfully affirmed in our textual data as well as through extensive interview and focus group research. For the women we spoke with (and, we would argue, for *many* women), food is not just a hobby or a means to an end, but a key way to articulate and embody femininity—to be "recognizably womanly" (Devault 1991: 118). The women in our study were particularly invested in food, but we contend that even women who care little about food construct their identities in a social context where idealized femininities are linked to skilled foodwork and successful body projects.

Women's identities relate to food in multiple realms—from feeding children to expressing politics—and for that reason, we theorize food femininities as multifaceted and make clear that they are not reducible to one trait, practice, or tendency. Also in accordance with other pieces of feminist research, we have found that the connection between food and femininity materializes in various forms of *work*—including the work of caring for children, caring for one's body, and caring for the planet—and that each of these forms of care-work is subject to scrutiny and judgment from others (e.g., Beagan et al. 2014; MacKendrick 2014). For the women in our study, feminine identities are deeply connected to the way they eat, shop, and cook dinner. Foodwork is a material practice, an important dimension of social reproductive labor; at the same time, it is also a symbolically laden process involving creativity, nourishment, political concern, and care for others. Our study makes clear that not all women have equal access to the material and the symbolic rewards of successful foodwork. Like other scholars, we have found that the connection between food and femininity reflects and perpetuates vast inequalities, not only in relation to gender but also in the classed and racialized power structures that position women with uneven access to hegemonic feminine ideals (e.g., Bordo 1993; Naccarato and LeBesco 2012). While these continuities may appear unsurprising to some feminist readers, we believe it is crucial to empirically document the persistence of gendered themes in women's contemporary food lives—particularly in a context where postfeminist claims of gender equality have gained strong cultural resonance.

While our research reveals significant continuity with previous gender and food scholarship, a central contribution of this book has been to examine how this food/femininity connection persists in a contemporary sociohistorical context. A close look at the North American foodscape reveals significant changes from decades past: this is a moment when gender inequality is widely regarded as a relic of history, when food has gained new cultural cachet for both men and women, when dieting discourse has been replaced with a focus on "healthy eating," and when food choices are celebrated as a site of political expression. Given these changes, the continuity we find with the research of DeVault and others is striking. At the same time, our book shows how the link between food and femininity is rearticulated within a contemporary context where postfeminist ideals hold particular influence. In this way, we document important new developments—such as the contemporary maternal ideal of raising an organic child, the "choice"-focused healthy eating discourse of the do-diet, and the challenge of pursuing both pleasure *and* care in the performance of food femininities.

There is no question that food remains a deeply gendered domain; yet, throughout the book we have also documented many instances where hegemonic food and gender ideals were openly identified, critiqued, mocked, and subverted. Think here of Beth and Daniella's critical reflections about "June Cleaver" and their assertion that mothering needs to move beyond a 1950s' distribution of gender labor (chapter 3). Or recall the example of Paige, who resisted the notion that pregnant women should obsess about "every bite you eat" (chapter 4), or Hilary who laughed at the idea of "power foods" women "must eat" (chapter 5). Consider the words of activists like Debbie, Lauren, and Vanessa, who pointed out that the public face of the food movement continues to be associated with a few white men, while women of color work tirelessly in neighborhood gardens and community kitchens (chapter 6). Or think about the newly evolving culture of feminine foodie-ism where women's culinary pleasures are embraced, food restrictions are rejected, and Carmen claims her rightful place as the BBQ master in her family (chapter 7). Finally, think of the case of Shannon, a low-income single mother who openly challenged the idea that good food was simply a commodity and demanded that the state do more to provide healthy food to all citizens. These examples represent the array of critical perspectives articulated by our participants, even as our research sheds light on the significant continuous links between food and femininity. As we have shown throughout the book, an *awareness* of gendered food inequities does not always mean that these inequities can be easily transcended in women's everyday food lives.

A second key contribution we make to feminist food scholarship is to deepen our understanding of the powerful role of emotions in feminine food-work. Throughout the book, we have documented gendered emotions relating to care and sacrifice—as documented in past scholarship (e.g., Devault 1991; Hochschild 2008)—but also *positive* emotions of pleasure and creative expression, excitement and empowerment, political passion and familial pride. Given the intensity of these emotional attachments to food, the women in our study found it difficult to step back from these responsibilities and take a more cavalier approach to food. It can *feel* awkward, or confrontational, or simply unrewarding to divest oneself of responsibility for food labor, especially in heterosexual relationships. Food is simply too symbolically loaded—with emotion, pleasure, cultural significance, and gender ideals—for many women to comfortably step back from the work of reading labels, making grocery lists, researching superfoods, and cooking dinner. Even if it were structurally and relationally possible for women in heterosexual relationships to redistribute the burden of foodwork to their male partners, it is important to acknowledge the emotional ties that bind women to food. The stakes of feminine failure at foodwork are high and can engender anxieties that maintain women's investment in food-work and body management. A certain kind of power arises from performing hegemonic femininity effectively through food, and our data affirms that women with economic resources, cultural capital, and racial privilege can more readily access this status.

A third contribution of our work relates to the concept of calibration, a process for managing the performance of femininity in relation to food ideals and in engagements with consumer culture more generally. We use the term *calibration* to describe practices wherein women actively manage their relationship to various extremes in an effort to perform acceptable middle-class femininities. Calibration involves a process of continual adjustment to meet an idealized and elusive feminine standard. When talking with women about their food practices, we repeatedly observed how women positioned themselves as conscientious and committed, but not rigid or fanatical. While previous feminist scholarship has shown how women actively negotiate gendered discourses (e.g., Carlson 2011; Press 2011), our research demonstrates how women distance themselves not only from the abject but also from an *overly perfect* performance of femininity. Even as neoliberal discourse promotes the acquisition of expert knowledge to control one's diet, the feminine subject who is *too* controlling in her shopping, eating, and foodwork is pathologized as a figure of feminine excess—a health nut, obsessive mother, food snob, or ethical-eating purist. The need to avoid the penalty of the *positive extreme* was striking—a theme we believe should be incorporated into theoretical understandings of femininity. At the same time, the feminine subject who is *too* relaxed about her eating and foodwork runs the risk of being perceived as unhealthy, self-indulgent, irresponsible, and/or a bad mother.

The calibration process highlights the challenge of successfully performing food femininities and also sheds light on the dynamic connection between discourse and subjectivity, opening the black box of subjectification. Feminist Foucauldian scholarship has made the important contribution of theorizing subjectivity formation as a socially situated process, analyzing how neoliberal discourse is negotiated in the context of gendered, classed, and racialized relations of power (Bordo 1993; Cairns 2013; McLeod and Yates 2006). Building on these insights, our analysis throughout this book demonstrates the ongoing discursive positioning required in the performance of femininities, paying attention to social location and structural inequality. As such, we identify gendered processes that make the performance of successful food femininities difficult to achieve—especially for disadvantaged women, and especially given the continual surveillance and evaluation of women's bodies and food practices.

Having laid out our intended contributions to the field, we next turn to a key question that undergirded much of our thought process when writing and researching this book: What would a feminist politics of foodwork look like?

1. Feminist ideals and foodwork routines

At the very time when we were writing this book, *New York Magazine* published a much-discussed article on "The Feminist Housewife" (Miller 2013). Profiling "feminists who say they're having it all—by choosing to stay at home," the piece added fuel to popular discussion about contemporary women embracing domestic activities—making jams, cooking from scratch, raising backyard chickens—a phenomenon that writer Emily Matchar (2013) dubs the "new domesticity." This shift has been the focus of heated debate, raising thorny questions about what a feminist politics of women's home-cooking might look like. Does the reclaiming of domestic foodwork represent a feminist win, giving value to a historically devalued site of women's labor? Or is this a repackaging of patriarchal relations as postfeminist success? Is it possible to move this debate beyond reductive narratives that designate women's home-cooking as wholly liberating or uniformly oppressive?

In a postfeminist, neoliberal climate that applauds the ideal of individual "choice," it is not entirely clear how to reconcile feminist ideals of equality with foodwork routines dominated by women's labor. Of course, we believe that women should have the choice to reclaim domestic spaces, especially when many find tremendous pleasure in tasks like putting up preserves, baking bread, or creatively decorating a child's birthday cake. To criticize domestic cooking as retrograde not only seems curmudgeonly but can also contribute to a patriarchal devaluing of women's foodwork. At the same time, we wonder about the gender implications of these patterns. As feminist food scholar Marjorie DeVault asked over 20 years ago, does the predominance of women cooking, baking, and cleaning in the kitchen inadvertently work to reinforce the idea that "giving service is part of being a woman, and receiving it fundamentally part of being a man" (1991: 234)? While we deeply respect the meaning and pleasure many women find in the kitchen, we also think it is important to pull back the analytic lens and look at broader gender relations. Food doyens like Michael Pollan, as well as innumerable voices in the food blogosphere (see chapter 5), suggest that home-cooking represents a kind of nutritional and environmental salvation. Is this a vision based on women doing most of the grunt-work—even if it is work that many women (including ourselves) have been socialized to find pleasurable and rewarding?

Our own research reveals a complex picture that does not fit neatly into the "emancipation-through-home-cooking" versus "oppressed-by-family-dinners" debate that dominates the popular media (e.g., Heffernan 2014). Throughout this book, we have seen many fond descriptions of cooking as a labor-intensive but also creative process. It is burdensome, but also satisfying. It is a way to express oneself and can also be a way to regain a sense of control in a food system dominated by corporate actors selling industrialized foods via globalized commodity chains. For many women, cooking provides moments of intense satisfaction, tangible pleasures, and a way to show love, care, and affection. Recall Alejandra's statement: "If I like you, I'll cook for you." While the pleasures of cooking can be vast, they emerge in a context where cooking is still very clearly a form of *labor*—labor that women are more likely to perform and that is particularly challenging when resources are limited (Bowen, Elliott, and Brenton 2014). Not only are women more often responsible for everyday foodwork in domestic kitchens, but they are also disproportionately represented in lower paid, lesser status jobs in food manufacturing, food service, and restaurant kitchens (Allen and Sachs 2007: 7; Barndt 1999); for every dollar earned by a white man in the food system, a white woman makes 63 cents, and a Black and Latina woman earns only 53 and 50 cents, respectively (Carolan 2012: 109).

Making sense of the relationship between feminist ideals and gendered foodwork routines brings us face to face with a thorny tension between individual choice and structural change. We argue that a feminist approach to food must attend simultaneously to personal meanings around food *and* structural political critique and must actively draw out the connections between these two levels. This is no easy feat. On the one hand, it requires an acknowledgment of enduring feminist issues of structure and patriarchy—the structural and cultural inequalities that devalue femininity and oppress women. On the other hand, it requires a simultaneous appreciation for women's desires and pleasures in the domestic sphere—a key insight of third-wave feminists, as well as a generation of born-again canners, pickle-makers, and cupcake bakers. This second insight might sound frivolous, but it has a solid feminist foundation, which involves long-standing struggles to reclaim the domestic sphere as a site of value, and not just a realm of degradation that women should flee once they are "liberated." Our interviews and focus groups suggest that these two insights are often intensely difficult to balance in everyday life and leave many women feeling conflicted about their relationship to foodwork.

Our own thinking on this issue has been deeply informed by our participants. In the next section we explore some of the tensions that manifested in everyday foodwork for the women in our study. Then, we build on these insights to make a claim about the key components of a feminist food politics.

2. Lived experiences: "I don't think that I have to boycott home-cooking as a feminist"

When asked if she thinks there have been changes in the gendered division of food labor, Hilary is emphatic. "Nowadays? Oh god, totally," she says, adding, "It helps that there are a lot of really famous chefs out there that are male. That just kind of normalizes that a little bit." In addition to the prominence of male celebrity chefs, Hilary suggests that public debates about work/life balance have also helped to facilitate change. Alejandra shares a similar view: "I think the more men wake up to the fact that women aren't there to basically be their maid, if the guy's enlightened even halfway, he understands that it's a part-nership." Alejandra notes that as a freelance writer, she did not have access to maternity leave, and her husband "stepped right in and stepped up" with foodwork when their daughter was born. She views this shared division of food labor as crucial to their daughter's socialization. "We want her to see mom and dad work together," she says.

While women like Hilary and Alejandra perceived substantial shifts in the gendered division of foodwork, the actual experiences of our participants tell a slightly different story. Of those who were married or partnered, most were in rela-tionships where woman did the majority of foodwork, and only a minority were in a relationship where it was shared evenly.[2] While men are clearly more involved in foodwork than they were in past decades, data on domestic practices (as opposed to *ideas* about shared labor) reinforce the impressions articulated by many of our participants (e.g., Bianchi et al. 2000; US Bureau of Labor Statistics 2012). "I think women still do the majority of cooking," says Shannon. "I think the majority of women are still thinking about the meal, planning ahead, doing prep work the night before." Kendra offers a similar perspective. "The friends I have, they are still cooking. I don't see the husband in the kitchen . . . So it's still tradi-tionally female." In keeping with the gendered division of cooking as labor versus leisure discussed in chapter 7, Kendra goes on to describe men's responsibility for their culinary specialty: "I have friends where the woman is from my country [Trinidad] and the man is from different cultures: White, Filipino, and French. So on occasions, the husband will cook something from their culture. That's the only time I see that and that's only when they're entertaining . . . Otherwise, no."

When considering the degree of change in cultural expectations and struc-tural relations linking femininity to domestic cooking, some women reflected critically upon the gendered division of foodwork in their own home. "When we were dating he'd cook," says Robin, a white graduate student who is married with a young son. "But now that I'm home at an hour that I can make supper and he's not, the roles have really fallen into these ridiculously gendered lines that kind of offend me as an ardent feminist." Even as this division of foodwork "offends" Robin's feminist sensibilities, she says, "it's practical and it works and I honestly am much better at it than he is." Robin was not the only woman who perceived a gap between her feminist principles and the gendered division of labor in her home. Deirdre describes herself as "an embarrassed feminist who cooks constantly" and explains that the commitment to feeding her family ethically sourced, home-cooked meals requires that she spend a great deal of time in the kitchen. "I still identify very strongly as a feminist yet here I am," says Deirdre, "I'm the one at home, I'm the one doing all the dishes. It hasn't been an easy transition. And I don't want to tell my daughters 'Oh become a homemaker sweetie! It's lovely.'" The tension Deirdre describes suggests that gendered inequities in foodwork are not necessarily the result of gendered *ideals* about cooking as women's responsibility. Rather, as we have seen throughout the book, gender inequities may persist despite women's commitment to feminist principles. This occurs not because women lack determination but because they negotiate ideals of gender equity alongside emotional investments in care-work, health, and ethics, as well as structural conditions that may make it "easier" for them to perform foodwork themselves (e.g., when partners have jobs with little flexibility and/or long hours). Recall that in chapter 6 Deirdre explained how her disproportionate share of the domestic foodwork came from her deep-seated commitment to providing ethical meals to her family (e.g., locally procured, home-cooked) and her realization that these ethical commitments would only be fulfilled if she personally put in the labor required to get these kinds of meals on the table.

While women like Robin and Deirdre reflect critically on this gendered division of food labor in relation to their feminist values, others emphasized that their foodwork was a personal *choice*, rather than an outcome of gender inequity. "As much as I would like to say we break all the gender stereotypes, we do [confirm traditional gender roles]," says Nina, explaining that she is the primary cook for her husband and children. Even though Nina says she would like to break gender norms, she uses the language of choice to emphasize her agency. Rather than "feeling bitter and resentful," Nina stresses that she cooks "because I enjoy it." She goes on to suggest that her own love of cooking is the cause for her husband's cluelessness in the kitchen. "I'm responsible for him having that learned helplessness issue," she says. "I'm a bit of a control freak. I'm the one in charge of doing the meals." Outing herself as a "control freak," Nina takes responsibility for the inequitable division of food labor within her home. Her words resonate with Beagan and colleagues' (2008) research exploring how women rationalize the division of family foodwork, as shown in their aptly titled article, "It's just easier for me to do it." Even though many women reject the idea that their foodwork results from oppressive gender ideologies, these same women are often left with a disproportionate share of food labor. In these alternate accounts, their own skill, standards, and enjoyment of cooking are deemed the greatest barrier to gender equality. Carol offers a similar assess-ment, suggesting that perhaps men do less domestic cooking because "maybe we let them. We give them an out." She continues:

> If we just went and they were forced to do it then they'd think about it more . . . Sometimes you fall into that pattern of, it's just easier for me to do it rather than tell you how to do it. 'Cause I'm tired, or they're starving or the kids

are screaming or something like that. Which isn't right but sometimes it's just faster. Just, oh, let me do it . . . I'm guilty of that.

Carol confesses that she is "guilty" of taking the lead on foodwork rather than demanding that her husband assume a more equitable share of this labor. She and Nina draw upon a similar discourse of the controlling woman whose special talents and proclivities create a feminine monopoly over kitchen space and food tasks.

Even though many women insist that they *choose* to do foodwork, the pathologized figure of the female "control freak" inadvertently naturalizes the association between femininity and domesticity. Outright gender inequality is rejected and replaced with alternate rationales for women's foodwork: *I'm just pickier / have higher standards / have more skills / know more about healthy food choices / don't want to start a fight*. Paradoxically, women are still positioned as gatekeepers of the kitchen, but they are now deemed responsible for their own oppression. This is a situation of women making individual choices, but one that is clearly structured by enduring gendered inequities—a situation that Beagan et al. describe as "gender gone underground" (2008: 666).

Given the way that gender is driven "underground" in the context of postfeminist individualism, it is not surprising that few of the women we spoke with explicitly referenced feminism when discussing gender and foodwork. Even so, shifting conceptions of feminist politics often surfaced in the background of our interviews and focus groups, as women articulated their own views and experiences in relation to broader ideas about gender (in)equality. While Robin and Deirdre claimed feminism as a site of empowerment, others were critical of what they perceived as prescriptive notions of gender equality that seemed to form a kind of judgmental feminist gaze. "I guess in the 21st century women think they shouldn't be cooking for the family," says Yin. "There are all these things that are labeled unequal, and this shouldn't be your job. And I see it differently." Yin describes how women's foodwork is valued in other countries— like China—and says:

> I don't think there is anything wrong with [home-cooking] as long as [women] are empowered to be what they want to be. I don't think we need to restrict ourselves to become less feminine or become less of a traditional female role than we chose to be. It's really a woman's choice about what she wants to do and if you like cooking, there is nothing wrong with it.

Yin's comments have clear resonance with a postfeminist sensibility that foregrounds personal choice as the means to women's empowerment.

Throughout the book, we have raised questions about the limitations (and neoliberal connections) of "choice" rhetoric and its potentially deleterious impact on collective mobilization and structural change. At the same time, we feel it is crucial to take seriously Yin's interpretation of gender equity struggles as a call to "become less feminine." Whether or not this is the intended message, the fact that women may experience feminism as demeaning of particular food femininities is itself a feminist issue. A judgmental feminist gaze clearly presents barriers to political mobilization and may inadvertently bolster patriarchal relations by devaluing particular femininities—and women—as lower status (thus elevating white professional women who outsource cooking as "better" feminists). From Yin's perspective, the claim that women's cooking is a site of inequality works to undermine the value and pleasure derived through cooking. "Women in my life, they want to take care of their family by providing them with food and all the nutrition they need. So I think that is a very noble call," she says. Her comments bring us back to the feminist dialectic we laid out at the beginning of the chapter and our argument that a feminist approach to foodwork must attend simultaneously to personal meanings *and* structural critique. Put differently, a feminist food politics must avoid demeaning women's foodwork at the same time that it pursues a collective politics of structural change.

Food activist Debbie Field spoke directly to this tension between valuing women's food knowledge and a feminist discomfort with what is perceived to be traditional, patriarchal gender roles. Positioning social reproduction at the heart of her feminist politics, Debbie attributes great value to the food knowledge she learned from her immigrant mother as a child. Describing the division of food labor when her own children were young, she insists that "even if I did slightly different work or maybe more than [my partner] did sometimes, it wasn't part of my oppression, it was part of my liberation." She continues: "Similarly cooking from scratch was part of my liberation and it's part of my connection to generations of my foremothers, so I don't think that I have to boycott home-cooking as a feminist. I think, in fact, I can urge my brothers to join with me in this home-cooking revolution." Rather than urging women to reject the pleasures of cooking, Debbie articulates a vision of foodwork as *feminist* work. In doing so, though, she is quick to caution against gender essentialisms. Debbie notes that just because foodwork has historically been a site for the performance of femininities, there is no inherent connection between domestic cooking and femininity. Noting that she has now passed on this food knowledge to her son, Debbie suggests that we are in the middle of an "exciting revolution around gender roles" that is creating new opportunities to do gender differently. "I'm not saying that only girl children should be taught to cook," she says, "all children should be taught in school. But I'm saying that it's okay to say that I can provide an insight on this as a woman and as a feminist."

3. Building a feminist food politics

In this final section, we build upon our participants' insights to stake a claim about key priorities of a feminist food politics. In addition to the need for collective mobilization to create change, we emphasize the importance of building alliances across food and gender scholarship and activism. We share Arlene Avakian and Barbara Haber's (2005) commitment to building a "feminist food studies" —a goal further elaborated by Patricia Allen and Carolyn Sachs (2007) in their perceptive analysis of women and food chains. Here, we build on the work of these and other feminist food scholars as we offer our own take on what a feminist food politics looks like.

To begin, we return to an original feminist precept: *the personal is political*. What does this phrase mean in the context of a postfeminist sensibility that valorizes women's individual, *personal* choices and dismisses collective feminist struggles as a thing of the past (McRobbie 2009)? We suggest that seeing the personal as political is not a call to retreat to our personal lives, enjoying our locally sourced salad, "happy meat" meat-loaf, homemade bread, or whatever else we enjoy cooking and eating. Such personal food choices may feel political at the level of reflecting our values and may go some distance toward supporting a more nourishing home environment; these measures can also be connected to larger projects to build more sustainable, socially just food production practices. Yet, a retreat to the "personal" politics of consumption is profoundly limiting. As food scholar, Julie Guthman writes, "[e]ating local, organic, seasonal food that you prepared yourself may be pleasurable but it is not universally so, nor is it tantamount to effecting social justice" (2011: 5). While personal consumption cannot simply be equated with social justice, neither can it be seen as completely disconnected. We see the "personal is political" mantra as a reminder that feminist politics must continually work on multiple levels: the level of personal feelings, meaning, and experience, as well as the larger, political context of power and inequality. Below we identify three planes that are deeply interrelated in the formation of feminist food politics: (1) the personal meaning attached to food, (2) the politics of struggling for food justice, and (3) academic studies of the food system. We argue that a committed feminist food politics must avoid getting stuck on a single plane and must continually work to see the connections—and tensions—between them.

Respecting the personal . . . but looking beyond the dinner plate

A key component of feminist struggles has been valuing the lived experiences of women and other marginalized groups. Attention to women's personal joys and struggles is crucial to developing an expanded conception of politics that includes everyday issues like making dinner. Throughout this book, we have argued that there are important insights to be gained by exploring the interplay between food and femininity in women's lives—in their identity formation, relations of care, pleasures and frustrations, and hopes for the future. Yet, at the current moment, we encounter a tension, as the feminist commitment to the "personal" is increasingly co-opted through a postfeminist narrative of individual choice as the paramount route to empowerment. The personal is no longer political when it is divorced from questions of power.

A feminist politics that works *only* at the level of the personal runs the risk of solipsism, lacking access to broader critiques of social inequalities—in the home and beyond. To achieve greater gender equality at a collective level, we need to take up food activist Debbie Field's call to not only celebrate the joy, passion, and expertise of women's foodwork but also encourage men to share in everyday food labor. Redistributing foodwork within the home is particularly important for equality in heterosexual relationships, but foodwork needs to be valued more generally as part of a restructured, counterhegemonic masculinity (see Szabo 2013, 2014).

Moving beyond individualized approaches to food politics is also important for a feminist politics that understands gender oppression in the context of intersecting inequalities. Working solely at the individual level can be tempting given the good feelings produced by successful foodwork—*I feel empowered when I make healthy food choices; I am a good parent because I make my child's meals from scratch; I feel responsible when I purchase local vegetables at the farmers market.* By getting stuck at the level of the individual, we risk not seeing the big picture of gender *and* food system inequality. In this bigger picture, not only are women positioned to do a disproportionate amount of a household foodwork, but women at a collective level are marginalized from multiple positions of power and authority in the food system (Sachs and Allen 2007: 6–9). Equally disturbing, the dominant food system—like much of corporate capitalism—has proven adept at exploiting social inequalities along lines of race, class, and citizenship and turning them into cheap sources of labor used to produce "cheap" food (Carolan 2011b; Holmes 2013). This is a food system that works in conjunction with a neoliberal mode of governance that prioritizes market relations and the voluntary sector over state responsibilities and state-mandated income redistribution. The results have proven catastrophic when it comes to meeting basic food needs. According to the US Department of Agriculture Statistics (USDA 2013), an estimated 15 percent of the American population is food-insecure; more shockingly, 20 percent of US households with children are food-insecure, suggesting that a tremendous degree of food-related care-work is done under conditions of extreme financial constraint. In Canada, the situation is not much better, with 12 percent of Canadian households experiencing food insecurity, a number that jumps to 27 percent for aboriginal households and 35 percent for lone-parent households headed by women (Tarasuk et al. 2013). A feminist food politics must take seriously the personal meaning that women find in foodwork while critiquing the injustices of a market-logic that denies equitable food access and emotional fulfillment.

Valuing collective struggle . . . but still caring what goes on the plate

On the other hand, a feminist politics that resides exclusively on the level of collective struggles for change—for gender equality, for fair pay, for food security—must avoid trampling on the meanings that connect women to food. As seen in Yin's comments above—and in many of our other interviews and focus groups—women may feel judged for their love of cooking and the pleasure they find in foodwork. Whether it is a fair assessment or not, these women perceive a judgmental feminist gaze looking down on them as they cook dinner. Yet, as we noted in chapter 2 and have highlighted throughout the book, food femininities need not *always* be hegemonic. Part of a feminist food politics is building a collective understanding that cooking dinner is not retrograde, but can be a feminist act.

We are on some tricky political ground with this statement. We do not want to romanticize a past where women (and a female serving class) were wedded to feeding roles, nor do we want to overstate the loss of cooking skills in a contemporary industrial foodscape (see Short 2006). As noted in our previous critique of the status distinctions performed through "ethical" eating (chapter 6), it is important to avoid fetishizing the choice of alternative food as "good food" and romanticizing simple solutions to complex, systemic problems (Biltekoff 2013; Freedman 2013; Guthman 2011). At the same time, our conversations with women from different class and racial backgrounds have led us to believe that cooking skills—when collectively supported and fostered among both men and women—are an important (albeit limited) tool of resistance to a corporate-dominated food system. Think here of Neela's community health center offering classes in which young immigrant men teach boys to cook (chapter 6). This belief in the importance of cooking skills stems from the understanding that many people lack the time, energy, interest, and knowledge to cook from whole foods, leaving them more vulnerable to the harmful practices of transnational corporations selling unhealthy, industrialized foods (Moss 2013). Here, it is important not to blame poor communities for poor nutrition, especially since many middle- and upper-middle-class families also lack basic cooking skills and rely on take-out and readymade meals. At the same time, it is equally important not to minimize the vulnerability of economically disadvantaged communities. As our interviewee Sarah said so clearly: "it's not fair that poor people suffer the most for the shit things that factory farming does."

Of course, teaching people how to cook will not magically provide them with tools to resist a corporate-dominated food system; people still need time, money, access, interest, collective support, and other goods that are unequally distributed across the population. However, the fact remains that the corporate food system has a for-profit orientation and razor-thin profit margins; together, these have generated a food industry with highly problematic ways of eating and producing food that have been well documented by critical nutritionists and political-economists (e.g., Moss 2013; Nestle 2007; Winson 2004, 2013). The industry has a deliberate strategy of evoking home-cooked meals in their marketing campaigns, without inspiring people to actually cook from scratch. In the words of one food industry executive:

> We want to trigger sentiments for home cooking [with our products] without triggering sentiments to make people want to do the home cooking themselves . . . you don't want them longing for actual home cooking too much. It would be bad for business if we started making people feel bad about eating food from large multi-national corporations (quoted in Carolan 2014).

Developing and *valuing* women's and men's cooking skills, and making alternatives to industrialized processed foods more viable, can give people more agency to navigate a corporate-dominated food system. We believe that a project of culinary reskilling can be defensible in feminist terms, but it must also take up a structural critique that identifies why domestic cooking is particularly difficult for marginalized populations, avoids fetishizing the food practices of privileged groups (e.g., whites, thin people, economic and cultural elites; as critiqued by Biltekoff 2013), and accounts for how taste patterns are shaped through our embodied engagement in industrial food systems (Carolan 2014; Hayes-Conroy and Hayes-Conroy 2008).

Building a feminist food studies . . . and avoiding sectarianism

In addition to bridging an analysis of food meanings and structures, building a feminist politics of foodwork also requires forging alliances across scholarly and political divides. Avakian and Haber (2005) note a long-standing and curious division between studies of gender and food. Until recently, scholarly investigations of food and femininity focused primarily on body image and associated issues like anorexia and bulimia. While these remain critical areas to investigate, an exclusive focus on these issues can inadvertently pathologize the relationship between femininity and food and draw attention away from the positive possibilities that come out of women's historical and continued connections to foodwork. Conversely, food studies has tended to neglect women, and very little of its purview has been explicitly feminist (Avakian and Haber 2005:2; Allen and Sachs 2007). In their review of the materialist literature on food production, Allen and Sachs note that with a few important exceptions (e.g,. Barndt 1999), "[g]ender analysis remains on the margins of the sociology of agriculture" (2007: 4). A similar pattern can be found in writing on consumer food politics. Many popular and academic critiques of the industrial food system call for people to "re-connect" to their food—perhaps by growing a garden, cooking home-made dinners, and avoiding processed goods that your "great-grandmother wouldn't recognize as food" (Pollan 2008: 148). Yet, such pleas tend to say little about the gendered implications of this advice, except in nostalgic appeals for hegemonic food femininities. For instance, Michael Pollan looks back on the last several decades and notes that "mom lost much of her authority over the dinner menu, ceding it to scientists and food marketers" (2008: 3).

Given the curious absence, or at least underestimation of gender issues in food scholarship, Avakian and Haber (2005) call for the development of a "feminist food studies"—an agenda that we have embraced in writing this book. They suggest that a feminist food studies can "help us to understand how women reproduce, resist, and rebel against gender constructions as they are practiced and contested in various sites, as well as illuminate the contexts in which these struggles are located" (2005: 2). To build such a feminist food studies, critical scholars must resist compartmentalizing the social world within academic silos. More specifically, food and agriculture scholars need to do more work to think through the gendered implications of their topics. This may seem obvious, but it remains a pressing issue. (Josée would note from her recent experiences in academia that it still seems possible to write a food-related dissertation that never once mentions gender.) Of course, in keeping with an intersectional approach, a feminist food studies must go beyond "adding in" gender, to explore how the gendering of foodwork intersects with systems of oppression such as race, which has been similarly neglected within food scholarship (see Slocum 2013). At the same time, gender scholars need to continue the push to take food seriously as a point of domination and resistance (Avakier and Haber 2005; Bowen, Elliott, and Brenton 2014; Brady, Gingras, and Power 2013; Hayes-Conroy and Hayes-Conroy 2008; Hollows 2003; hooks 1992; Meah 2013). Among the important insights yielded by this push is a richer understanding of how foodwork fits into domestic routines, identities, and shifting concepts of masculinity and femininity (e.g., Szabo 2013).

The intersection of food and femininity generates multiple examples of injustice and activism—examples that we have explored in the previous chapters and many more that have been raised by scholars working on transnational food issues (e.g., Bain 2010; Barndt 2001; Federici 2004; Preibisch and Encalada Grez 2010). For example, recall the gendered nature of food activism explored in chapter 6, a tendency that too often leaves men in charge of food policy decisions. At a more personal level, consider the gendered dimension of "voting with your fork," a narrative that bolsters neoliberal ideology and individualizes responsibility for ecosocial change in highly feminized ways. Many additional examples can be found beyond the pages of this book. For instance, consider issues of sexual harassment and lower wages that face women farm workers (Ontiveros 2007; Waugh 2010), or the higher rates of hunger that women and girls experience on a global scale (Food and Agriculture Organization of the United Nations 2005). There are many—too many—examples of gendered food injustice, creating multiple opportunities for mobilization at the intersection of food and femininity. Many of these issues—like women's disproportionate share of food labor—require collective awareness and collective action, not just a reliance on individual choice or interpersonal negotiating skills. It is not enough to place the burden on individual women, encouraging them to "lean-in" and ask for more (hooks 2013). This kind of individualized politics is not only limited in creating social change but also works to reproduce inequalities by celebrating the choices of a privileged few.

By documenting the complexities and inequalities underlying the relationship between food and femininity, we hope that our research can be one piece of a broader effort to forge a collective feminist food politics. This vision builds from personal stories told by women who care passionately about the place of food in their lives, families, relationships, and communities. While a feminist food politics builds on women's experiences with food, it also pays keen attention to broader food struggles. This dual commitment requires that we ask difficult questions of the collectivity: Who has the creativity, the care, the resources, and the commitment to cook up a "good" dinner? (That is, a dinner that is sustainable, healthy, socially just, and delicious?) If the answer to this question is mainly "women"—and particular, privileged groups of women—then a feminist food politics clearly has work to do.

We would like to conclude this book by returning to a question we asked in the introduction, namely, why do so many women care so much about food? After hours talking with women and men in their homes, analyzing their impassioned food narratives, and situating these personal stories in the context of broader structural critique, the answer we have come to is this: because conceptualizations of femininity are still profoundly connected to food. As explored throughout the book, this is not a singular food femininity. Rather, femininities are expressed in the multiple ways a woman cares for people and the earth, moderates her diet, and nourishes loved ones. From our research, we conclude that meeting (or at least approximating) contemporary standards of normative femininity requires tremendous attention to food. For a woman to ignore food is to risk being deemed a failure, pushed outside the boundaries of hegemonic femininity—a woman who does not care about her kids' health; who puts herself and her family at risk for disease and obesity; who lacks knowledge, good taste, and pleasure in the kitchen; and who does not care about the planet when she is at the grocery store. Yes, men are starting to care more about food, but their sense of masculinity is not as intimately connected to food in these same demanding, penalizing, and emotionally potent ways.

By highlighting the powerful connections between food and femininity, we do not mean to end this book on a pessimistic note. To the contrary, we believe that the present moment of *caring about food* is one of rich political possibilities. Allen and Sachs state that "[a]s women work to reshape the food system in the interest of better health, social justice, and environmental soundness, they are also creating possibilities for women to gain control of their bodies and their lives" (2007: 15). We have seen these possibilities through many conversations about women and food—in our research for this book, in classroom discussions with students, and in dinner table conversations with friends and family. Food is an arena where many women think critically about the corporate industrial food system, reflect on everyday food routines, bump up against gender and class inequality, and often feel motivated to make change. At a moment when so many people are striving to "eat for change," a feminist food politics must work to expand this conversation—by shining a light on persistent connections between food and femininity and revitalizing collective movements for gendered social justice.

Notes

1. Significantly, research suggests that the division of household labor in lesbian rela-tionships is relatively equitable when compared to heterosexual couples and gay men (Dunne 2000; Kurdek 2007; but see Carrington 1999). Our sample is not large enough to offer definitive confirmation of greater equality in same-sex couples. However, we did observe that the division of household labor appeared more contentious in the heterosexual couples we interviewed, with greater room for flexibility among LGBTQ participants. Indeed, as we discuss, heterosexual women struggle to reconcile their belief in gender equality, with greater practical and emotional connections to food-work than their male partners.

2. Of all our partnered participants, 49 were in a relationship where a woman did most of the foodwork. Seventeen were in a relationship were foodwork was shared evenly. In five couples, a man was primarily responsible for foodwork, and that included one gay male couple who shared foodwork evenly.

Appendix A

Participant demographics

Focus group participants

Pseudonym	Age	Race/ethnicity	Highest degree	Occupation	Household income	Gender	Sexual orientation	Kids (Y/N)
Abby	40	White	Bachelor's	Retail	30,000–39,999	F	Heterosexual	N
Agnes	39	White	Bachelor's	Grocery cashier	40,000–59,999	F	Heterosexual	Y
Aiden	27	White	Graduate degree	Architect	60,000–99,999	M	Heterosexual	N
Alex	23	White	College diploma	Bartender	40,000–59,999	M	Heterosexual	N
Alyssa	23	White	College diploma	Actress, server	30,000–39,999	F	Heterosexual	N
Anissa	25	Mixed race	Master's	Part-time librarian	<9,000	F	Heterosexual	N
Anne	42	White	College diploma	Stay-at-home mom	100,000–199,999	F	Heterosexual	Y
Axel	70	White	Professional degree	Retired	60,000–99,999	M	Heterosexual	Y
Beth	60	White	High school	Corporate counselor	60,000–99,999	F	Heterosexual	Y
Brad	36	White	Bachelor's	Investment advisor	>200,000	M	Heterosexual	N
Brenda	46	White	Trade school	Unemployed	40,000–59,999	F	Heterosexual	Y
Carl	60	White	High school	Corporate counselor	60,000–99,999	M	Heterosexual	Y
Carmen	33	Asian	Master's	Librarian	60,000–99,999	F	Unknown	Y
Cassandra	31	White	Bachelor's	Filmmaker	60,000–99,999	F	Heterosexual	N
Chris	Late twenties	White	Master's	Student, engineering	40,000–59,999	M	Unknown	N
Christine	36	White	Bachelor's	Part-time nurse	100,000–199,999	F	Heterosexual	N
Cynthia	55	Asian	College diploma	Retail (part-time)	60,000–99,999	F	Heterosexual	Y

Pseudonym	Age	Race/ethnicity	Highest degree	Occupation	Household income	Gender	Sexual orientation	Kids (Y/N)
Daniella	66	White/Jewish	Bachelor's	Retired	40,000–59,999	F	Heterosexual	N
Deb	43	Indigenous	High school	Unemployed	10,000–19,000	F	Heterosexual	Y
Derek	26	White	High school	General contractor	40,000–59,999	M	Heterosexual	Y
Elaine	33	Asian	Bachelor's	Research analyst (on maternity leave)	40,000–59,999	F	Heterosexual	Y
Ellen	47	White	Graduate degree	Nurse practitioner	100,000–199,999	F	Heterosexual	N
Elspeth	51	White	Graduate degree	Executive director of a business association	100,000–199,999	F	Heterosexual	N
Eric	41	White	Bachelor's	Musician	>200,000	M	Heterosexual	Y
Erin	52	White	High school	Recreational tourism	60,000–99,999	F	Heterosexual	N
Fiona	57	White	College diploma	Grocery customer service manager	40,000–59,999	F	Heterosexual	Y
Grace	53	White	High school	Management consultant	60,000–99,999	F	Heterosexual	Y
Haley	26	White	Bachelor's	Architectural model maker	60,000–99,999	F	Unknown	N
Hannah	24	White	MBA	Student	30,000–39,999	F	Heterosexual	N
Heather	28	White	Graduate student	Part-time chef, student	40,000–59,999	F	Homosexual	N
Jessie	25	West Indian	Graduate degree	Architect	40,000–59,999	F	Unknown	N
Jill	27	White	High school	Unemployed cook	10,000–19,999	F	Heterosexual	N
Joan	60	White/Jewish	High school	Grocery customer service	30,000–39,999	F	Heterosexual	Y
Julia	26	White	Graduate degree	Self-employed information specialist	60,000–99,999	F	Heterosexual	N

Name	Age	Ethnicity	Education	Occupation	Income	Gender	Sexual orientation	
Kelly	28	White	Graduate degree	Fashion marketer	60,000–99,999	F	Unknown	N
Kerri	36	White	Master's	Occupational therapist	60,000–99,999	F	Heterosexual	N
Kim	33	Asian	Master's	Teacher	100,000–199,999	F	Unknown	N
Lee	57	White	Bachelor's	Tax consultant	60,000–99,999	M	Heterosexual	N
Li	47	Asian	Bachelor's	Personal life coach	40,000–59,999	M	Heterosexual	N
Lois	65	White	High school	Retired nurse	40,000–59,999	F	Heterosexual	N
Lucia	42	Hispanic	Master's	Social worker	60,000–99,999	F	Heterosexual	Y
Mai	30	Asian	Graduate degree	Unemployed	<9,000	F	Heterosexual	N
Manuela	39	Hispanic	High school	Real estate sales rep	60,000–99,999	M	Heterosexual	Y
Martha	47	White	Graduate degree	Catering/bakery	30,000–39,999	F	Heterosexual	N
Matilda	54	White	Law degree	Adjudicator/mediator	100,000–199,999	F	Heterosexual	Y
Nadia	27	White	Bachelor of Education	Occasional teacher	30,000–39,999	F	Heterosexual	N
Nancy	44	White	Postgraduate degree	Education officer	100,000–199,999	F	Heterosexual	Y
Natalie	27	White	Bachelor's	Editor	30,000–39,999	F	Unknown	N
Nate	40	White	Master's	College instructor	60,000–99,999	M	Queer	N
Nicole	51	Indigenous	High school	Outreach worker	<9,999	F	Heterosexual	Y
Nina	42	White	Graduate degree	Writer and editor	100,000–199,999	F	Heterosexual	Y
Olga	27	White	Graduate degree	Urban planner	60,000–99,999	F	Heterosexual	N
Olive	27	Black	Graduate degree	Magazine editor	40,000–59,999	F	Heterosexual	N
Oliver	24	White	Bachelor's	Student	<9,999	M	Queer	N
Paige	32	White	Bachelor's	Community food program coordinator	20,000–29,999	F	Heterosexual	Y

Pseudonym	Age	Race/ethnicity	Highest degree	Occupation	Household income	Gender	Sexual orientation	Kids (Y/N)
Pam	29	White	Bachelor's	Unemployed	30,000–39,999	F	Heterosexual	N
Pasha	28	White	Bachelor's	Program assistant at transportation organization	30,000–39,999	M	Heterosexual	N
Patrick	31	White	Master's	College instructor	60,000–99,999	M	Queer	N
Patty	64	White	Master's	Teacher (on disability leave)	30,000–39,999	F	Unknown	U
Peter	32	White	Bachelor's and professional degree	Music teacher	100,000–199,999	M	Heterosexual	Y
Rachel	27	White	Bachelor's	Student	10,000–19,000	F	Queer	N
Richard	48	White	Bachelor's	Sales manager at butcher	60,000–99,999	M	Heterosexual	N
Rob	32	White	Professional degree	Architect	60,000–99,999	M	Heterosexual	N
Robin	32	White/Jewish	Master's	PhD student	100,000–199,999	F	Heterosexual	Y
Rose	28	White	Bachelor's	Musician	10,000–19,999	F	Unknown	N
Rosita	25	Chinese, Hispanic, Indigenous	Bachelor's	Food co-op coordinator	20,000–29,999	F	Queer	Y
Roy	32	White	Master's	Teacher	100,000–199,999	M	Unknown	N
Ruth	24	White	High school	Singer	<9,000	F	"Open"	N
Ryan	24	White	Master's	Graduate student	20,000–29,999	M	"Ambivalent"	N
Sadie	49	White	High school	School lunchroom supervisor	30,000–39,999	F	Heterosexual	Y

Name	Age	Ethnicity	Education	Occupation	Income	Gender	Sexuality	
Sally	25	White	Bachelor's	Part-time web designer	10,000–19,000	F	Heterosexual	N
Selena	29	White	Postgraduate degree	Student	30,000–39,999	F	Heterosexual	Y
Seth	24	White	College diploma	Musician	10,000–19,999	M	Heterosexual	N
Sitara	49	South Asian	Master's	Social services	40,000–50,999	F	Heterosexual	Y
Sophie	32	White	Master's	Teacher	60,000–99,999	F	Heterosexual	N
Stacey	26	White	Master's	Teacher in training	10,000–19,999	F	Bisexual	N
Sue	40	White	Graduate degree	Family support worker	60,000–99,999	F	Heterosexual	Y
Svetlana	26	White	Bachelor's	Program assistant at university faculty	40,000–59,999	F	Heterosexual	N
Syd	26	White/Jewish	College diploma	Actor, baker	<9,999	F	Heterosexual	N
Tammy	33	White	Bachelor's	Home daycare provider	60,000–99,999	F	Heterosexual	Y
Tara	36	White	High school	Unemployed (on disability leave)	20,000–29,999	F	Bisexual	Y
Theresa	52	Mixed race	High school	Unemployed	20,000–29,999	F	Heterosexual	Y
Tiffany	28	White	Bachelor's	Student	10,000–19,000	F	Heterosexual	N
Tim	29	White	Bachelor's	City employee	20,000–29,999	M	Unknown	N
Tom	42	White	Did not finish high school	Filmmaker	60,000–99,999	M	Heterosexual	Y
Vicky	50	White	Master's	Occasional teacher	60,000–99,999	F	Heterosexual	Y
Yvonne	54	White	Bachelor's	High school teacher	100,000–199,999	F	Heterosexual	Y
Zhara	44	South Asian	Graduate degree	Writer	100,000–199,999	F	Heterosexual	Y
Zoe	26	White	Bachelor's	City employee	10,000–19,999	F	Queer	N

Interview participants

Pseudonym	Age	Race/ethnicity	Highest degree	Occupation	Household income	Gender	Sexual orientation	Kids (Y/N)
Alejandra	42	Hispanic	Posgraduate diploma	Freelance writer	100,000–199,999	F	Heterosexual	Y
Arielle	25	White	Bachelor's	Communications (fashion)	60,000–99,999	F	Heterosexual	N
Camilla	54	White	Graduate degree	Writer	60,000–99,999	F	Heterosexual	N
Carol	42	White	Trade school	Producer	100,000–199,999	F	Heterosexual	Y
Cindy	44	White	Bachelor's	Personal trainer	100,000–199,999	F	Heterosexual	Y
Claudette	49	White	Trade school	Chef	60,000–99,999	F	Heterosexual	N
Dierdre	51	White	High school	Farmers' market manager	60,000–99,999	F	Heterosexual	Y
Donna	46	Black	Master's	E-learning trainer	60,000–99,999	F	Heterosexual	N
Eva	43	White/Jewish	Graduate degree	Foundation grant-writer	100,000–199,999	F	Heterosexual Trans family	Y
Fran	31	White/Creole	High school	Accounts receivables admin (on maternity leave)	40,000–59,999	F	Bisexual	Y
Gail	33	White	Trade school	Acupuncture	60,000–99,999	F	Lesbian	Y
Gina	54	White	Graduate degree	Investment fund manager	100,000–199,999	F	Heterosexual	Y
Harsha	28	South Asian	High school	Unemployed	10,000–19,999	F	Heterosexual	N
Hilary	28	White	Bachelor's	Coffee barista	30,000–39,999	F	"Open"	N
Ingrid	46	White/Jewish	Bachelor's	Unemployed	20,000–29,999	F	Heterosexual	N

Joanne	60	Mixed race	Bachelor's	Retired	40,000–59,999	F	Lesbian	N
Judy	56	White/Jewish	Law degree	Editor in legal publisher	60,000–99,999	F	Heterosexual	N
Kalise	26	Black	High school	Retail	20,000–29,999	F	Heterosexual	N
Kelsey	27	White	Bachelor's	Marketer	60,000–99,999	F	Heterosexual	N
Kendra	48	Black	High school	Unemployed	<9,000	F	Heterosexual	N
Lisa	42	White	Bachelor's	Product developer	100,000–199,999	F	Heterosexual	Y
Maria	32	Hispanic	Graduate degree	Health policy analyst	60,000–99,999	F	Heterosexual	N
Marisa	43	Black	Bachelor's	Project manager	100,000–199,999	F	Heterosexual	Y
Nadine	48	White	Bachelor's	Unemployed (on disability leave)	10,000–19,999	F	Heterosexual	N
Petra	38	White	Bachelor's	Personal trainer	30,000–39,999	F	Queer	N
Sarah	23	Asian	Bachelor's	Student/part-time librarian	20,000–29,999	F	Heterosexual	N
Shannon	45	White	High school	Unemployed (on disability leave)	10,000–19,999	F	Heterosexual	Y
Wei	40	Asian	Graduate degree	Communications industry	100,000–199,999	F	Heterosexual	N
Yin	33	Asian	Bachelor's	Environmental fundraiser	100,000–199,999	F	Heterosexual	N

Activists¹

Pseudonym	Age	Race/ethnicity	Highest degree	Occupation	Household income	Gender	Sexual orientation	Kids (Y/N)
Bronwyn	36	White	Master's	Community food programmer	40,000–59,999	F	Heterosexual	Y
Carly	34	White	Law degree	Food lawyer	60,000–90,000	F	Heterosexual	N
Cassia	46	White	Bachelor's	Writer and chef	100,000–199,999	F	Bisexual	Y
Cecilia								
Chandra	48	Mixed race	PhD	Self-employed	10,000–19,999	F	Heterosexual	Y
Debbie	60	White/Jewish	Graduate degree	Executive director of FoodShare	60,000–99,999	F	Heterosexual	Y
Jackie	30	Middle eastern	Bachelor's	Student	<9,000	F	Queer	N
Lauren	41	White	PhD	Food policy coordinator		F	Heterosexual	Y
Marnie	30	White	Master's	Student, college instructor	60,000–99,999	F	Queer	N
Neela	26	South Asian	Master's	Health promoter	40,000–59,999	F	Heterosexual	N
Vanessa	32	Asian	Master's	Director at FoodSpokes	40,000–59,000	F	Heterosexual	N

1 The food activists we interviewed were given the option of using their real name, rather than a pseudonym, given that they were speaking on a topic in which they have expertise. Some of the names used in this table are pseudonyms, and some are the activists' real first names.

Appendix B

Methods

Our analysis draws on a dataset comprised of detailed narratives obtained from focus groups and in-depth interviews with 129 food-oriented consumers in Toronto, Canada. Our data collection and research questions were focused on women, but we also spoke with men to provide some comparative leverage in our analysis. We primarily spoke with people who viewed food as important to their identities and who were interested in talking about food. We asked participants to discuss food shopping and meal preparation, as well as to identify the priorities guiding their food choices. Focus groups allowed us to explore, through a moderated discussion, how participants conceptualize the significance of their food practices, while interviews allowed us to examine this conceptualization more closely. Interview respondents were recruited through advertisements in grocery stores and food-related listservs. For focus groups, initial contacts were recruited through a large survey distributed at grocery stores and farmers' markets throughout the city. Across both focus groups and interviews, over 80 percent of participants were women.

Focus groups were held at a participant's home and were comprised of that participant's friends and/or acquaintances. Groups consisted of four to six participants, and one or more of the authors moderated discussion (sometimes with the help of a research assistant). Focus groups lasted 1.5 to 2 hours. Interviews were held in respondents' homes or at the university, lasted roughly 1 hour, and were conducted by one of the authors. Participants were given an honorarium in the form of a $25 grocery gift card to a shopping venue of their choice. All participants were asked to complete a short survey to record basic sociodemographic information. We conducted 20 focus groups with a total of 69 women and 20 men and conducted in-depth interviews with 40 women (11 of whom we specifically targeted as prominent Toronto-based food activists). Across focus groups and interviews, 77 participants identified as married or partnered, and 21 identified as gay, lesbian, bisexual, or queer. Seventy-nine of our participants were middle or upper middle class, and 50 were working class or poor. Class designations were made based on an interpretive reading that factored in participant's household income, education, and occupational prestige (Gilbert 2008; Lamont 1992).

In both the focus groups and interviews, we started with broad questions to identify the basic priorities that guide respondents' food choices and then asked respondents to comment on the importance of specific issues (e.g., health, ethics, price, cooking). We asked participants if they experienced tensions between any of these factors (e.g., health vs. price) or found it difficult to "stay true to" their food values in everyday life (e.g., ethics vs. convenience). Prior to the interviews, we asked interviewees to bring photos that reflected the significance of food in their lives and then discussed these photos with participants. Interviews with food activists included questions regarding their motivations for becoming involved in food activism, as well as current struggles and goals/hopes for the future. Each focus group and interview ended with a discussion of the relationship between food and social change. We asked all participants if they viewed their food shopping as political and whether they believed consumer food choices could promote social and environmental change. All focus groups and interviews were digitally recorded and professionally transcribed, and we coded the transcripts to identify major themes.

Focus group guide

Introduction

We are interested in understanding women and/or men's food shopping decisions and everyday food practices. We are particularly interested in understanding the kinds of tensions that can arise when balancing various factors, like taste, cost, time, and food values. The focus groups are meant to provide a comfortable space to share and discuss these issues with friends. Please do not worry about being judged—we struggle with these very tensions ourselves!

Opening discussion

1. To get us started, can you each briefly introduce yourself and tell us a bit about who does the **food shopping and cooking** in your household? [Probes: Gendered burdens and gender labor in the family, likes/dislikes, general practices]

2. Moderator places six items (or large color photos of items) on a table within view of all participants:
   (a) apple
   (b) banana

(c) bottle of olive oil
(d) dark chocolate bar
(e) picture of a steak
(f) an egg carton

What *factors* might shape your decision of whether or not to purchase these products? [Probe on issues raised during this initial discussion]

Motivations/ideals/practices

1. **Meat**: How often do you eat meat? Where do you shop for meat? What factors do you consider when purchasing meat? Are there types of meat that you find delicious or unappealing? [If you do not purchase meat, why not?]

   It comes up in a lot of our discussions that women seem to be more open to restricting or eliminating meat from their diets. What do you think is going on there?

2. **Health/body**: To what extent do issues of health influence your food shopping?

   Do you think food-related concerns about health or body-image are different for men and women? (e.g., do men care about health/body-image as much as women?)

3. **Shopping**: How do you feel about food shopping? Is it something you enjoy, or is it more of a chore? Do you think it matters *where* you buy your food, and where do you like to shop? What is the shopping experience like in these different places? Where do you *primarily* shop, and where might you go occasionally? Do you enjoy shopping more or less than your partner?

4. **Parenting**: For those of you who have children, how do children shape your food shopping practices? Did your shopping and cooking habits change when you got pregnant or when you started cooking for children? How does your partner feel about this? Do they help out with feeding the kids? If you were shopping for only yourself, do you think you would shop differently? If you were to have children in the future, do you think you would shop differently?

5. **Gendered labor**: Many women in heterosexual relationships we have spoken with have said that they take primary responsibility for researching and guiding family food decisions, even when their male partners are supportive and helpful with grocery shopping or other household chores. Why do you think the roles tend to get divided this way?

6. **Cooking**: Do you enjoy cooking? How is your cooking influenced by the food preferences of your kids and/or partner?

   In the past, women did most of the cooking in many families. To what extent do you think this is changing? (e.g., women who never cook, and men who love cooking)? Can you think of concrete examples of how this is changing (or not changing)?

7. **Eating out**: What inspires you to eat out, instead of cooking inside the home? Where do you like to eat out? How do your children and/or partner influence where you eat out?

8. **Knowledge**: Where do you look for food knowledge? Why these places? How do you learn about food and cooking?

Tensions/constraints/contradictions

We have been discussing various factors that may shape your food practices to varying degrees. Now I want to move to discuss some of the tensions or challenges that may arise when food shopping.

1. **Competing factors**: Of all the factors that shape your food consumption (e.g., cost, taste, health, convenience, environment, social concerns), which has the greatest impact on your shopping practices? That is, what is your number one priority? Where do you feel the biggest tensions?

2. **Cost**: If money were not an issue, do you feel you would shop differently?

3. **Identity**: Do you feel that food is important to your identity?

4. **Practices vs. values**: One of the things we were interested in understanding is whether people ever feel as though their actual shopping practices conflict with their values when it comes to food. Think about a day when you were happy with you food practices, and a day when you were unhappy with your food practices. What are some of the key differences? Are there certain shopping locations or stores where you feel it is easier to satisfy your values when shopping?

5. **Pleasure/health**: Are there foods or restaurants that you think are delicious but you feel conflicted about eating at because they seem unhealthy?

Social change/political eating

Many of you have stated that your shopping decisions reflect your desire to promote particular kinds of goals, be they environmental, social, or health-related. In our field of research, there is a debate around whether this kind of "ethical" or "green" shopping constitutes a form a political action—equivalent to voting or participating in a letter-writing campaign, for example. I want to open this up to discussion. Can food shopping be considered a form of political action?

1. **Change**: What kinds of changes would you like to see in our current food system? What would a perfect food system look like to you? How about a perfect meal?

2. **Responsibility**: Who is responsible for making these changes? How do you feel about the responsibility that is given to consumers? (e.g., frustrated, empowered, guilty, etc.) More generally, who do you think should be responsible for ensuring the safety of the food system and the safety of our environment? Do you see a role for government in all of this?

3. **Political eating**: Do you view your own food shopping as political? To what extent do you think shopping can create social and environmental change? How can people have the most influence? Are you familiar with the phrase "voting with your dollar"?

4. **Signs of change**: Are there things that make you feel optimistic about change in the food system? Signs or hope or potential?

Conclusion

Moderator stops discussion. Thanks participants. Distributes honorarium.

Interview guide

Introduction

To start with, can you tell me a bit about yourself and your living situation?

How and when did you become interested in food?
Can you tell me about the pictures you took of food in your life?
How is food shopping and cooking done in your household? (Probes: Who? Where? How often? How is it decided what should be bought?)

Identity

You responded to our call for participants, which targeted women who view food as an important part of their identity. How is food part of your identity?

Motivations

Now I would like to ask a few questions about the kinds of issues that influence how you shop and cook. First, tell me about what kinds of things are most important to you and have the biggest impact on your food decisions. (*Let participant provide an answer and then probe for specifics below.*)

Ethics: In what ways are your shopping and eating practices affected by concerns about ethical issues? Prompts: How important is environment, labor or fair trade, local, organic, sustainability, others? For any of these, why is that important to you?

> Do you ever feel as though you must choose between different ethical commitments? How do you make these decisions? How do you balance ethics alongside other factors such as cost, taste, health, and convenience?

Health: To what extent do issues of health or body-image influence your food shopping? Examples? What does the term "healthy eating" mean to you?

> Do you read labels? If so, what kinds of things are you looking for?
> Are there foods or restaurants that you think are delicious but you feel conflicted about eating at because they seem unhealthy?
> How do you balance health and other priorities such as taste, cost, convenience, ethics?
> Do you feel pressure to be careful about what you eat for *body-image reasons*? Do you think that women still feel pressure to restrict calories, to not eat too much, and to avoid fattening foods? Do you think food-related concerns about health or body-image are different for men and women? Are they different for mothers with kids?

Meat: How often do you eat meat? Where do you shop for meat? What factors do you consider when purchasing meat? (If you do not purchase meat, why not?)

> During our focus group research, we found that women seem to be more open to restricting or eliminating meat from their diets. What do you think is going on there?

Parenting: Are you shopping for children?

> *No*: If you were to have children, do you think you would shop differently?
> *Yes*: To what extent does your family influence your choice to shop a certain way? Did your shopping and cooking habits change when you started

feeding children? How does your partner feel about this? Do they help out with feeding the kids? If you were shopping for only yourself, do you think you would shop differently?

Do you think people with/without children shop differently? (does having children affect how they think about food?) Do you feel mothers are pressured to shop and feed their children in specific ways?

Shopping experience: How do you feel about food shopping? Is it something you enjoy, or is it more of a chore?

Does it change depending on where you buy your food? What is the shopping experience like in these different places?

Do you enjoy shopping more or less than your partner? Do you enjoy it with children, with your partner/friends, or on your own?

Gendered labor: (*Especially for participants who are partnered*)

Many women in heterosexual relationships we have spoken with have said that they take primary responsibility for researching and guiding family food decisions, even when their male partners are helpful with grocery shopping or other household chores. Why do you think the roles tend to get divided this way?

Cooking: Do you enjoy cooking?

Can you give me an example of a relatively simple meal you might serve? What about a relatively complex meal? In your mind, what is an ideal meal?

Do you like to cook for yourself, or do you enjoy cooking more for other people? How is your cooking influenced by the food preferences of your kids and/or partner? In the past, women did most of the cooking in many families. To what extent do you think this is changing? Can you think of concrete examples of how this is changing (or not changing)?

Eating out: What inspires you to eat out, instead of cooking at home? Where do you like to eat out? Can you tell me about the kind of restaurant you avoid and have disliked in the past?

[How do your children and/or partner influence where you eat out?]

Food media: How do you inform yourself about food issues (e.g., shopping, cooking, health, food trends, politics, etc.)?

Do you ever read food magazines or watch food TV shows or read food-blogs? Which ones?

Cost/financial constraints: How do you think your eating patterns are influenced by your economic situation? If money were not an issue, do you feel you would shop differently?

Practices vs. values: How often do you feel like there is a contradiction between your beliefs and your food choices? Can you think of an example of when this happens? (e.g., a particular constraint on shopping location, product choice by a family member?)

> Think about a day when you were happy with your food practices and a day when you were unhappy with your food practices. What are some of the key differences?
> Are there certain shopping locations or stores where you feel it is easier to satisfy your values when shopping?

Beliefs: Are people ever skeptical of your beliefs about food (e.g., health, ethics, kids)? What is your response to their skepticism?

> Will your partner put in a similar amount of effort to buy foods to meet the kinds of standards that you have described?
> Do you think women are more concerned about food issues than men?

Shifts: Can you think of a time when you made a significant change to your shopping or eating practices? (e.g., a time when you decided to stop buying/eating a particular product, or stopped shopping at a particular venue)

Social change/political eating

You have talked about several ways in which your shopping decisions reflect your desire to promote particular kinds of goals, be they environmental, social, or health-related.

Change: What kinds of changes would you like to see in our current food system? What would a perfect food system look like to you?

> What do you think is the best way to make change when it comes to food issues?

Responsibility: Who is responsible for making these changes? Who do you think should be responsible for ensuring the safety and sustainability of the food system?

How do you feel about the responsibility that is given to consumers? (e.g., frustrated, empowered, guilty, etc.) What is government's role in all of this? What should be their role?

Politics: Do you view your own food shopping as political? To what extent do you think shopping can create social and environmental change?

Are you familiar with the phrase "voting with your dollar"? Is this more or less effective than what we might call "traditional" political action aimed at creating change (e.g., attending a protest, voting, or supporting a nonprofit group that is lobbying for regulatory change)?

Do you see your own actions as a consumer as promoting change—in the form of social justice, environment, health, etc.?

What other actions might affect change? Beyond individual shopping decisions, what strategies do you think might be effective for creating social and environmental changes within our food system?

Wrap-up

Thank you, we have come to the end of the interview. Do you have any questions for me? Anything I did not ask that you wish I had? Any other comments?

[Honorarium]

Appendix C

Discourse analysis of food media

Textual sources were selected to reflect the multiple realms in which food femininities are performed (as guided by our focus group and interview research), including parenting, health and body, pleasure/cooking, and food politics.

In order to select online sources with a wide North American readership, we drew insight from lists of top food-blogs relating to health, cooking, and parenting. After a round of initial coding, we developed a detailed code list relating to core themes. Coding was conducted by the authors with the support of a research assistant.

Blogs (coded one randomly selected entry from each month of 2012)

100 Days of Real Food
Eating Bird Food
Family Bites
Jan's Sushi Bar
The Locavore (now SarahElton.com)
Making Love in the Kitchen
Oh She Glows
Queen of Green
Peas and Thank You
Pioneer Woman
Seven Spoons
Smitten Kitchen
Sweet Potato Chronicles

Magazines (a minimum of six issues were coded between 2011 and 2012)

Bon Appétit
Chatelaine Magazine
Cooking Light
O, The Oprah Magazine
Parents
Real Simple
Whole Living

Newspapers

Globe and Mail, "Life" section. Selections from January 2011 to December 2011.

New York Times, "Dining" section and "Well" blog. Selections from January 2011 to December 2011.

References

Abarca, M. E. (2004), "Authentic or Not, It's Original," *Food and Foodways*, 12(1): 1–25.

Abarca, M. E. (2007), "Charlas Culinarias: Mexican Women Speak from Their Public Kitchens," *Food and Foodways*, 5(3–4): 183–212.

Acker, J. (2006), "Inequality Regimes: Gender, Class, and Race in Organizations," *Gender & Society*, 20(4): 441–64.

Adams, C. (1990), *The Sexual Politics of Meat: A Feminist-Vegetarian Critical Theory*, New York: Continuum International Publishing Group.

Adkins, L. (2003), "Reflexivity Freedom or Habit of Gender?" *Theory, Culture & Society*, 20(6): 21–42.

Adler, T. (1981), "Making Sunday on Pancakes: The Male Cook in Family Tradition," *Western Folklore*, 40(1): 45–54.

Alkon, A. H. and McCullen, C. G. (2011), "Whiteness and Farmers Markets: Performances, Perpetuations . . . Contestations?" *Antipode*, 43(4): 937–59.

Allen, P. and Guthman, J. (2006), "From 'Old School' to 'Farm-to-School': Neoliberalization from the Ground Up," *Agriculture and Human Values*, 23: 401–15.

Allen, P. and Sachs, C. (2007), "Women and Food Chains: The Gendered Politics of Food," *International Journal of Sociology of Food and Agriculture*, 15(1): 1–23.

Allen, P. and Sachs, C. (2012), "Women and Food Chains: The Gendered Politics of Food," in P. Williams-Forson and C. Counihan (eds), *Taking Food Public*, New York: Routledge.

Andrews, M. (2003), "Nigella Bites the Naked Chef: The Sexual and the Sensual in Television Cookery Programmes," in J. Floyd and L. Forster (eds), *The Recipe Reader: Narratives, Contexts, Traditions*, Burlington: Ashgate.

Arendell, T. (2000), "Conceiving and Investigating Motherhood: The Decade's Scholarship," *Journal of Marriage and Family*, 62(4): 1192–207.

Armstrong, P. and Armstrong, H. (2001), *Thinking it Through: Women, Work and Caring in the New Millennium*, Halifax: Healthy Balance Research Program.

Arnot, M., Walkerdine, V., Letherby, G., and Seidler, V. J. (2011), "Review Symposium: Angela McRobbie, *The Aftermath of Feminism: Gender, Culture and Social Change*," London: Sage, 2009, 184, *Sociology*, 45(4): 700–6.

Atkinson, L. (2012), "Buying into Social Change: How Private Consumption Choices Engender Concern for the Collective," *The Annals of the American Academy of Political and Social Science*, 644(1): 191–206.

Avakian, A. V. and Haber, B. (2005), *From Betty Crocker to Feminist Food Studies: Critical Perspectives on Women and Food*, Amherst: University of Massachusetts Press.

Bain, C. (2010), "Structuring the Flexible and Feminized Labor Market: GlobalGAP Standards for Agricultural Labor in Chile," *Signs*, 35(2): 343–70.

Baker, L. (2004), "Tending Cultural Landscapes and Food Citizenship in Toronto's Community Gardens," *Geographical Review*, 94: 305–25.

Banet-Weiser, S. (2012), "'Free Self-Esteem Tools?': Brand Culture, Gender, and the Dove Real Beauty Campaign," in R. Mukherjee and S. Banet-Weiser (eds), *Commodity Activism: Cultural Resistance in Neoliberal Times*, New York: New York University Press.

Banet-Weiser, S. and Mukherjee, R. (2012), "Introduction: Commodity Activism in Neoliberal Times," in R. Mukherjee and S. Banet-Weiser (eds), *Commodity Activism: Cultural Resistance in Neoliberal Times*, New York: New York University Press.

Banet-Weiser, S. and Portwood-Stacer, L. (2006), "'I Just Want to Be Me Again!' Beauty Pageants, Reality Television and Post-feminism," *Feminist Theory*, 7(2): 255–72.

Barndt, D. (1999), *Women Working the NAFTA Food Chain: Women, Food and Globalization*, Toronto: Sumach Press.

Barndt, D. (2001), "On the Move for Food: Three Women Behind the Tomato's Journey," *Women's Studies Quarterly*, 1&2: 131–43.

Barnett, B. (2006), "Health as Women's Work: A Pilot Study on How Women's Magazines Frame Medical News and Femininity," *Women and Language*, 29(2): 1–12.

Barnett, C., Cloke, P., Clarke, N., and Malpass, A. (2005), "Consuming Ethics: Articulating the Subjects and Spaces of Ethical Consumption," *Antipode*, 37: 23–45.

Barnett, C., Clarke, N., Cloke, P., and Malpass, A. (2008), "The Elusive Subjects of Neo-liberalism: Beyond the Analytics of Governmentality," *Cultural Studies*, 22(5): 624–53.

Bartky, S. L. (1997), "Foucault, Femininity, and the Modernization of Patriarchal Power," in K. Conboy, N. Medina, and S. Stanbury (eds), *Writing on the Body: Female Embodiment and Feminist Theory*, New York: Columbia University Press.

Bassett, R., Beagan, B., and Chapman, G. E. (2008), "Grocery Lists: Connecting Family, Household and Grocery Store," *British Food Journal*, 110(2): 206–17.

Beagan, B., Chapman, G. E., Johnston, J., McPhail, D., Powers, E., and Valliantos, H. (2014), *Acquired Tastes*, Vancouver: UBC Press.

Beagan, B., Chapman, G. E., D'Sylva, A., and Bassett, B. R. (2008), "'It's Just Easier for Me to Do It': Rationalizing the Family Division of Foodwork," *Sociology*, 42(4): 653–71.

Becker, H. (1963), *Outsiders: Studies in the Sociology of Deviance*, New York: Free Press.

Bellows, A. C., Alcaraz, G., and Hallman, W. K. (2010), "Gender and Food, a Study of Attitudes in the USA towards Organic, Local, U.S Grown and GM-Free Foods," *Appetite*, 55(3): 540–50.

Beynon, J. (2002), *Masculinities and Culture*, Buckingham: Open University Press.

Bianchi, S. M., Milkie, M. A., Sayer, L. C., and Robinson, J. P. (2000), "Is Anyone Doing the Housework? Trends in the Gender Division of Household Labor," *Social Forces*, 79(1): 191–228.

Biltekoff, C. (2013), *Eating Right in America: The Cultural Politics of Food and Health*, Durham, NC: Duke University Press.

Black, P. (2004), *The Beauty Industry: Gender, Culture, Pleasure*, London: Routledge.

Blair-loy, M. (2009), "Cultural Constructions of Family Schemas: The Case of Women Finance Executives," *Gender and Society*, 15(5): 687–709.

Bobrow-Strain, A. (2012), *White Bread: A Social History of the Store-Bought Loaf*, Boston: Beacon Press.

Bodenhorn, B. (1990), "'I'm Not the Great Hunter, My Wife Is': Iñupiat and Anthropological Models of Gender," *Étude/Inuit/Studies*, 14(1–2): 55–74.

Boler, M. (1999), *Feeling Power: Emotions and Education*, New York: Routledge.

Bordo, S. R. (1989), "The Body and the Reproduction of Femininity: A Feminist Appropriation of Foucault," in A. M. Jaggar and S. R. Bordo (eds), *Gender/Body/Knowledge: Feminist Reconstructions of Being and Knowing*, New Brunswick, NJ: Rutgers University Press.

Bourdieu, P. (1977), *Outline of a Theory of Practice*, Cambridge: Cambridge University Press.

Bourdieu, P. (1984), *Distinction: A Social Critique of the Judgement of Taste*, Cambridge, MA: Harvard University Press.

Bourdieu, P. (1986), "The Forms of Capital," in J. Richardson (ed.), *Handbook of Theory and Research for the Sociology of Education*, New York: Greenwood Press.

Bourdieu, P. and Wacquant, L. J. (1992), *An Invitation to Reflexive Sociology*, Chicago: University of Chicago Press.

Bordo, S. R. (1993), *Unbearable Weight: Feminism, Western Culture, and the Body*, Berkeley, CA: University of California Press.

Bowen, S., Elliot, S., and Brenton, J. (2014), "The Joy of Cooking?" *Contexts*, 13(3): 20–5.

Boyd, E. M., Reynolds, J. R., Tillman, K. H., and Martin, P. Y. (2011), "Adolescent Girls' Race/Ethnic Status, Identities, and Drive for Thinness," *Social Science Research*, 40(2): 667–84.

Brady, J., Gingras, J., and Power, E. (2012), "Still Hungry: A Feminist Perspective on Food, Foodwork, the Body, and Food Studies," in M. Koc, J. Sumner, and A. Winson (eds), *Critical Perspectives in Food Studies*, New York: Oxford University Press.

Brickell, C. (2005), "Masculinities, Performativity, and Subversion," *Men and Masculinities*, 8(1): 24–43.

Brightman, R. (1996), "The Sexual Division of Foraging Labor: Biology, Taboo and Gender Politics," *Comparative Studies in Society and History*, 38: 687–729.

Brown, K. R. (2009), "The Social Dynamics and Durability of Moral Boundaries," *Sociological Forum*, 24(4): 854–76.

Bugge, A. B. and Almås, R. (2006), "Domestic Dinner Representations and Practices of a Proper Meal among Young Suburban Mothers," *Journal of Consumer Culture*, 6(2): 203–28.

Burgard, D. (2009), "What Is Health at Every Size?" in E. Rothblum and S. Solovay (eds), *Fat Studies Reader*, New York: New York University Press.

Burman, E. and Stacey, J. (2010), "The Child and Childhood in Feminist Theory," *Feminist Theory*, 11(3): 227–4.

Butler, J. (1997), *Excitable Speech: A Politics of the Performative*, New York: Routledge.

Cairns, K. (2012), "Partnering Power: Questions Posed from Governmentality," in B. L. Spencer, K. D. Gariepy, K. Dehli, and J. Ryan (eds), *Canadian Education: Governing Practices and Producing Subjects*, Calgary: Sense Publishers.

Cairns, K. (2013), "The Subject of Neoliberal Affects: Rural Youth Envision their Futures," *The Canadian Geographer*, 57(3): 337–44.

Cairns, K. and Johnston, J. (2015), "Choosing Health: Embodied Neoliberalism, Postfeminism, and the 'Do-diet,'" *Theory and Society*, 44(2): 153–75.

Cairns, J. and Sears, A. (2013), *The Democratic Imagination: Envisioning Popular Power in the 21st Century*, Toronto: University of Toronto Press.

Cairns, K., Johnston, J., and Baumann, S. (2010), "Caring About Food: Doing Gender in the Foodie Kitchen," *Gender & Society*, 24(5): 591–615.

Cairns, K., Johnston, J., and MacKendrick, N. (2013), "Feeding the 'Organic Child': Mothering through Ethical Consumption," *Journal of Consumer Culture*, 13(2): 97–118.

Cairns, K., DeLaat, K., Johnston, J., and Baumann, S. (2014), "The Caring, Committed Eco-Mom: Consumer Ideals and Lived Realities," in B. Barendregt and R. Jaffe (eds), *Green Consumption: The Global Rise of Eco-Chic*, London: Bloomsbury Publishing.

Campos, P., Saguy, A., Ernsberger, P., Oliver, E., and Gaesser, G. (2006), "The Epidemiology of Overweight and Obesity: Public Health Crisis or Moral Panic?" *International Journal of Epidemiology*, 35(1): 55–60.

Cappeliez, S. and Johnston, J. (2013), "From Meat and Potatoes to 'Real-Deal' Rotis: Exploring Everyday Culinary Cosmopolitanism," *Poetics*, 41: 433–55.

Carfagna, L., Dubois, E. A., Fitzmaurice, C., Laidley, T., Ouimette, M., Schor, J., and Willis, M. (2014), "An Emerging Eco-Habitus: The Reconfiguration of High Cultural Capital Practices among Ethical Consumers," *Journal of Consumer Culture*, doi: 10.1177/1469540514526227.

Carlson, J. (2011), "Subjects of a Stalled Revolution: A Theoretical Consideration of Contemporary American Femininity," *Feminist Theory*, 12(1): 75–91.

Carolan, M. (2011a), *Embodied Food Politics*, Burlington, VT: Ashgate Publishing Company.

Carolan, M. (2011b), *The Real Cost of Cheap Food*, Washington, DC: Earthscan.

Carolan, M. (2012), *The Sociology of Food and Agriculture*, New York: Routledge.

Carolan, M. (2014), "Affective Sustainable Landscapes and Care Ecologies: Getting a Real Feel for Alternative Food Communities," *Sustainability Science*, doi: 10.1007/s11625–014–0280–6.

Carrington, C. (1999), *No Place Like Home: Relationship and Family Life Among Lesbians and Gay Men*, Chicago: University of Chicago Press.

Castañeda, M. (2012), "Changing the World One Orgasm at a Time: Sex Positive Retail Activism," in R. Mukherjee and S. Banet-Weiser (eds), *Commodity Activism: Cultural Resistance in Neoliberal Times*, New York: New York University Press.

Charles, N. and Kerr, M. (1988), *Women, Food and Families*, Manchester and New York: Manchester University Press.

Choo, H. Y. and Ferree, M. M. (2010), "Practicing Intersectionality in Sociological Research: A Critical Analysis of Inclusions, Interactions, and Institutions in the Study of Inequalities," *Sociological Theory*, 28(2): 129–49.

Christopher, K. (2012), "Extensive Mothering: Employed Mothers' Constructions of the Good Mother," *Gender & Society*, 26: 73–96.

Christopher, K. (2013), "African Americans' and Latinas' Mothering Scripts: An Intersectional Analysis," *Advances in Gender Research*, 17: 187–208.

Cockburn-Wootten, C., Pritchard, A., Morgan, N., and Jones, E. (2008), "'It's Her Shopping List!' Exploring Gender, Leisure, and Power in Grocery Shopping," *Leisure/Loisir*, 32(2): 407–36.

Collins, P. H. (1994), "Shifting the Center: Race, Class and Feminist Theorizing about Motherhood," in D. Bassin, M. Honey, and M. Kaplan (eds), *Representations of Motherhood*, New Haven, CT: Yale University Press.

Coltrane, S. (2000), "Household Labor and the Routine Production of Gender," in M. S. Kimmel (ed.), *The Gendered Society Reader*, New York: Oxford University Press.

Connell, R. W. (1995), *Masculinities*, Berkeley: University of California Press.

Connell, R. W. and Messerschmidt, J. W. (2005), "Hegemonic Masculinity: Rethinking the Concept," *Gender & Society*, 19(6): 829–59.

Connolly, J. and Prothero, A. (2008), "Green Consumption: Life-politics, Risk and Contradictions," *Journal of Consumer Culture*, 8(1): 117–45.

Cook, D. T. (2009a), "Children's Subjectivities and Commercial Meaning: The Delicate Battle Mothers Wage when Feeding their Children," in A. James, A. Kjorholt, and V. Tingstad (eds), *Children, Food and Identity in Everyday Life*, 112–29, Basingstoke: Palgrave.

Cook, D. T. (2009b), "Semantic Provisioning of Children's Food: Commerce, Care and Maternal Practice," *Childhood*, 16(3): 317–34.

Coveney, J. (2000), *Food, Morals and Meaning: The Pleasure and Anxiety of Eating*, New York: Routledge.

Crawford, R. (1980), "Healthism and the Medicalization of Everyday Life," *International Journal of Health Services*, 10(3): 365–88.

Crawford, R. (2006), "Health as a Meaningful Social Practice," *Health: An Interdisciplinary Journal for the Social Study of Health, Illness and Medicine*, 10(4): 401–20.

Crawshaw, P. (2007), "Governing the Healthy Male Citizen: Men, Masculinity and Popular Health in Men's Health Magazine," *Social Science & Medicine*, 65(8): 1606–18.

Cruikshank, B. (1996), "Revolutions Within: Self-government and Self-esteem,"
    in B. Osborne and N. Rose (eds), *Foucault and Political Reason: Liberalism,
    Neo-liberalism & Rationalities of Government*, Chicago: University of Chicago Press.

Curry, D. (1997), "Decoding Femininity: Ads and Their Teenage Readers," *Gender &
    Society*, 4(11): 453–77.

Cutler, D. M., Glaeser, E. L., and Shapiro, J. M. (2003), "Why Have Americans Become
    More Obese?" *Journal of Economic Perspectives*, 17(3): 93–118.

Dean, M. (1999), *Governmentality: Power and Rule in Modern Society*, London and
    Thousand Oaks, CA: Sage Publications.

Deutsch, F. M. (2007), "Undoing Gender," *Gender & Society*, 21(1): 106–27.

Deutsch, T. (2010), *Building a Housewife's Paradise: Gender, Politics, and American
    Grocery Stores in the Twentieth Century*, Chapel Hill: University of North Carolina
    Press.

de Solier, I. (2013), *Food and the Self: Consumption, Production and Material Culture*,
    London: Bloomsbury.

DeVault, M. L. (1991), *Feeding the Family: The Social Organization of Caring as
    Gendered Work*, Chicago and London: University of Chicago Press.

Dorfman, C. J. (1992), "The Garden of Eating: The Carnal Kitchen in Contemporary
    American Culture," *Feminist Issues*, 12(1): 21–38.

Doucet, A. (2013), "A 'Choreography of Becoming': Fathering, Embodied Care, and
    New Materialisms," *Canadian Review of Sociology*, 50(3): 284–305.

Douglas, M. (1966), *Purity and Danger: An Analysis of Concepts of Pollution and Purity*,
    London: Routledge.

Duffy, M. (2005), "Reproducing Labor Inequalities: Challenges for Feminists
    Conceptualizing Care at the Intersections of Gender, Race, and Class," *Gender &
    Society*, 19(1): 66–82.

Dunn, G. A. (2000), "Opting into Motherhood: Lesbians Blurring the Boundaries and
    Transforming the Meaning of Parenthood and Kinship," *Gender and Society*, 14: 11–35.

DuPuis, M. and Goodman, D. (2005), "Should We Go 'Home' to Eat? Toward a Reflexive
    Politics of Localism," *Journal of Rural Studies*, 21: 359–71.

Durkheim, E. and Mauss, M. (1963), *Primitive Classification*, Chicago: University of
    Chicago Press.

Dworkin, S. L. and Wachs, F. L. (2009), *Body Panic: Gender, Health, and the Selling of
    Fitness*, New York: New York University Press.

Eichler, M. (1997), *Family Shifts: Families, Policies, and Gender Equality*, Toronto: Oxford
    University Press.

Eliasoph, N. (1997), "'Close to Home': The Work of Avoiding Politics," *Theory and
    Society*, 26: 605–47.

Elliott, R. (2013), "The Taste for Green: The Possibilities and Dynamics of Status
    Differentiation through 'Green' Consumption," *Poetics*, 41: 294–322.

Erickson, R. J. (2005), "Why Emotion Work Matters: Sex, Gender, and the Division of
    Household Labor," *Journal of Marriage and Family*, 67: 337–51.

Eskes, T. B., Duncan, M. C., and Miller, E. M. (1998), "The Discourse of Empowerment: Foucault, Marcuse, and Women's Fitness Texts," *Journal of Sport & Social Issues*, 22(3): 317–44.

Everts, J. (2010), "Consuming and Living the Corner Shop: Belonging, Remembering, Socializing," *Social & Cultural Geography*, 11(8): 847–63.

Federici, S. (2004), "Women, Land-struggles, and Globalization: An International Perspective," *Journal of Asian and African Studies*, 39(1–2): 47–62.

Ferguson, S. (1999), "Building on the Strengths of the Socialist Feminist Tradition," *Critical Sociology*, 7(2): 1–15.

Ferguson, S. (2008), "Canadian Contributions to Social Reproduction Feminism," *Race, Gender and Class*, 15(1–2): 42–57.

Food and Agriculture Association of the United Nations (FAO) (2005), *The State of Food Insecurity in the World*, Rome: FAO.

Foucault, M. (1977), *Discipline and Punish: The Birth of the Prison*, New York: Vintage Books.

Foucault, M. (1994a [1974]), "Prisons et Asiles dans le Mécanisme du Pouvoir," in *Dits et Ecrits* (Vol. 11), Paris: Gallimard.

Foucault, M. (1994b), "The Political Technology of Individuals," in J. Faubion (ed.), *Michel Foucault: Power*, New York: The New Press.

Fox, B. (1988), "Conceptualizing 'Patriarchy,'" *Canadian Review of Sociology and Anthropology*, 25(2): 163–82.

Fox, B. (2001), "The Formative Years: How Parenthood Creates Gender," *Canadian Review of Sociology and Anthropology*, 38(4): 373–90.

Fox, B. (2009), *When Couples Become Parents: The Creation of Gender in the Transition to Parenthood*, Toronto: University of Toronto Press.

Freedman, D. (2013), "How Junk Food Can End Obesity," *Atlantic Monthly*, http://www.theatlantic.com/magazine/archive/2013/07/how-junk-food-can-end-obesity/309396/

Friedan, B. (1967), *The Feminine Mystique*, New York: Dell Pub. Co.

Fusco, C. (2006), "Inscribing Healthification: Governance, Risk, Surveillance and the Subjects and Spaces of Fitness and Health," *Health & Place*, 12(1): 65–78.

Gantt, P. M. (1991), "Taking the Cake: Power Politics in Southern Life and Fiction," in S. Innes (ed.), *Cooking Lessons: The Politics of Food and Gender*, Toronto: Rowman and Littlefield.

Giddens, A. (1991), *Modernity and Self-identity: Self and Society in the Late Modern Age*, Stanford, CA: Stanford University Press.

Gilbert, D. L. (2008), *The American Class Structure in an Age of Growing Inequality*, London: Sage Publications.

Gill, R. (2007), "Postfeminist Media Culture: Elements of a Sensibility," *European Journal of Cultural Studies*, 10(2): 147–66.

Gill, R. and Scharff, C. (2011), "Introduction," in R. Gill and C. Scharff (eds), *New Femininities: Postfeminism, Neoliberalism and Subjectivity*, Hampshire and New York: Palgrave Macmillan.

Gillis, S. and Hollows, J. (eds) (2009), *Feminism, Domesticity and Popular Culture*, New York: Taylor & Francis.

Glenn, E. (1992), "From Servitude to Service Work: In the Racial Historical Continuities of Paid Reproductive Division Labor," *Signs*, 18(1): 1–43.

Glenn, E. (1994), "Social Constructions of Mothering: A Thematic Overview," in E. Glenn, G. Chang, and L. R. Forcey (eds), *Mothering: Ideology, Experience, and Agency*, New York: Routledge.

Gonzalez, J. A. (2009), "Market Trends and Consumer Profile at the Organic Farmers Market in Costa Rica," *British Food Journal*, 111(5): 498–510.

Goodman, M., Maye, D., and Holloway, L. (2010), "Ethical Foodscapes? Premises, Promises and Possibilities," *Environment and Planning A*, 42: 1782–96.

Goodman, D., Dupuis, M., and Goodman, M. K. (2011), *Alternative Food Networks: Knowledge, Practice and Politics*, Abingdon: Routledge.

Gough, B. (2007), "'Real Men Don't Diet': An Analysis of Contemporary Newspaper Representations of Men, Food and Health," *Social Science & Medicine*, 64: 326–37.

Green, A. I. (2008), "Erotic Habitus: Toward a Sociology of Desire," *Theory and Society*, 37(6): 597–626.

Greer, G. (1970), *The Female Eunuch*, London: Harper Perennial.

Grosz, E. A. (1994), *Volatile Bodies: Toward a Corporeal Feminism*, Bloomington, IN: Indiana University Press.

Gupta, S., Evertsson, M., Grunow, D., Nermo, M., and Sayer, L. (2010), "Economic Inequality and Housework," in J. Tres and S. Drobni (eds), *Dividing the Domestic: Men, Women, and Household Work in Cross-National Perspective*, Stanford: Stanford University Press.

Guthman, J. (2003), "Fast Food/Organic Food: Reflexive Tastes and the Making of 'Yuppie Chow,'" *Social and Cultural Geography*, 4(1): 45–58.

Guthman, J. (2008), "Neoliberalism and the Making of Food Politics in California," *Geoforum*, 39: 1171–83.

Guthman, J. (2009), "Teaching the Politics of Obesity: Insights into Neoliberal Embodiment and Contemporary Biopolitics," *Antipode*, 41(5): 1110–33.

Guthman, J. (2011), *Weighing In: Obesity, Food Justice, and the Limits of Capitalism* (Vol. 32), Berkeley, CA: University of California Press.

Guthman, J. and DuPuis, M. (2006), "Embodying Neoliberalism: Economy, Culture, and the Politics of Fat," *Environment and Planning D: Society and Space*, 24: 427–48.

Hadlock, C. (2013), "Consumer Trends," *Food and Drink Magazine*, http://www.fooddrink-magazine.com/index.php/articles/blog/641-a-nation-of-foodies.

Hardine, J. and Pribram, E. D. (2009), "Introduction: The Case for a Cultural Emotion Studies," in J. Hardine and E. D. Pribram (eds), *Emotions: A Cultural Studies Reader*, London and New York: Routledge.

Harding, K. (2009), "Michael Pollan Wants You Back in the Kitchen," *Salon*, August 1, http://www.salon.com/2009/08/01/pollan_on_child/.

Harvey, D. (2005), *A Brief History of Neoliberalism*, New York: Oxford University Press.

Hayes, S. (2010), *Radical Homemakers: Reclaiming Domesticity from a Consumer Culture*, Richmandville, NY: Left to Write Press.

Hayes-Conroy, A. and Hayes-Conroy, J. (2008), "Taking Back Taste: Feminism, Food and Visceral Politics," *Gender, Place and Culture*, 15(5): 461–73.

Hays, S. (1996), *The Cultural Contradictions of Motherhood*, New Haven, CT: Yale University Press.

Heffernan, V. (2014), "What if You just Hate Making Family Dinner?" *The New York Times Magazine*, http://www.nytimes.com/2014/10/12/magazine/what-if-you-just-hate-making-dinner.html

Heldke, L. (2003), *Exotic Appetites: Ruminations of a Food Adventurer*, New York: Routledge.

Hill, H. and Lynchehaun, F. (2002), "Organic Milk: Attitudes and Consumption Patterns," *British Food Journal*, 104(7): 526–42.

Hinrichs, C. C. (2000), "Embeddedness and Local Food Systems: Notes on Two Types of Direct Agricultural Market," *Journal of Rural Studies*, 16(3): 295–303.

Hochschild, A. (2003 [1989]), *The Second Shift*, Toronto: Penguin Books.

Hollows, J. (2000), *Feminism, Femininity and Popular Culture*, Manchester: Manchester University Press.

Hollows, J. (2003a), "Feeling Like a Domestic Goddess: Postfeminism and Cooking," *European Journal of Cultural Studies*, 6(2): 179–202.

Hollows, J. (2003b), "Oliver's Twist Leisure, Labour and Domestic Masculinity in the Naked Chef," *International Journal of Cultural Studies*, 6(2): 229–48.

Hollows, J. (2007), "The Feminist and the Cook: Julia Child, Betty Friedan and Domestic Femininity," in E. Casey and L. Martens (eds), *Gender and Consumption: Domestic Cultures and the Commercialisation of Everyday Life*, Vermont: Ashgate Publishing Company.

Holmes, S. (2013), *Fresh Fruit, Broken Bodies: Migrant Farmworkers in the United States*, Berkeley, CA: University of California Press.

Holt, D. (1997), "Distinction in America? Recovering Bourdieu's Theory of Tastes from its Critics," *Poetics*, 25: 93–121.

Holt, D. (1998), "Does Cultural Capital Structure American Consumption?" *Journal of Consumer Research*, 25: 1–25.

hooks, b. (1992), "Eating the Other: Desire and Resistance," *Black Looks: Race and Representation*, Boston: South End Press.

hooks, b. (2004), *The Will to Change: Men, Masculinity and Love*, New York: Astria Books.

hooks, b. (2013), "Dig Deep: Beyond Lean In," *The Feminist Wire*, http://thefeministwire.com/2013/10/17973/

Hope Alkon, A. (2013), "Man Can Cook: Michael Pollan, the Food Movement, and Feminism 101," *Feministing*, http://community.feministing.com/2013/05/01/man-can-cook-michael-pollan-the-food-movement-and-feminism-101/

Huggan, G. (2001), *The Post-Colonial Exotic: Marketing the Margins*, New York: Routledge.

Illouz, E. (2008), *Saving the Modern Soul: Therapy, Emotions, and the Culture of Self-Help*, Berkeley: University of California Press.

Illouz, E. (2009), "Emotions, Imagination and Consumption: A New Research Agenda," *Journal of Consumer Culture*, 9(3): 377–413.

Inness, S. A. (2001a), *Cooking Lessons: The Politics of Gender and Food*, New York: Rowman & Littlefield Publishers, Inc.

Inness, S. A. (2001b), *Dinner Roles: American Women and Culinary Culture*, Iowa City, IA: University of Iowa Press.

Isenhour, C. and Ardenfors, M. (2009), "Gender and Sustainable Consumption: Policy Implications," *International Journal of Innovation and Sustainable Development*, 4(2–3): 135–49.

James, A., Jenks, C., and Prout, A. (1998), *Theorizing Childhood*, Cambridge: Polity Press.

Jeleniewski Seidler, V. (2011), "Review Symposium on Angela McRobbie," *Sociology*, 45(4): 700–6.

Johnston, J., Rodney, A., and Chong, P. (2014), "Making Change in the Kitchen? A Study of Celebrity Cookbooks, Culinary Personas, and Inequality," *Poetics*, http://dx.doi.org/10.1016/j.poetic.2014.10.001

Johnston, J. and Baumann, S. (2010), *Foodies: Democracy and Distinction in the Gourmet Foodscape*, New York: Routledge.

Johnston, J. and Cairns, K. (2012), "Eating for Change," in S. Banet-Weiser and R. Muhkerjee (eds), *Commodity Activism: Cultural Resistance in Neoliberal Times*, New York: New York University Press.

Johnston, J. and Cairns, K. (2013), "Searching for the 'Alternative', Caring, Reflexive Consumer: A Commentary on Alternative Food Networks: Knowledge, Practice and Politics," *International Journal of Sociology of Agriculture and Food*, 20(3): 403–8.

Johnston, J. and Cairns, K. (2014), "Food Shopping: A Chore or a Pleasure?" *Contexts*, 13(3): 6.

Johnston, J. and Cappeliez, S. (2012), "You Are What You Eat: Enjoying (and Transforming) Food Culture," in M. Koc, J. Sumner, and T. Winson (eds), *Critical Perspectives in Food Studies*, Don Mills, ON: Oxford University Press.

Johnston, J. and Szabo, M. (2011), "Reflexivity and the Whole Food Market Shopper: Shopping for Change, or Cruising for Pleasure?" *Agriculture and Human Values*, 28: 303–19.

Johnston, J. and Taylor, J. (2008), "Feminist Consumerism and Fat Activists: A Comparative Study of Grassroots Activism and the Dove Real Beauty Campaign," *Signs*, 33(4): 941–66.

Johnston, J., Baumann, S., and Cairns, K. (2010), "The National and the Cosmopolitan in Cuisine: Constructing America Through Gourmet Food Writing," in D. Inglis and D. Gimlin (eds), *The Globalization of Food*, New York: Berg.

Johnston, J., Szabo, M., and Rodney, A. (2011), "Good Food, Good People: Understanding the Cultural Repertoire of Ethical Eating," *Journal of Consumer Culture*, 11(3): 293–318.

Johnston, J., Szabo, M., and Rodney, A. (2012), "Place, Ethics, and Everyday Eating: A Tale of Two Neighbourhoods," *Sociology*, 46(6): 1091–108.

Judkins, B. and Presser, L. (2008), "Division of Eco-friendly Household Labor and the Marital Relationship," *Journal of Social and Personal Relationship*, 25(6): 923–41.

Keddie, A., Mills, C., and Mills, M. (2008), "Struggles to Subvert the Gendered Field: Issues of Masculinity, Rurality and Class," *Pedagogy, Culture & Society*, 16(2): 193–205.

Kellner, D. (1995), *Media Culture*, New York: Routledge.

Kelly, T. M. (1991), "Honoring Helga, 'The Little Lefse Maker': Regional Food as Social Market, Tradition, and Art," in S. Innes (ed.), *Cooking Lessons: The Politics of Food and Gender*, Toronto: Rowman and Littlefield.

Ketchum, C. (2005), "The Essence of Cooking Shows: How the Food Network Constructs Consumer Fantasies," *Journal of Communication Inquiry*, 29(3): 217–34.

Kimura, A. H. (2011), "Food Education as Food Literacy: Privatized and Gendered Food Knowledge in Contemporary Japan," *Agriculture and Human Values*, 28: 465–82.

King, S. (2012), "Civic Fitness: The Body Politics of Commodity Activism," in R. Mukherjee and S. Banet-Weiser (eds), *Commodity Activism: Cultural Resistance in Neoliberal Times*, New York: New York University Press.

Koch, S. L. (2012), *A Theory of Grocery Shopping: Food, Choice, and Conflict*, London: Berg.

Krais, B. (2006), "Gender, Sociological Theory and Bourdieu's Sociology of Practice," *Theory, Culture & Society*, 23(6): 119–34.

Krashinsky, S. (2013), "How Foodies Influence the Things We Eat," *Globe & Mail*, August 27.

Kroska, A. (2004), "Divisions of Domestic Work: Revising and Expanding Theoretical Explanations," *Journal of Family Issues*, 25(7): 900–32.

Kurdek, L. A. (2007), "The Allocation of Household Labor by Partners in Gay and Lesbian Couples," *Journal of Family Issues*, 28(1): 132–48.

Kwan, S. (2010), "Navigating Public Spaces: Gender, Race, and Body Privilege in Everyday Life," *Feminist Formations*, 22(2): 144–66.

Lachance-Grzela, M. and Bouchard, G. (2010), "Why Do Women Do the Lion's Share of Housework? A Decade of Research," *Sex Roles*, 63: 767–80.

Lake, A. A., Hyland, R. M., Mathers, J. C., Rugg-Gunn, A. J., Wood, C. E., and Adamson, A. J. (2006), "Food Shopping and Preparation among the 30-Somethings: Whose Job is It? (The ASH30 Study)," *British Food Journal*, 108(6): 475–86.

Lamont, M. (1992), *Money, Morals, and Manners: The Culture of the French and the American Upper-Middle Class*, Chicago, IL: University of Chicago Press.

Lamont, M. (2000), *The Dignity of Working Men: Morality and the Boundaries of Race, Class and Immigration*, Cambridge, MA: Harvard University Press.

Lamont, M. and Fournier, M. (1992), *Cultivating Differences: Symbolic Boundaries and the Making of Inequality*, Chicago: University of Chicago Press.

Lareau, A. (2002), "Invisible Inequality: Social Class and Childrearing in Black Families and White Families," *American Sociological Review*, 67(5): 747–76.

Lareau, A. (2011), *Unequal Childhoods: Class, Race and Family Life*, Berkeley, CA: University of California Press.

Lavin, C. (2013), *Eating Anxiety: The Perils of Food Politics*, Minneapolis, MN: University of Minnesota Press.

Lawler, S. (2004), "Rules of Engagement: Habitus, Power and Resistance," in L. Adkins and B. Skeggs (eds), *Feminism After Bourdieu*, Oxford: Blackwell Publishing.

Lazar, M. M. (2009), "Entitled to Consume: Postfeminist Femininity and a Culture of Post-critique," *Discourse & Communication*, 3(4): 371–400.

Lea, E. and Worsley, T. (2005), "Australians' Organic Food Beliefs, Demographics and Values," *British Food Journal*, 107(11): 855–69.

LeBesco, K. (2011), "Neoliberalism, Public Health, and the Moral Perils of Fatness," *Critical Public Health*, 21(2): 153–64.

Levenstein, H. (1988), *Revolution at the Table*, New York: Oxford University Press.

Little, J., Ilbery, B., and Watts, D. (2009), "Gender, Consumption and the Relocalisation of Food: A Research Agenda," *Sociologia Ruralis*, 49(3): 201–17.

Lockie, S. (2009), "Responsibility and Agency within Alternative Food Networks: Assembling the 'Citizen Consumer,'" *Agriculture and Human Values*, 26: 193–201.

L'orange Furst, E. (1997), "Cooking and Femininity," *Women's Studies International Forum*, 20(3): 441–9.

Lupton, D. (1995), *The Imperative of Health: Public Health and the Regulated Body*, London: Sage Publications.

Lupton, D. (1996a), "Food, Memory and Meaning—The Symbolic and Social Nature of Food Events," *The Sociological Review*, 42(4): 664–85.

Lupton, D. (1996b), *Food, the Body and the Self*, London: Sage Publications.

Lupton, D. (1999), *Risk*, London: Routledge.

Luxton, M. (1980), *More than a Labour of Love: Three Generations of Women's Work in the Home*, Toronto: The Canadian Women's Educational Press.

Macgregor, S. (2004), "From Care to Citizenship: Calling Ecofeminism back to Politics," *Ethics and the Environment*, 7(1–2): 85–96.

Macgregor, S. (2006), *Beyond Mothering Earth: Ecological Citizenship and the Politics of Care*, Vancouver: UBC Press.

MacKendrick, N. A. (2010), "Media Framing of Body Burdens: Precautionary Consumption and the Individualization of Risk," *Sociological Inquiry*, 80(1): 126–149.

MacKendrick, N. A. (2011), "The Individualization of Risk as Responsibility and Citizenship: A Case Study of Chemical Body Burdens" (PhD NR78295), University of Toronto, Canada.

MacKendrick, N. A. (2013), "Protecting Ourselves from Chemicals: A Study of Gender and Precautionary Consumption," in D. N. Scott (ed.), *"Consuming" Chemicals: Law, Science & Policy for Women's Health*, Vancouver: University of British Columbia Press.

MacKendrick, N. A. (2014), "More Work for Mother: Chemical Body Burdens as Maternal Responsibility," *Gender & Society*, doi: 10.1177/0891243214529842.

Magnusson, M. K., Arvola, A., and Hursti, U. K. (2001), "Attitudes Towards Organic Foods Among Swedish Consumers," *British Food Journal*, 103(3): 209–26.

Maniates, M. (2002), "Individualization: Plant a Tree, Buy a Bike, Save the World?" in T. Princen, M. Maniates, and K. Conca (eds), *Confronting Consumption*, Cambridge: The MIT Press.

Marcotte, A. (2011), "Men Buy Groceries like This, Women Buy Groceries like That," *Slate*, www.slate.com/blogs/xx_factor/2011/12/28/marketers_blow_smoke_trying_to_convince_stores_that_male_shoppers_need_special_treatment_.html

Martin, N. K. (2007), "Porn Empowerment: Negotiating Sex Work and Third Wave Feminism," *Atlantis: Critical Studies in Gender, Culture & Social Justice*, 31(2): 31–41.

Matchar, E. (2013), *Homeward Bound: Why Women Are Embracing the New Domesticity*, New York: Simon & Schuster.

McIntyre, L. and Rondeau, K. (2011), "Individual Consumer Food Localism: A Review Anchored in Canadian Farmwomen's Reflections," *Journal of Rural Studies*, 27: 116–24.

McLeod, J. and Yates, L. (2006), *Making Modern Lives: Subjectivity, Schooling, and Social Change*, New York: State University of New York Press.

McPhail, D., Beagan, B., and Chapman, G. E. (2012), "'I Don't Want to be Sexist But. . .': Denying and Re-Inscribing Gender Through Food," *Food, Culture and Society: An International Journal of Multidisciplinary Research*, 15(3): 473–89.

McRobbie, A. (2004), "Post-Feminism and Popular Culture," *Feminist Media Studies*, 4(3): 255–64.

McRobbie, A. (2009), *The Aftermath of Feminism: Gender, Culture and Social Change*, Los Angeles, CA: Sage Publications.

Meah, A. (2013), "Reconceptualizing Power and Gendered Subjectivities in Domestic Cooking Spaces," *Progress in Human Geography*, doi:10.1177/0309132513501404.

Mears, A. (2010), "Size Zero High-End Ethnic: Cultural Production and the Reproduction of Culture in Fashion Modeling," *Poetics*, 38(1): 21–46.

Metzl, J. (2010), "Introduction: Why 'Against Health'?" in J. Metzl and A. Kirkland (eds), *Against Health: How Health Became the New Morality*, New York: New York University Press.

Micheletti, M. (2003), *Political Virtue and Shopping: Individuals, Consumerism and Collective Action*, New York: Palgrave Macmillan.

Mikkonen, J. and Raphael, D. (2010), "Social Determinants of Health: The Canadian Facts," doi:10.1016/B978–012288145–9/50048–6.

Milkie, M. (1999), "Social Comparisons, Reflected Appraisals, and Mass Media: The Impact of Pervasive Beauty Images on Black and White Girls' Self-Concepts," *Social Psychology Quarterly*, 62(2): 190–210.

Miller, D. (1998), *A Theory of Shopping*, Ithaca, NY: Cornell University Press.

Miller, J. (2012), "Food: Shared, Prepared, Organic and Genetically Modified," *The Generation X Report: Quarterly Research Report From the Longitudinal Study of American Youth*, 1(3): 1–8.

Miller, L. (2013), "The Feminist Housewife: Can Women Have it All by Choosing to Stay at Home?" *New York Magazine*, http://nymag.com/news/features/retro-wife-2013–3/

Moloney, M. and Fenstermaker, S. (2002), "Performance and Accomplishment: Reconciling Feminist Conceptions of Gender," in S. Fenstermaker and C. West (eds), *Doing Gender, Doing Difference: Inequality, Power, and Institutional, Change*, New York: Routledge.

Molz, J. G. (2004), "Tasting an Imagined Thailand: Authenticity and Culinary Tourism in Thai Restaurants," in L. M. Long (ed.), *Culinary Tourism*, Lexington, KY: University Press of Kentucky.

Moore, S. E. (2010), "Is the Healthy Body Gendered? Toward a Feminist Critique of the New Paradigm of Health," *Body & Society*, 16(2): 95–118.

Moss, M. (2013), *Salt, Sugar, Fat: How the Food Giants Hooked Us*, Toronto: McClelland & Stewart.

Mundy, J. (2013), "The Gay Guide to Wedded Bliss," *Atlantic Monthly*, May 22.

Murcott, A. (1983), "'It's a Pleasure to Cook for Him': Food, Mealtimes and Gender in Some South Wales Households," in E. Gamarnikow, D. Morgan, J. Purvis, and D. Taylorson (eds), *The Public and the Private*, London: Heinemann.

Murphy, E. (2000), "Risk, Responsibility, and Rhetoric in Infant Feeding," *Journal of Contemporary Ethnography*, 29(3): 291–325.

Naccarato, P. and LeBesco, K. (2012), *Culinary Capital*, New York: Berg.

Nestle, M. (2007), *Food Politics: How the Food Industry Influences Nutrition and Health*, Berkeley, Los Angeles, and London: University of California Press.

Neuhaus, J. (2003), *Manly Meals and Mom's Home Cooking: Cookbooks and Gender in Modern America*, Baltimore, MD: John Hopkins University Press.

Ontiveros, M. L. (2007), "Harassment of Female Farmworkers: Can the Legal System Help?" in S. Harley (ed.), *Women's Labor in the Global Economy: Speaking in Multiple Voices*, New Brunswick, NJ: Rutgers University Press.

Orbach, S. (1978), *Fat Is a Feminist Issue*, Berkeley, CA: Berkeley Publishing.

Orenstein, P. (2010), "The Femivore's Dilemma," *New York Times Magazine*, March 11.

O'Shaughnessy, S. and Kennedy, E. H. (2010), "Relational Activism: Reimagining Women's Environmental Work as Cultural Change," *Canadian Journal of Sociology*, 35(4): 551–72.

O'Sullivan, G., Hocking, C., and Wright-St. Clair, V. (2008), "History in the Making: Older Canadian Women's Food-Related Practices," *Food and Foodways*, 16(1): 63–87.

Parsons, J. (2014), "'Cheese and Chips out of Styrofoam Containers': An Exploration of Taste and Cultural Symbols of Appropriate Family Foodways," *M/C Journal*, 17(1).

Patil, V. (2013), "From Patriarchy to Intersectionality: A Transnational Feminist Assessment of How Far We've Really Come," *Signs*, 38(4): 847–67.

Patterson, M. and Johnston, J. (2012), "Theorizing the Obesity Epidemic: Health Crisis, Moral Panic and Emerging Hybrids," *Social Theory & Health*, 10(3): 265–91.

Peterson, R. A. (2005), "Problems in Comparative Research: The Example of Omnivorousness," *Poetics: Journal of Empirical Research on Culture, the Media and the Arts*, 33: 257–82.

Peterson, R. A. and Kern, R. M. (1996), "Changing Highbrow Taste: From Snob to Omnivore," *American Sociological Review*, 61(5): 900–7.

Pini, B. (2002), "Focus Groups, Feminist Research and Farm Women: Opportunities for Empowerment in Rural Social Research," *Journal of Rural Studies*, 18(3): 339–51.

Pollan, M. (2008), *In Defense of Food: An Eaters Manifesto*, Toronto: Penguin.

Power, E. (2005), "The Unfreedom of Being Other: Canadian Lone Mothers' Experiences of Poverty and 'Life on the Cheque,'" *Sociology*, 39(4): 643–60.

Preibisch, K. L. and Encalada Grez, E. (2010), "The Other Side of el Otro Lado: Mexican Migrant Women and Labor Flexibility in Canadian Agriculture," *Signs*, 35(2): 289–316.

Probyn, E. (2000), *Carnal Appetites: Foodsexidentities*, New York: Routledge.

Pugh, A. (2009), *Longing and Belonging: Parents, Children, and Consumer Culture*, Berkeley, CA: University of California Press.

Pugh, A. (2013), "What Good Are Interviews for Thinking About Culture? Demystifying Interpretive Analysis," *American Journal of Cultural Sociology*, 1(1): 42–68.

Pyke, K. D. and Johnson, D. L. (2003), "Asian American Women and Racialized Femininities: 'Doing' Gender Across Cultural Worlds," *Gender and Society*, 17(1), 33–53.

Rafferty, K. (2011), "Class-based Emotions and the Allure of Fashion Consumption," *Journal of Consumer Culture*, 11(2): 239–60.

Razack, S. (1998), *Looking White People in the Eye: Gender, Race, and Culture in Courtrooms and Classrooms*, Toronto: University of Toronto Press.

Reay, D. (1995), "'They Employ Cleaners to Do That': Habitus in the Primary Classroom," *British Journal of Sociology of Education*, 16(3): 353–71.

Reel, J. J., SooHoo, S., Franklin Summerhays, J., and Gill, D. L. (2008), "Age Before Beauty: An Exploration of Body Image in African-American and Caucasian Adult Women," *Journal of Gender Studies*, 17(4): 321–30.

Reinharz, S. (1992), *Feminist Methods in Social Research*, New York: Oxford University Press.

Richardson, N. (2010), "'The 'Buck' Stops with Me'—Reconciling Men's Lay Conceptualisations of Responsibility for Health with Men's Health Policy," *Health Sociology Review*, 19(4): 419–36.

Ridgeway, C. L. (2008), "Framed Before We Know it: How Gender Shapes Social Relations," *Gender & Society*, 23(2): 145–60.

Ridgeway, C. L. and Correll, S. (2004), "Unpacking the Gender System: A Theoretical Perspective on Gender Beliefs and Social Relations," *Gender & Society*, 18(4): 510–31.

Ringrose, J. and Walkerdine, V. (2008), "Regulating the Abject," *Feminist Media Studies*, 8(3): 227–46.

Risman, B. J. (2009), "From Doing to Undoing: Gender as We Know it," *Gender & Society*, 23(1), 81–4.

Ristovski-Slijepcevic, S., Chapman, G. E., and Beagan, B. (2010), "Being a 'Good Mother': Dietary Governmentality in the Family Food Practices of Three Ethnocultural Groups in Canada," *Health*, 14(5): 467–83.

Roff, R. J. (2007), "Shopping for Change? Neoliberalizing Activism and the Limits to Eating Non-GMO," *Agriculture and Human Values*, 24: 511–22.

Rose, N. (1999), *Powers of Freedom: Reframing Political Thought*, New York: Cambridge University Press.

Sachs, C. E. (1996), *Gendered Fields: Rural Women, Agriculture, and Environment*, Boulder, CO: Westview Press.

Said, E. (1978), *Orientalism*, New York: Vintage Books.

Saguy, A. (2013), *What's Wrong with Fat?*, New York: Oxford University Press.

Saguy, A. C. and Gruys, K. (2010), "Morality and Health: News Media Constructions of Overweight and Eating Disorders," *Social Problems*, 57(2): 231–50.

Salvio, P. M. (2012), "Dishing it Out: Food Blogs and Post-feminist Domesticity," *Gastronomica: The Journal of Food and Culture*, 12(3): 31–9.

Sassatelli, R. (2004), "Body Politics," in K. Nash and A. Scott (eds), *The Blackwell Companion to Political Sociology*, Oxford and Malden, MA: Blackwell Publishing Ltd.

Scharff, C. M. and Gill, R. (2010), "Introduction," in R. Gill and C. Scharff (eds), *New Femininities: Post-feminism, Neoliberalism and Subjectivity*, Hampshire and New York: Palgrave Macmillan.

Schenone, L. (2003), *A Thousand Years Over a Hot Stove: A History of American Women Told Through Food, Recipes, and Remembrances*, New York: W.W. Norton and Company.

Scheper-Hughes, N. (1993), *Death Without Weeping: The Violence of Everyday Life in Brazil*, Berkeley, CA: University of California Press.

Schippers, M. (2007), "Recovering the Feminine Other: Masculinity, Femininity, and Gender Hegemony," *Theory and Society*, 36: 85–102.

Schneider, T. and Davis, T. (2010), "Fostering a Hunger for Health: Food and the Self in 'The Australian Women's Weekly,'" *Health Sociology Review*, 19(3): 285–303.

Scrinis, G. (2013), *Nutritionism: The Science and Politics of Dietary Advice*, New York: Columbia University Press.

Seccombe, W. (1992), *A Millennium of Family Change: Feudalism to Capitalism in North-Western Europe*, London: Verso.

Sewell, W. F. (1992), "A Theory of Structure: Duality, Agency, and Transformation," *The American Journal of Sociology*, 98(1): 1–29.

Seyfang, G. (2005), "Shopping for Sustainability: Can Sustainable Consumption Promote Ecological Citizenship?" *Environment Politics*, 14: 290–306.

Shapiro, L. (2001), *Perfection Salad: Women and Cooking at the Turn of the Century*, Berkeley, CA: University of California Press.

Shapiro, L. (2004), *Something from the Oven: Reinventing Dinner in 1950s America*, New York: Penguin.

Short, F. (2006), *Kitchen Secrets: The Meaning of Cooking in Everyday Life*, New York: Berg.

Shove, E. (2010), "Beyond the ABC: Climate Change Policy and Theories of Social Change," *Environment and Planning A*, 42(6): 1273–85.

Shove, E., Pantzar, M., and Watson, M. (2012), *The Dynamics of Social Practice: Everyday Life and How it Changes*, Thousand Oaks, CA: Sage Publications.

Skeggs, B. (2004a), "Exchange, Value and Affect: Bourdieu and 'the Self,'" in L. Adkins and B. Skeggs (eds), *Feminism After Bourdieu*, Oxford: Blackwell Publishing.

Skeggs, B. (2004b), "Introducing Pierre Bourdieu's Analysis of Class, Gender and Sexuality," in L. Adkins and B. Skeggs (eds), *Feminism After Bourdieu*, Oxford: Blackwell Publishing.

Skeggs, B. (2004c), *Class, Self, Culture*, New York: Routledge.

Slater, D. (1997), *Consumer Culture and Modernity*, Cambridge: Polity Press.

Slocum, R. (2007), "Whiteness, Space and Alternative Food Practice," *Geoforum*, 38(3): 520–33.

Slocum, R. (2008), "Thinking Race Through Feminist Corporeal Theory: Divisions and Intimacies at the Minneapolis Farmers' Market," *Social and Cultural Geography*, 9(8): 849–86.

Slocum, R. (2013), "Introduction. Geographies of Race and Food: Fields, Bodies, Markets," in R. Slocum and A. Saldanha (eds), *Geographies of Race and Food*, Burlington, VT: Ashgate Press.

Smith, A. (2005), "Native American Feminism, Sovereignty and Social Change," *Feminist Studies* 31(1): 116–32.

Smith, D. E. (1987), *The Everyday World as Problematic: A Feminist Sociology*, Milton Keynes: Open University Press.

Smithers, J., Lamarche, J., and Joseph, A. E. (2008), "Unpacking the Terms of Engagement with Local Food at the Farmers' Market: Insights," *Ontario Journal of Rural Studies*, 24(3): 337–50.

Sobal, B. (2005), "Men, Meat and Marriage: Models of Masculinity," *Food and Foodways*, 13(1–2): 135–58.

Spade, D. (2013), "Intersectional Resistance and Law Reform," *Signs*, 38(4): 1031–55.

Spitzack, C. (1990), *Confessing Excess: Women and the Politics of Body Reduction*, Albany, NY: State University of New York Press.

Stansell, C. (1987), *City of Women*, New York: Albert Knopf.

Starr, A. (2010), "Local Food: A Social Movement?" *Cultural Studies, Critical Methodologies*, 10(6): 479–90.

Statistics Canada (1998, 2006, 2011), *Overview of the Time Use of Canadians*, Ottawa: Minister of Industry.

Strauss, E. (2011), "Yuppy, Hippie Artifice," *North West Edible Life*, http://www.nwedible.com/2011/04/yuppie-hippie-artifice.html

Swarns, R. (2014), "When Their Workday Ends, More Fathers Are Heading into the Kitchen," *New York Times*, http://www.nytimes.com/2014/11/24/nyregion/when-the-workday-ends-more-fathers-are-heading-to-the-kitchen.html?_r=0

Swartz, D. (1997), *Culture and Power: The Sociology of Pierre Bourdieu*, Chicago: University of Chicago Press.

Swenson, R. (2009), "Domestic Divo? Televised Treatments of Masculinity, Femininity and Food," *Critical Studies in Media Communication*, 26(1): 36–53.

Swidler, A. (2001), *Talk of Love: How Culture Matters*, Chicago: University of Chicago Press.

Szabo, M. (2011), "The Challenges of 'Re-engaging with Food': Connecting Employment, Household Patterns and Gender Relations to Convenience Food Consumption in North America," *Food, Culture and Society: An International Journal of Multidisciplinary Research*, 14(4): 547–566.

Szabo, M. (2013), "Food, Work or Play? Men's Domestic Cooking, Privilege and Leisure," *Sociology*, 47(4): 623–38.

Szabo, M. (2014), "Men Nurturing Through Food: Challenging Gender Dichotomies Around Domestic Cooking," *Journal of Gender Studies*, 23(1): 18–31.

Szasz, A. (2007), *Shopping Our Way to Safety*, St. Paul, MN: University of Minnesota Press.

Tannahill, R. (1973), *Food in History*, New York: Stein and Day.

Tarasuk, V. S., Mitchell, A., and Dachner, N. (2013), "Research to Identify Policy Options to Reduce Food Insecurity," http://nutritionalsciences.lamp.utoronto.ca/wp-content/uploads/2014/01/foodinsecurity2011_final.pdf

Tasker, Y. and Negra, D. (2007), *Interrogating Postfeminism: Gender and the Politics of Popular Culture*, Durham, NC: Duke University Press.

Taylor, J., Johnston, J., and Whitehead, K. (2014), "A Corporation in Feminist Clothing? Young Women Discuss the Dove 'Real Beauty' Campaign," *Critical Sociology*, doi:10.1177/0896920513501355.

Taylor, V. (1996), *Rock-a-by Baby: Feminism, Self Help, and Postpartum Depression*, New York: Routledge.

Thompson, B. (1994), *A Hunger So Wide and So Deep*, Minneapolis, MN: University of Minnesota Press.

Thompson, C. J. (1996), "Caring Consumers: Gendered Consumption Meanings and the Juggling Lifestyle," *Journal of Consumer Research*, 22: 388–407.

Thompson, C. J. and Coskuner-Balli, G. (2007), "Enchanting Ethical Consumerism: The Case of Community Supported Agriculture," *Journal of Consumer Culture*, 7(3): 275–303.

US Bureau of Labor Statistics. (2012), "American Time Use Survey: 2011," http://www.bls.gov/news.release/pdf/atus.pdf.

US Department of Agriculture (2013), "Food Security in the US: Key Statistics and Graphics," http://www.ers.usda.gov/topics/food-nutrition-assistance/food-security-in-the-us/key-statistics-graphics.aspx#householdtype.

Vaisey, S. (2009), "Motivation and Justification: A Dual-process Model of Culture in Action," *American Journal of Sociology*, 114(6): 1675–715.

Vijayasiri, G. (2011), "The Allocation of Housework: Extending the Gender Display Approach," *Gender Issues*, 28(3): 155–74.

Vinz, D. (2009), "Gender and Sustainable Consumption: A German Environmental Perspective," *European Journal of Women's Studies*, 16(2): 159–79.

Wakefield, S., Yeudall, F., Taron, C., Reynolds, J., and Skinner, A. (2007), "Growing Urban Health: Community Gardening in Southeast Toronto," *Health Promotion International*, 22(2): 92–101.

Warde, A. and Martens, L. (2000), *Eating Out: Social Differentiation, Consumption and Pleasure*, Cambridge: Cambridge University Press.

Warin, M. (2011), "Foucault's Progeny: Jamie Oliver and the Art of Governing Obesity," *Social Theory and Health*, 9(1): 24–40.

Waugh, I. M. (2010), "Examining the Sexual Harassment Experiences of Mexican Immigrant Farmworking Women," *Violence Against Women*, 16(3): 237–61.

Wellesley (Mass.) Congregational Church Parlor Fund Committee. (1890), *The Wellesley Cook Book*, Prepared by the Ladies Congregational Society, Boston: C. J. Peters & Son. http://books.google.ca/books?id=SlsEAAAAYAAJ&printsec=frontcover#v=onepage&q&f=false

West, C. and Zimmerman, D. (1987), "Doing Gender," *Gender & Society*, 1(2): 125–51.

West, C. and Zimmerman, D. (2009), "Accounting for Doing Gender," *Gender & Society*, 23(1): 112–22.

West, E. (2009), "Doing Gender Difference Through Greeting Cards: The Construction of a Communication Gap in Marketing and Everyday Practice," *Feminist Media Studies*, 9(3): 285–99.

Wilkinson, S. (1998), "Focus Groups in Feminist Research: Power, Interaction, and the Co-Construction of Meaning," *Women's Studies International Forum*, 21(1): 111–25.

Williams-Forson, P. A. (2001), "'Sucking the Chicken Bone Dry': African American Women, Fried Chicken, and the Power of a National Narrative," in S. Innes (ed.), *Cooking Lessons: The Politics of Food and Gender*, Toronto: Rowman and Littlefield.

Williams, C. (2006), *Inside Toyland*, Berkeley, CA: University of California Press.

Williams, P., Hubbard, P., Clark, D., and Berkeley, N. (2001), "Consumption, Exclusion and Emotion: The Social Geographies of Shopping," *Social & Cultural Geography*, 2(2): 203–20.

Willis, M. M. and Schor, J. B. (2012), "Does Changing a Light Bulb Lead to Changing the World? Political Action and the Conscious Consumer," *The Annals of the American Academy of Political and Social Science*, 644(1): 160–90.

Winson, A. (2004), "Bringing Political Economy into the Debate on the Obesity Epidemic," *Agriculture and Human Values*, 21: 299–312.

Winson, A. (2013), *The Industrial Diet: The Degradation of Food and the Struggle for Healthy Eating*, Vancouver: UBC Press.

Wolf, N. (1990), *The Beauty Myth*, Toronto: Vintage Books, Random House.

Wright, J., O'Flynn, G., and Macdonald, D. (2006), "Being Fit and Looking Healthy: Young Women's and Men's Constructions of Health and Fitness," *Sex Roles*, 54(9–10): 707–16.

Zeisler, A. (2008), *Feminism and Pop Culture*, Berkeley, CA: Seal Press.

Zinn, M. B. (1990), "Family, Feminism, and Race in America," *Gender & Society*, 4(1): 68–82.

Zukin, S. (2004), *Point of Purchase: How Shopping Changed American Culture*, New York: Routledge.

Zukin, S. and Maguire, J. S. (2004), "Consumers and Consumption," *Annual Review of Sociology*, 30(1): 173–97.

Index